Corporate Impact

Measuring and Managing Your Social Footprint

Adrian Henriques

publishing for a sustainable future

London • Washington, DC

First published in 2010 by Earthscan

Earthscan Ltd, Dunstan House, 14a St Cross Street, London EC1N 8XA, UK
Earthscan LLC, 1616 P Street, NW, Washington, DC 20036, USA

Earthscan publishes in association with the International Institute for Environment and Development

For more information on Earthscan publications, see www.earthscan.co.uk or write to earthinfo@earthscan.co.uk

ISBN: 978-1-84407-653-6

Typeset by MapSet Ltd, Gateshead, UK
Cover design by Rogue Four Design

A catalogue record for this book is available from the British Library

Library of Congress Cataloging-in-Publication Data

Henriques, Adrian, 1954-
  Corporate impact : measuring and managing your social footprint / Adrian Henriques.
      p. cm.
  Includes bibliographical references and index.
  ISBN 978-1-84407-653-6
  1. Social responsibility of business. 2. Sustainability. I. Title.
  HD60.H468 2010
  658.4'08—dc22

                                                        2009032172

At Earthscan we strive to minimize our environmental impacts and carbon footprint through reducing waste, recycling and offsetting our CO_2 emissions, including those created through publication of this book. For more details of our environmental policy, see www.earthscan.co.uk.

Printed and bound in the UK by TJ International, an ISO14001 accredited company. The paper used is FSC certified and the inks are vegetable based.

Contents

Boxes, Figures and Tables

BOXES

FIGURES

TABLES

Acknowledgements

I would like to thank Mathis Wackernagel, Chris Tuppen, Janet Williamson, Alison Ball, Adam Richards and David York for the help that they gave in the course of preparing this book. Deborah Seamark and Judy Kuszewski were also both very helpful indeed in reading drafts of the book and giving feedback.

Abbreviations

CR	Corporate Responsibility
CSR	Corporate Social Responsibility
EU	European Union
EPZ	Export Processing Zone
FDI	Foreign Direct Investment
GDP	Gross Domestic Product
GRI	Global Reporting Initiative
HRIA	Human Rights Impact Assessment
IFRS	International Financial Reporting Standards
ISO	International Standards Organisation
MDGs	Millennium Development Goals
NGO	Non-Governmental Organization
NHS	National Health Service
PR	Public Relations
ROI	Return on Investment
SEC	Sexual Exploitation of Children
SIA	Social Impact Assessment
SRI	Socially Responsible Investment
SROI	Social Return on Investment
UDHR	Universal Declaration of Human Rights
UNEP	United Nations Environment Programme

1

Introduction

At university I studied sociology. At that time (the 1970s), remarkably little attention was paid to the role of companies in shaping our world. Of course, Adam Smith had warned against the dangers of businessmen (Smith, 1999a,b) and Wallerstein (Wallerstein, 1974, 1980, 1989) and others were explaining the role of economics in the pattern of nations and the growing inequalities of the world. But the result was an account of how economic activity was changing the world, not of how to understand the role of an individual company in doing it (EC, 2002).

Today, I am a professor at a Business School, and the situation in Business Schools seems to have some unfortunate parallels to what was going on in the 1970s. There is (naturally) much attention paid to business activity and how to enhance it, but little work on how to understand the impact of a given company, for good or ill, on the world.

Yet it seems fairly clear that, after the family, companies are perhaps *the* major unit of modern society since they influence almost every aspect of our lives. It follows that without understanding the role and impact of a company, it is not possible to understand what is going on in society, much less to control or manage it. So governments, which like to demand an 'evidence base' for their policies, do not have a systematic understanding of the impact of individual companies or even know how to measure it – far less do they have an adequate basis of evidence on which to found their business, economic or social policies.

And yet we know companies are large and getting larger. In the 1930s Berle and Means found companies to be spectacularly large (Berle and Means, 1933) and, as predicted, they stagger the imagination today. In 2008 Walmart's revenue was nearly US$350 billion. That is larger than the GDP of Venezuela and exceeds the *combined total* of the world's smallest 94 countries, up to and including Jamaica (CIA-USA, 2007; WalMart, 2007). Yet it is still not possible to discover what the overall impact of Walmart is (or, more strictly, what the overall impact on society of all the economic activity represented by the goods Walmart sells is).

Why is this? There are perhaps three key explanations. One is that any full-scope understanding of the impact of companies has been displaced by an endless dedication to understanding their financial consequences. This is necessary, but it is not enough. A central theme of this book will be that while the financial impact of companies is obviously *part* of their impact, it is very far indeed from being the total of their impact, which includes other social and environmental consequences. In many cases a company's financial impact is not even the most important of their social consequences.

A further explanation is that companies are not passive players in the development of society. They are actively and consciously involved in its development. And they are very powerful. Unfortunately, companies do not on the whole find it in their interests for their full social consequences to be known and available. Since they are powerful, they can prevent full disclosure. The recent rise of 'CSR' (or Corporate Social Responsibility) might seem to suggest that I am wrong in this. The number of large companies, at least in Europe, which have produced a report on their impacts beyond the financial impacts is significant. But as I have argued in *Corporate Truth* (Henriques, 2007), the delivery of transparency by companies is fatally mismatched with the interests of their stakeholders. The insight that stakeholders need into the power that companies have over them is rarely permitted. In other words where companies exert power over their stakeholders, the need for transparency is greatest – and that is precisely where it is typically lacking.

A final explanation is that understanding and measuring the impact of a company is actually a hard thing to do. Of course this may be exacerbated by the fact that the academic community has not devoted sufficient attention to it. But it is also because it is intrinsically a complex problem. This book is addressed particularly to this problem, seeking to understand the nature of this complexity and to appraise and suggest ways in which the social impact of companies has been and can be measured and assessed.

SOCIAL IMPACT?

I consider nothing that is human to be alien to me.
Publius Terentius Afer, c150 BCE

Social impact concerns social issues. So what counts as a social issue? The first things that come to mind may be problems such as obesity, drinking to excess, health issues, religious conflict, human rights and poverty. All these issues – and many more – have a social feel to them. What gives them that feel? And how does that relate to the social impact of corporations? I believe a variety of factors can make a social issue social, and the edge of the concept is blurred.

One of the things which makes obesity, for example, a specifically social issue is that it concerns a large proportion of the population of a number of countries, including the USA and the UK and, increasingly, 'undeveloped' countries. Companies can be involved in the issue through selling food, selling diets or in selling obesity remedies of some kind. This connection with large sections of societies is part of what gives an issue a social 'feel'. Of course, obesity can also affect those who may have little or no formal or direct connection with any company that might be involved. The partners of those who are clinically obese may fall into this category.

Yet environmental issues can also affect large numbers of people. Does that make them social issues? I shall be arguing just this: because they affect *people*, environmental issues are also *social* issues. Yet environmental issues appear to be different, because they involve more technical matters connected with the physical environment, and also because some aspects of certain environmental issues can be quantified and measured precisely. Carbon dioxide emissions, for example, can be quantified and the corresponding global temperature can also be assessed, although neither measurement is straightforward and the calculations involved can be complex.

Another key factor which makes an issue count as a social one concerns responsibility. One feature of some social issues which can distinguish them from environmental issues is whether or not those impacted have some responsibility for the issue. Obesity, for example, can be blamed on companies pushing junk food on the public and particularly on the young. Yet many people also feel that those who over-consume should bear some responsibility. Exactly how responsibility for the outcome of obesity on a particular person should be shared between that person and a company selling food, for example, is not clear. One of the factors which makes assigning responsibility to any companies involved more difficult is that they will rarely have targeted any particular person, despite the best efforts of marketing departments. Most advertising is aimed at large numbers of people. And of course some of these will not have become obese, even if they have consumed the products of the food company in question. But it is also clear that neither company nor consumer can escape all blame. The question of responsibility for environmental issues, such as exposure to pollution, is weighted the other way round. Those who suffer from pollution will not have chosen that fate. But the question of responsibility is not clear-cut, as those who suffer from pollution may well be very reluctant to give up the goods whose production leads to the pollution.

A COMPANY'S ROLE

What should a company's role be in this? If Walmart is such a big player, does that have particular consequences for Walmart's responsibility? We expect governments to take responsibility for the social welfare of their citizens. But on the whole we do not expect companies to take very much responsibility for their social impacts. Why not?

To its credit, Walmart has made some effort to address its environmental impacts. It acknowledges the major environmental problem of our time: 'Climate change is an urgent threat not only to our business but also to our customers, communities, and the life support systems that sustain our world' (WalMart, 2008). What it is doing on this front may or may not be sufficient, given the scale of its impact. Yet Walmart is still widely attacked, mostly for its record on wider social issues and its anti-union stance in particular. Is this simply on account of its size and success, as some (Nordlinger, 2004) claim? Or does its pre-eminent economic position justify any proportionately greater ethical burden on the company? How much do its social impacts matter – and how far should responsibility for them be shared with other groups?

A comparison of social issues and environmental issues facing companies can be helpful. As we have seen, environmental issues on the whole have the possibility of 'scientific' appraisal. Not only can they usually be clearly measured (or we at least know what measurement should look like), but we can know when they have been addressed. They may raise political issues in the determination of how to address them, but these typically cross traditional party lines. Social issues are rarely like this. Above all they seem to raise political issues from the start. How Walmart relates to its staff is a central part of its social responsibility, but it is also regarded as an inherently political matter, raising all the prejudices around unions. This is actually quite natural, since the issues that matter in company-stakeholder relations are particularly those which concern the relative power of the company and its stakeholders. The central question is perhaps 'How much control should Walmart staff expect to have over their conditions of employment?'

Social responsibility is also wrapped up in some confusing way with 'sustainability'. So that even though it is now accepted that there is a social dimension to sustainability, there is little clear understanding of what that really means or how it might be measured by companies. There is no agreement as to the appropriate measures of social impact and a general unease that what is being measured does not always capture what matters.

This is important to companies not only because they now profess a much greater concern with sustainability, but because corporate social impacts affect how well and how profitably a company can be run. The social impact and nature of companies is in fact closely connected to the nature of their stakeholder relationships. In general, good stakeholder relationships lead to better business relationships. Good relations with customers, for example, will lead to better sales or more loyal customers. This is both commercial common sense – as well as an area which has been minutely studied.

But what happens when a stakeholder has little power, no direct commercial relationship with the company and is generally in a vulnerable position? The business case, although it can sometimes be made, is much less direct. And because the proper measurement of corporate social impacts is always hard, such vulnerable stakeholders are likely to be doubly neglected. For those seeking to understand the impact and consequences of companies, there is therefore a need to scrutinize current company-stakeholder relationship measurement techniques relevant to all stakeholders.

THE ELUSIVENESS OF THE SOCIAL

Expectations of the extent to which social impact can be measured will always be too high. When all the quantitative techniques have done their work, there will always be left over those matters which lie beyond them. The impact of a mobile phone or fashion trainer, for example, is partly captured by the numbers sold, an analysis of those to whom they are sold and so on. But their full impact also includes how they shape the lives of those who wear them – and also of those who do not wear them, perhaps because they cannot afford it. It includes the jealousies they may arouse and also the crimes to which they can lead: when one young person mugs another one in order to possess the trainers (or phone) in question. While it might be possible to capture the volumes of these incidents, no set of such numbers will capture how the victim and aggressor felt. Yet the complete social impact of trainers includes these feelings, as well as many others, such as the comfort felt by older wearers of trainers, for whom other shoes just don't do it!

What are the reasons for this elusiveness? In addition to the technical difficulties in finding suitable measures, together with the resource requirement necessary to measure them appropriately, I believe the main factors underlying it are:

- the range and complexity of social issues, which typically result from the interaction of many different parties;
- the inherently subjective nature of social issues, which involve people who have their own views on the matter.

There are many different techniques for measuring social impact, some of which this book will describe. While it is possible to list a set of procedures or methods which can collectively capture many of the social impacts of a company, there is no single tool which captures them all.

BUSINESS CASES

What stakeholder engagement can do for you: boost brand, boost sales and motivate employees. (EC, 2008)

The European Commission has a marvellously straightforward view of the benefits of understanding social impact – or at least the engagement aspect of it. While on its own unconvincing, what such unbridled optimism can do is to prompt a closer look at the issue of understanding the business consequences of an organization understanding its own social impact.

The context of the business case for understanding social impact needs to be set in a moral frame which should guide action. As Geoffrey Chandler, one of the chief pioneers of the drive to put human rights on the corporate agenda, has put it:

> *I believe our train of thought should be this: business is part of society; society has agreed certain international values and principles; business needs to reflect these in its operations if it is to be acceptable. Its social purpose is to provide products and services profitably and responsibly, the boundaries of that responsibility being determined by the extent of its impact on its stakeholders, the nature of that responsibility being determined by society's values.*
> (BT, 2003)

This means that certain actions which are wholly immoral should be prevented on moral grounds alone. Slavery was once a profitable enterprise – and in some forms, it still is. But the argument for its abolition relied on moral grounds as well as economic challenges. And no business today would argue that because it could make money out of slavery, it should be allowed to do so. A key part of a business's 'licence to operate' is that it is not operating outside the zone of moral acceptability as determined by society. Unfortunately, sometimes in practice a company's fear of finding out about, and having to remedy, its dependence on immoral activity can actually prevent efforts to discover the role such practices are playing. For this reason it has sometimes been suggested that a company should not look too hard into its potentially more dubious activities. That is one side of the argument for businesses to understand their social impact.

The other side of the business case for a company to understand its impact is justifying what positive courses of action, including efforts to determine its impact, *should* be undertaken. While a business case will not always be necessary to justify social responsibility, it is always sufficient. So there remains the challenge of justifying to its shareholders a particular means for a business to determine its social impact. The remainder of this section will look at some of the main kinds of argument employed. None of the processes for understanding social impact come cost free; all of them require some kind of investment, at least in management time. However, the focus below will be on benefits, which can be harder to articulate than costs.

There are some areas for which the advantage of understanding corporate social impact are clear. This is especially true for 'human capital' (Kingsmill, 2003). It is usually quite apparent to most organizations that the level of training and competence of their staff directly affects how well they can perform. However, the overall social impact of a company is often thought about as if it excluded such well-understood areas as human capital. And of course, justification is still demanded for action in relation to areas in which social impact is not so obvious.

It is useful to note first that the most common form of general justification of social responsibility, that it enhances a company's reputation, does not directly underwrite its efforts to understand its social impact. An enhanced reputation results primarily from good social performance. It does not flow automatically from simply understanding all areas in which social performance might be improved. On the other hand, systematic improvement in social performance, which will lead to lasting reputation benefits, is unlikely to be possible without a systematic understanding of social impact. But the connection remains indirect.

Nevertheless, there are some business arguments for understanding social impact. The first of these is connected with trust. In general, an increase in stakeholders' trust in a company is a sign of an increase in 'social capital'. It might seem that, just as with reputation, trust increases with good social performance, rather than with understanding social impact. And this is of course true: nothing increases trust like trustworthiness. However, the process of understanding social impact, which must involve stakeholders, can also have a role to play. The process of engagement that underlies an understanding of social impact is a social process in which the company and its stakeholders get to know each other. This alone can increase trust, provided it is undertaken sensitively. Simply getting to know your stakeholders/company is likely to increase trust.

The virtue of greater trust is quite widespread. Typically an increase in trust will lower the cost of doing business. For example, part of the cost of dealing with suppliers is the legal costs of arranging appropriate contracts. Now much of the work that lawyers do is to pin down what happens should things go wrong with a commercial contract. Lawyers are driven in their perception of risk partly by their own experience and partly by the concerns expressed by the two sides of the contract. It follows that where each side expresses trust and confidence in the other party, less time and therefore cost will be expended by contract lawyers. This can be very significant, particularly in the extractive sectors, where permission to operate can be granted far more quickly if the local communities are on board. Analogous arguments can be made about the relationship between a company and almost any stakeholder.

The second argument for a positive business case for a company to understand its social impact can be summed up in one word: intelligence. Companies' activities can be described as facilitating the interactions between their various stakeholders. It should therefore be obvious that a company needs to keep in close contact with its stakeholders to maximize its business advantage. And indeed, most companies are keen to be in close touch with their main commercial stakeholders, especially customers. That interest, depending on the nature of the business, may extend to suppliers, shareholders and competitors. But with staff, somewhat surprisingly, there is an ambivalence about how close companies wish to be. And companies are often very cautious as to how closely they wish to work with hostile stakeholders.

However, one thing which stakeholders can provide is information, or early warning, about issues which may be – or may become – of significant concern to the company. NGOs, for example, are often amongst those who raise issues to prominence. Campaigning NGOs such as Oxfam brought the issue of access to pharmaceutical medicines in the South to the attention of the press. This has remained a key issue for pharmaceutical companies for nearly 10 years. By working with NGOs, rather than ignoring them for as long as possible, a company has access to key sources of intelligence. Of course, no stakeholder will tolerate simply being pumped for information. If a stakeholder is to be a source of intelligence it needs to be treated as a partner, not a problem.

The third argument concerns risk and uncertainty. To some extent it builds on the advantages of stakeholder intelligence. While access to intelligence can help with strategic planning, connection to stakeholders in general can reduce uncertainty. It is important here to distinguish between risk and uncertainty. Risk can be characterized by a set of known alternatives against which probabilities can be assigned. Many commercial strategies are based on the close analysis of alternative strategies in the face of such risks. Uncertainty is a more profound lack of knowledge than simply facing a set of defined risks, encompassing context as well as specific outcomes. Uncertainty characterizes the 'unknown unknowns' of the future.

Companies often approach such uncertainty through the use of scenarios. Scenarios are coherent stories which map out plausible possible futures the company may face. The use of scenarios is common when trying to plan (prepare may be a more accurate word) for the more distant future. What is interesting here, as the *Financial Times* economist John Kay has pointed out (Kay, 2008) is that the way to tackle uncertainty is through stories. Of course there is a danger that the stories are simply fantasies which satisfy our hopes, rather than offering any predictive value. The key is to assess the stories with common sense. And that sense is to be found in the intelligence which stakeholders can provide.

The exploration of social impact and the narrative communication of it which stakeholders may provide is thus an essential input into a coherent approach to the uncertainty of the future. In practice this means that companies should seek the wisdom of their stakeholders, rather than using cunning to exploit them. Stakeholders should be consulted in the sense in which, in a personal capacity, we might consult someone wise and with much relevant experience. That can only be done if stakeholders are treated with respect.

FRAMEWORK OF THIS BOOK

This book attempts to provide a coherent framework within which the issues of social impact can be understood, measured and assessed. This will involve exploring some basic issues, such as what 'social impact' actually means as well as reviewing the practical ways in which it has been measured. The first four chapters therefore provide a theoretical framework for understanding social impact. Social impact is compared to environmental impact and the differences which affect its measurement are highlighted. It is argued that the role of the stakeholder is central to any assessment of impact.

To measure the social purpose of companies it is important to know what they are for – in particular, what sort of impact they are intended to have. In other words, what is the purpose of companies? Is it to make money, perhaps by selling bread, or to deliver on some social outcome, such as producing food? Chapter 2 will explore this dilemma through stakeholder relationships looking at social need and practical issues, such as legal constraints. The dilemma is actually not as acute as it may first appear: on the one hand economic outcomes are also social ones and on the other, economic outcomes may be necessary to support positive social impacts.

Chapter 3 provides a case study of social impact. It explores the difficult issue of the sexual exploitation of children. This is obviously a social issue. But it is not obvious how the activities of companies contribute to it or prevent its occurrence.

If social issues are part of sustainability, it is necessary to understand how social impact and environmental impact are related. And in order to lay the ground for later chapters, it is necessary to understand how environmental and social issues each relate to sustainability. At one level this concerns causal connections between these apparently different domains – such as the (false) argument that wealth is necessary before sustainability can be addressed. Yet social and environmental issues are much more closely connected than this: in Chapter 4 it will be argued that environmental concerns are always at the same time social ones. This book will not describe methods of environmental measurement, as this area is very well catered for.

Since stakeholders, as I will argue, are central to understanding social impact, how should we understand stakeholders? Chapter 5 will cover the difficulties of identifying stakeholders and will also confront very practical issues which are rarely covered in the CSR world, such as what engagement with staff means in the context of active union representation. While not providing a manual of stakeholder consultation, this chapter will discuss a range of techniques which have been used to 'engage' stakeholders – and how and why they may be beneficial or inappropriate in practice. Stakeholder identification and engagement is central to almost all techniques of social impact assessment and measurement.

Chapters 5 to 13 describe a variety of techniques for assessing social impact. The advantages and disadvantages of each are set out and also the contribution each can make to understanding sustainability, together with suitable examples. One feature of most of the techniques described is that they have been used exclusively for one kind of organization. Social Return on Investment (SROI), for example, which is covered in Chapter 10, has been used largely for the social enterprise sector, rather than for private companies. Others are used mainly by the private sector. One of the purposes of the book is to demonstrate how all of them can be useful to measure the impact of private enterprise.

This range of techniques falls into three main approaches:

- stakeholder-centred techniques to measure social impact, focusing on the subjective experience of stakeholders;
- direct measurements of social impacts;
- economic measures of social impacts.

At one level this book is a collection and explanation of a set of techniques for measuring social impact. Running through the descriptions of most of these techniques is the issue of the role of the stakeholder and the tension between objective measures of impact and its subjective nature. Stakeholders are important not only because the social impact of a company *is* its impact on stakeholders, but also because stakeholders themselves have a voice and can tell their story. Without this story, any account of social impact will be incomplete. Therefore one of the techniques, 'narrative analysis' or looking at stories, is different from the others in that it is the main technique that has a primary focus on what stakeholders themselves have to say. This is explored in Chapter 6.

Chapter 7 addresses the history of social impact assessment and 'social capital', a concept which has been historically applied mainly to local communities and is concerned with the nature of the interconnections between individuals within society. The history and application of the concept will be discussed prior to exploring how the concept of social capital can be applied to companies.

Chapter 8 discusses the nature of indicators and which indicators have in practice been used to measure various aspects of social impact. Chapter 9 covers the reporting of social impact. It addresses the usefulness of the Global Reporting Initiative (GRI) in identifying social impact measures. The GRI is an important reference point as it represents the largest exercise to date to arrive at consensus over social measurement. This chapter also analyses a typical example of reporting on social issues.

Chapter 10 addresses a concrete example of a social measurement technique. SROI attempts to measure social impact in financial terms. The measurement of SROI will be discussed in detail, including its history, the pitfalls of finding data and the appropriateness of its calculations.

Economic impacts are also social impacts. There are some examples of companies trying to understand their overall economic impact, beyond shareholder returns. Chapter 11 describes these together with a particularly practical tool for capturing corporate economic impact.

Is there one measure which somehow captures the overall social impact of an organization? Chapter 12 explores the possibilities of a social footprint on the analogy of the ecological footprint. A number of attempts to produce a social footprint measure are discussed and Chapter 12 will present an additional one. However, while the goal of a single measure which somehow captures all aspects of social impact in one measure looks possible, it is probably doomed to be unsatisfying. Nevertheless, the discussion raises crucial issues for understanding the social aspects of sustainability in a coherent way.

Chapter 13 reviews the approach and relevance of financial accounting techniques to the measurement of social impact. Companies enjoy a fairly complete framework for measuring financial impacts, encompassing capital and revenue accounting. This chapter explores how far this model can be applied to the social aspects of sustainability accounting. The discussion draws on the various techniques which have been covered in earlier chapters showing how they might fit into such a framework.

The conclusion, Chapter 14, draws the threads of analysis and discussion together. It describes the relative merits and problems of each main approach to assessing corporate impacts.

Finally, a note on what this book is *not*. This book is not about the impact of the discipline or practice of corporate responsibility or even of corporate social responsibility. CSR has led companies to address some of their impacts, including social ones (although ironically the specifically social impacts are the least well addressed by companies' CSR). There will therefore be many references to CSR throughout the book. But the various impacts which happen to be addressed by companies when they 'do' CSR, must not be taken to delimit the boundaries of their actual social impact. Of course, the impact of what companies do in addressing their responsibilities under the name of CSR (or CR) is an interesting question, see (Blowfield and Murray, 2008) for example. But it is a far narrower issue than the impact of companies on society. And it is not the subject of this book.

TERMINOLOGY

Much of the discussion in this book uses the work 'impact'. For some, this word carries negative associations. For these people, a word such as 'effect' would be more neutral. While it is true that the word 'impact' implies 'hitting' or the active assertion of a result, it is not inherently negative. To imply that all impacts are in some way negative is simply wrong. For clarity, then, impacts can be positive (such as the provision of needed goods or services) or negative (such as obesity or pollution).

The word 'issue', as used in the phrase 'social issue' refers to a set of outcomes in society of some kind, such as obesity. Clearly, not all social issues are the result of corporate activity, although a good proportion are exactly that.

2

The Social Purpose of Companies

Where do you start to look to measure the social impact of a company? To measure the impact of a company, it is very helpful to know what it is 'for' and what it is trying to do. A company's declared purpose is unlikely to exhaust the range of its impacts, but if companies have a social purpose, then it could be expected that at least that part of their impact which relates to their purpose will be clearly identifiable, if not easily measurable, since it will be clearly related to its core business. That of course still leaves the question of how far the social impact of a company extends beyond its core business.

A large telecommunications company, with a long history of concern over its impact, both environmental and social, had a history of giving to social causes. One day it was asked to contribute financially to a project to save endangered whales. The manager involved was taken aback: in his view, while whales were obviously a deserving cause, what had whales to do with telephones? The purpose of the company was to provide telephone services. The company also gave money to good causes, but this request seemed particularly far from the 'real' purpose of the company. Wouldn't a company with some connection to the sea, perhaps, be a more suitable donor? Or did the fact that the company had a large amount of money qualify it as a suitable saviour of the whale? Should the whales have got the money? Or what *are* companies for?

This chapter will address the following series of issues:

- Are companies simply there to make money? Or do they have some other, social, purpose?
- If the purpose of companies is to address social needs, then what are 'social needs'? And how can they be distinguished from 'mere wants'?
- The public sector and civil society appear to have a clear social purpose. How do companies relate to those sectors – and to society in general? The relationship of companies to these other sectors throws light on the purpose of companies.

- Companies have social impacts quite outside their acknowledged purpose. If it is supposed that a given company is not 'responsible' for the entirety of the outcomes to which their activities contribute, because they do not act alone, what is the boundary of their responsibility?

Before addressing these matters, it will be useful to gain some historical perspective on how the social purpose of companies has been handled in the past – and companies have a past at least 1,000 years old. After addressing them it will be useful to describe the formally different types of companies which are available and in common use today.

A BRIEF HISTORY OF COMPANIES

Over 1,000 years ago, in the seventh and eighth centuries in England, the dominant power outside the kings and their lords was the church. The oral rules of inheritance worked well enough for the king and for identifiable families, but it was not at all clear how it applied to the monasteries. A particular abbot and his monks came and went, but they wanted the monastery to survive beyond them. The solution was a charter document proclaiming the rights which the monastery should enjoy indefinitely. The first charters given to institutions were designed to provide more secure rights to the church than the contemporary legal system could provide. Trade guilds, schools and other social institutions all faced the same problem of longevity (or its lack) and all found a similar legal solution which effectively granted them immortality.

The process of applying for a charter was expensive and difficult, requiring at first an approach to the monarch, although this was subsequently changed to involve 'only' parliament, rather than the monarchy. Nevertheless, there were just a few dozen charters in active use by the end of the seventeenth century (Ireland, 1996). The main sorts of enterprise which were chartered were railways, canals and bridges – those largely responsible for what is now regarded as part of the public infrastructure. At this stage, charters conferred limited liability, but only in return for a social dividend which could be delivered by the company's profit seeking activity.

The chartered company perhaps reached its zenith with the East India Company. This was incorporated in 1600 and granted a monopoly in all trade between England and 'the lands beyond the Cape of Good Hope' (Robins, 2006, p27). However the East India Company was granted its charter for only 20 years at a time and provided it was adequately serving the public interest. Serving the public interest in this case meant particularly taking full advantage of the economic possibilities which its monopoly enabled.

Along with the monopoly went a number of astonishingly wide powers. These included the civil administration of India (including the territory of the modern states of Pakistan and Bangladesh as well as modern India), the right to mint coins in India, the administration of justice and the right to wage war. The East India Company did all of these things in its pursuit of profit.

What is interesting – and unusual – about the East India Company was not that it was required to align the private interests of its shareholders with the state, but that it was permitted to *be* the state in India. It may have been only in order to underpin its profitability and it may have been undertaken in a ruthless and cruel way, but the purpose of the company was not achievable without assuming some of the functions of the state; that is, having a social function.

Until the nineteenth century, it remained difficult to form companies. The series of Companies Acts throughout the nineteenth and twentieth centuries dramatically changed this, making it much easier to form a company, particularly by requiring only registration with a public body to form a company and by removing the need to perform a public good. This may have been helped by the rising acceptance of the belief that all economic activity was socially beneficial. The majority of the companies which were publicly traded during the nineteenth century were involved with the same services such as the railways, utilities and others, which had once enjoyed charters.

The establishment of legal personality, which is crucial not only from a company perspective in order to hold property but also in order to hold them to account morally (Henriques, 2007) was also accomplished by the series of Companies Acts throughout the nineteenth and twentieth centuries. It was aided by the rise of share trading which ensured that there was a difference between a company and its members, who could trade their rights in the company (Ireland, 1996).

In summary, companies today, in most parts of the world, enjoy three things: limited liability, property rights and immortality. Limited liability enables the shareholder to limit their risk to the value of their investment. The law provides that companies themselves may own property and enjoy whatever rights any individual can have in their property. But it is immortality which takes companies beyond the powers of ordinary individuals. Companies, while they can be closed down, need never die. They can survive not only their management and staff, but also their shareholders. Perhaps more significant than any of these positive benefits of forming a company is the lack of a need to have a social objective of any kind. Under recent UK legislation it is not even necessary to state a purpose at all.

This is an attractive proposition. There may be some 200 million companies in the world today. If, as corporate citizens, they formed a state, it would be roughly the size of Brazil, the sixth most populous nation in the world. At the same time, the functions directly performed by (actual) states are being reduced in many parts of the world. Services such as the railways, utilities and others, which in the twentieth century were usually seen as natural functions of the state, are now routinely contracted out to private companies. Whatever your view of the wisdom or justice of this, it presumes that the companies that take on these social functions have a social purpose. Yet this can easily come to be in direct conflict with the nature of the modern company, which is entirely controlled by the shareholder. In the great majority of cases, any wider social purpose a company may have is ancillary to the shareholders' prime purpose of commercial gain. This is consistent with the European Commission's definition of corporate responsibility as an essentially voluntary activity (EC, 2001, p6).

The problems with this arrangement have not gone entirely unnoticed by governments, however. One of the remedies is regulation. The general purpose of regulation is to ensure that the activities regulated are conducted in a manner that is helpful to society, rather than operating against general social interests. Unfortunately, for the purposes of much regulation today, the interests of society are interpreted in almost purely economic terms. The function of regulators, in other words, is to ensure that the market is operating as well as possible and that no actors are in a position to abuse it. The remit of the UK Competition Commission is a prime example. Recent legislation has removed its requirement to take the wider public interest into account and ensures its focus is exclusively concerned with economic competition (CC, 2009).

In some cases the social function of regulators is also acknowledged. The regulation of water utilities provides an example: OFWAT, the UK water regulator, describes itself as an 'economic regulator' yet it also 'approves companies' codes of practice to help them deliver a better service, for example, to customers who need special services or customers who are in debt' (OFWAT, 2008).

So the history of companies has come full circle. The earliest companies were required to have a social purpose in order to enjoy the advantages of incorporation. The nineteenth and twentieth centuries saw the rise of very large numbers of companies devoted only to their own ends. By the beginning of the twenty-first century, however, some companies had come to take over state functions, and while largely under the control of shareholders, were also under constraints as a result of regulation.

WHAT ARE COMPANIES FOR?

The large pharmaceutical company Roche has written that 'We perform an essential function in society, from which we obtain our licence to operate' (Roche, 2007, p60). Yet if you ask most people what companies are for, the usual, cynical, answer is that they are simply there to make money – nothing more, nor anything less. And if we want companies to do anything else, we should just get over it.

Clearly there is a contrary point of view which Geoffrey Chandler has expressed eloquently: 'If we are to preserve the most effective mechanism the world has known for the provision of goods and services – that is the market economy with the public limited company its main instrument – then it has to be underpinned by principle. Financial failure can destroy individual companies. Moral failure will destroy capitalism' (Chandler, 2002).

Of course most, if not all, companies are indeed concerned with making money. But this response begs a series of important questions as to what it means to say that a company has a purpose at all, or if the purpose in question is not that of the company, then exactly whose is it? And when it comes to impacts, how far can you go in claiming responsibility? In other words, what is the boundary of responsibility of a company?

Now there are of course companies set up deliberately with a non-financial purpose. These companies have an explicit social or environmental purpose, but they also have financial constraints. In other words, they must not lose money indefinitely while meeting their non-financial objectives. This is the reverse of 'ordinary' companies, which usually see themselves as having financial objectives together with social and environmental constraints. But what is the difference between avoiding a constraint and having an objective? It is possible to see all companies as having social and environmental objectives together with financial constraints – it is only a matter of perspective.

Anyone who has tried to work out a strategy for a company will have run across this issue. Is the strategic objective of a manufacturing company, for example, just about making money – or is it about making products – things which society, hopefully, may need? If your answer to this question is 'money', then you can go no further with the strategy. From that premise alone, you will have no idea *how* the money is to be made. You may come to the conclusion that the best thing to do is to strip the assets and sell the company for as much as possible, because you will have no idea how to develop the business or its products. So there is clearly something wrong with having money *alone* as a strategic objective even from a business perspective. Conversely, it is entirely possible to position making money as a constraint. Nevertheless, financial appraisals of product strategy are obviously still a good idea.

At one level this is about ends and means. Companies make money *as a result* of selling products which they produce. But there is also an almost psychological question at stake. Even if your idea of the purpose of a company is that it is solely to make money, should you concentrate on that end alone you will take your eye off the practical ball of actual production – which is what in fact leads to making money. There is a parallel with happiness: notwithstanding the American Declaration of Independence, the pursuit of happiness can only be approached indirectly through the pursuit of something else.

Nevertheless, the view of orthodox economics is that the financial interest of shareholders is – and should be – pre-eminent, as Milton Friedman has forcefully argued:

> *Businessmen believe that they are defending free enterprise when they declaim that business is not concerned 'merely' with profit but also with promoting desirable 'social' ends; that business has a 'social conscience' and takes seriously its responsibilities for providing employment, eliminating discrimination, avoiding pollution and whatever else may be the catchwords of the contemporary crop of reformers. In fact they are — or would be if they or anyone else took them seriously – preaching pure and unadulterated socialism. Businessmen who talk this way are unwitting puppets of the intellectual forces that have been undermining the basis of a free society these past decades ... In a free-enterprise, private-property system,*

a corporate executive is an employee of the owners of the business. He has direct responsibility to his employers. That responsibility is to conduct the business in accordance with their desires, which generally will be to make as much money as possible. (Friedman, 2007)

Friedman's view seems to assume, rather oddly, that 'social ends' have nothing to do with a company's core business, but derive entirely from socialism. Apart from the political jibe, this is to take for granted that the social needs which a company's products may fulfil can be measured entirely by the economic demand for its products.

This view, which has many adherents, and which is at the heart of traditional economics, has also actually made a subtle shift from considering the purpose of a business to that of the purposes of its shareholders. In fact Friedman considered that 'the business' was only an artificial construct: 'What does it mean to say that "business" has responsibilities? Only people can have responsibilities. A corporation is an artificial person and in this sense may have artificial responsibilities, but "business" as a whole cannot be said to have responsibilities, even in this vague sense' (Friedman, 2007). Of course it simply does not follow that because businesses are artificial persons that therefore their responsibilities are artificial. Those responsibilities are quite real, as any court will affirm. As I have argued in some detail elsewhere (Henriques, 2007), the view that companies don't really exist is not consistent with common usage and is not ultimately tenable. Furthermore, Friedman himself goes on to acknowledge that businessmen should '[conform] to the basic rules of the society, both those embodied in law and those embodied in ethical custom' (Friedman, 2007) in running their business.

From the perspective of society, companies may therefore be said to have a functional purpose which concerns delivering goods and services. From the perspective of shareholders, the reason (purpose) to invest in companies will usually be to make money. Yet unless companies fulfil their social purpose then shareholders' main motivation will not be satisfied. Notwithstanding Milton Friedman, it is also possible to argue that companies *themselves* may have a reason to act in the way that they do. This 'reason' does not have to be the same as that of their shareholders. Of course, typically, shareholders are indeed the dominant stakeholder and often have the power to impose their will on their company. But it is, firstly, possible to establish companies that have a different purpose. Secondly, even companies whose ostensible purpose is simply to make money may be 'captured' by different stakeholder groups, such as senior management. This may distort or fundamentally alter the purpose of the company.

But do companies, in fact, produce what is needed? Or only what they can sell? These questions throw into relief some basic questions about the way the world economy works. In particular, how can humanity's colossal productive capacity be reconciled with the vast needs of so many people on earth? This is clearly a fundamental requirement of any stable global society.

WHAT ARE 'SOCIAL NEEDS'?

This section addresses the extent of the ethical content of goods and the nature of the needs that goods may be designed to satisfy. It is also necessary to think about the nature of desire itself – is it based on real need or 'mere wants'? Finally, even if companies are capable of delivering what is needed, are they actually the best way of doing that?

Are all goods good?

The Body Shop is often held up as a good company. It is true that from the late 1980s the Body Shop definitely pioneered a committed and ethical approach to doing business, starting from the position that it was not necessary to test its products on animals. As a result of efforts by its founder, Anita Roddick, it not only built up a global business, it has also changed the parameters of what is regarded as a possible business model. As a result of the Body Shop, the organic and fair-trade movements and other ethical businesses such as the Co-Operative Group, it is now credible to mainstream investors to invest in businesses which are designed to operate with concern for their stakeholders and the environment. So credible that the Body Shop was sold to L'Oreal, the world's largest cosmetics company, in 2006.

But the Body Shop produces cosmetics. Are cosmetics a good thing? There is clearly an extremely large demand for them – estimated at some US$180 billion (Euromonitor, 2004) – but does that make them a good thing? From some perspectives, especially in the face of the obvious need for basic items such as food in many parts of the world, cosmetics are unnecessary. Yet this view seems to come from a very ascetic and puritanical approach, particularly since there would appear to be relatively little contention for resources between these two sectors.

Or consider powdered baby milk, such as produced by Nestlé. This seems obviously a good thing; few people are against feeding babies. And of course some women find it hard to breastfeed their children. There is, however, overwhelming evidence that breast milk is far better for babies, especially very young ones (UNICEF, 2008). As a result, and because of the dominance of Nestlé in this market and its marketing practices, there has been a very long-running campaign against Nestlé (BabyMilkAction, 2008) by NGOs, despite Nestlé's protestations of good practice.

Finally, what about basic commodities like steel? Tata Steel of India is the world's fifth biggest steelmaker. Steel is used for everything from constructing new buildings to making knives and forks. But of course it is also used for weapons and arms manufacture – though not by Tata Steel itself. Is steel a good good, or is it somehow tainted by some of the uses to which it can be put?

The main lesson from these examples is that it is not possible to judge the ethical nature of a product from its nature alone. Things which seem useful can be put to questionable uses and the context in which apparently harmless goods are used can make them seem undesirable. While this may seem obvious, there is a strong tendency for companies to presume that unless their product is inherently unsustainable, then it is entirely without moral challenge. This is untrue.

How much is enough?

The unsustainability of the world economic system on environmental grounds is clear: the ecological conditions are simply not there to continue to supply indefinitely the services which the world economy requires – whether it is for energy, waste absorption or the simple availability of raw materials. Indeed they could never be there, for any economy which depends on continual growth. Are there any comparable arguments in relation to social aspects of sustainability?

Suppose we assume, for a moment, that we live in utopia. If, in this utopia, there are no undesirable products and there are no questionable contexts or modes of production involved in making or using them, how much of any given utopian product should be produced? The standard response from economics runs like this: if the market for utopian products is in equilibrium, then the amount being produced is exactly what is being demanded. Furthermore, if the market for utopian goods increases – that is, there is more being produced and consumed, then even more of what is needed is being produced – and there is still no waste!

Of the many problems with this view, one issue is that it is based on the economist's assumption that in general the price of goods adequately reflects the quantity of social benefit or welfare delivered by that product. This idea that human need can be satisfactorily quantified, and furthermore captured properly in financial units, is one to which we will be returning again in the course of analysing some of the practical methods for measuring social impact. What is important is to point out here is that it is in fact, just that: an assumption.

Perhaps the critical problem with this view is that it assumes that the demand for a product is independent of influence. Of course in the real world, companies work very hard to get their customers to buy their products. Through advertising and publicity, demand that did not exist before is created. It simply does not therefore follow that an increase in sales merely reflects an increase in satisfied need. More work needs to be done before that case is proven.

Whatever the cause, the fact is that we, as consumers, do think that we 'need' ever more, and more expensive, goods and services. We get ourselves into more and more debt as a result. Are we complicit in our own destruction? Or should we be able to recognize that we have enough? One problem is that if we suggest that consumers are over-consuming, then we are not respecting their autonomy and capacity to judge for themselves what they want. Who is to say what someone else should want?

The traditional answer from Marxists to this dilemma is to say that consumers are suffering from 'false consciousness'. In other words, while they

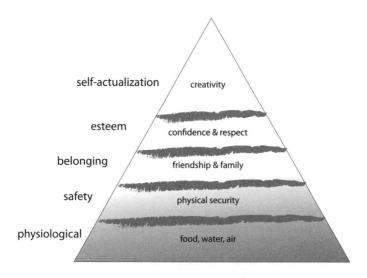

Figure 2.1 *Maslow Hierarchy*

think they know what they want, they have been deceived, and may indeed be complicit, at some level, in their own deceit. That argument is helpful if you know you have a guaranteed connection to the truth of what is *really* needed. However while it may be clear that many perceived needs are in fact generated by corporate activity and are not necessarily genuine in that sense, it is extraordinarily hard to determine what the 'real' level of need may be. There is however some help from social psychology, which we examine next.

The hierarchy of desire

A. H. Maslow, writing during the Second World War (Maslow, 1943), set out a hierarchy of needs that has been extremely influential in many fields, from assessing aid for the developing world to psychology. His basic insight was that human needs can be classified into a number of different types that can be placed in a hierarchy, as shown in Figure 2.1.

The hierarchy is such that the categories of needs – physiological, safety, love, esteem, and self-actualization – need to be satisfied from the bottom up: food and shelter come before social esteem, for example. However Maslow was at pains to point out that the overall picture can be quite complex:

> *Man is a perpetually wanting animal. Ordinarily the satisfaction of these wants is not altogether mutually exclusive, but only tends to be. The average member of our society is most often partially satisfied and partially unsatisfied in all of his wants. The hierarchy principle is usually empirically observed in terms of increasing percentages of non-satisfaction as we go up the hierarchy. Reversals*

of the average order of the hierarchy are sometimes observed. Also it has been observed that an individual may permanently lose the higher wants in the hierarchy under special conditions. There are not only ordinarily multiple motivations for usual behavior, but in addition many determinants other than motives ... Any thwarting or possibility of thwarting of these basic human goals, or danger to the defenses which protect them, or to the conditions upon which they rest, is considered to be a psychological threat. With a few exceptions, all psychopathology may be partially traced to such threats. A basically thwarted man may actually be defined as a 'sick' man, if we wish. (Maslow, 1943, p395)

While Maslow's hierarchy does provide a very useful prioritization of real needs, it does not provide a neat distinction between 'real needs' and 'artificial wants'. It also raises the question of whether the profusion of generated wants in a modern economy actually manages to thwart some of the higher needs, such as self-actualization. If we assume that happiness is the outcome of the degree to which all the needs in the hierarchy are satisfied – rather than only the material needs which modern economies can be so good at satisfying (and producing) – then it is interesting to look at measures of overall happiness over time.

Of course, traditional economics is supposed to be all about maximizing welfare, so there ought to be some connection to happiness. One of the problems with economic measures, however, is that (bad) things which cause unhappiness, but happen to make money are all counted together with those things which do improve welfare. William Nordhaus and James Tobin therefore suggested revizing the calculation of GNP to remove all the money spent on 'bads', such as removing environmental pollution or healthcare following road accidents. Their issue was whether economic growth should be curtailed because of environmental damage. Their conclusion was:

At present there is no reason to arrest economic growth to preserve natural resources, although there is good reason to provide proper economic incentives to conserve resources which currently cost their users less than their true social cost. (Nordhaus and Tobin, 1973, p532)

A further question is whether there actually had been a net gain in welfare with increasing economic growth. Herman Daly and John Cobb therefore proposed the idea of an Index of Sustainable Economic Welfare, as a replacement for GDP. The New Economics Foundation subsequently calculated this for the UK (Jackson, Marks et al., 1997) and concluded that while GDP has broadly risen since 1950, a measure which removes the 'bads' had peaked in 1976 and has subsequently declined. This is broadly confirmed by other work such as that of Richard Layard who reports that happiness levels have been broadly static for a long time (Layard, 2003) and Oliver James, who has looked more directly at happiness (James, 2007) and also finds it in decline.

It follows that companies cannot assume that their products are fulfilling a genuine social need. Marketing used to be thought of as concerned with discovering the needs of customers. But marketing is now much closer to sales. Modern marketing strategies such as those of Saatchi and Saatchi, have followed the lead of pioneers such as Edward Bernays to manipulate people through their emotions. The point is, quite explicitly, not just to satisfy demand but to create it. Saatchi and Saatchi do it with 'lovemarks':

> *Lovemarks are brands that inspire loyalty beyond reason. People love them because of what they are, not because of what they do. Their appeal is emotional. Companies may own brands. But Lovemarks are owned by the people who love them … find out what Saatchi & Saatchi knows about unlocking consumers' hearts and making them fall in love with a brand.* (Saatchi, 2008)

But it seems unlikely that lovemarks, such as Versace perhaps, are satisfying true needs for love, for example. It is salutary on a personal basis to identify our needs, review how many of our needs are actually being met and then consider how many can be met using money or economic wealth. The connection between money and happiness is tenuous. It is therefore not surprising in our economic culture, that people can buy what they don't need. Saatchi and Saatchi have been very successful. The real tragedy is that there are people who can't buy what they really do need.

An economic presumption

In the Western world, the public sector is responsible for about 40 per cent of GDP, leaving 60 per cent of economic activity to the private sector, to be delivered through companies. Over the world as a whole, the proportion available to the private sector is very likely higher, as many countries cannot support as high a level of state activity as the West.

At the same time, the level of inequality in the world is high and rising. According to the World Bank:

> *the average citizen in Luxembourg enjoys monetary resources 62 times higher than the average Nigerian. While the average Nigerian may find it difficult to afford adequately nutritious meals every day, the average citizen of Luxembourg need not worry too much about buying the latest generation cell phone on the market.* (WB, 2005, p6)

So how effective are companies in meeting social needs and closing the gap between rich and poor? First, it is important to acknowledge that the gap between rich and poor has been widening. As the Worldwatch Institute puts it, 'the global economy has grown sevenfold since 1950. Meanwhile, the disparity in per capita gross domestic product between the 20 richest and 20 poorest nations more than doubled between 1960 and 1995. Of all high-income nations, the United States has the most unequal distribution of income, with over 30 percent of income in the hands of the richest 10 percent and only 1.8 percent going to the poorest 10 percent.' (WI, 2003)

In fact globally the gap between rich and poor would be widening much more rapidly if it were not for China's impact on the numbers (Sala-i-Martin, 2002). Ironically, socialist China has managed to raise the standard of living of its population through the introduction of free markets more effectively than many other countries. In most of the world however, greater economic growth is not very effective in raising living standards for the majority of the population.

It follows that in assessing the impact of a given company it is no help to appeal to economic growth alone as the whole justification for the activities of a specific company. Any appeal to economic benefits needs to be supported by an analysis of what the specific economic outcome of the activity of a particular company has been and who has benefited from it.

COMPANIES AND SOCIETY

How do companies in practice relate to society? First we need, from a straight-forward sociological perspective, to be clear what we mean by 'society'. 'Society' is usually thought of as the people, institutions and patterns of action located within a particular territory. Institutions here include the full range of organizations – from local clubs, to companies as well as the institutions of the state. This has two crucial implications for understanding and measuring the social impact of companies. The first implication is that *companies are part of society*. The second implication is that the effects, or 'social impact' of a company is the set of impacts it has on the rest of society, including the land on which they live. This may seem obvious, but it defines the scope of corporate impact on society to include their effects on their stakeholders and on the environment.

By far the dominant way in which the relationship between companies and society is understood today is through traditional economic thought and the practice of market regulation. Both of these activities take for granted that a well-functioning market has an unquestioned place in society. Of course, if it really is 'well-functioning', then there may be some truth in that. And as we have seen, what has received attention is the extent to which companies discharge their economic role properly and efficiently. But how do we know whether this is happening?

It is a well established result of traditional economics that full efficiency is only achieved if the relevant markets are 'undistorted'. Distortions can arise from market imperfections, such as can result from monopolies, but also, and very importantly, as a result of externalities, such as the production of pollution without any recompense. Regulation, economic or social, can be a means to correct both these distortions. Yet however well an economy may be function-ing in economic terms, the relationship of markets (including companies) to society is unquestioned – and often simply not properly explored.

The basic assumption made by most writers is that the role of companies is confined to making money. And companies are good at making things which can be sold – a position blessed by traditional economics. Yet even taking this perspective, there are issues about the morality of that role and about how companies discharge it. Is it morally acceptable to make money? It is necessary to distinguish the getting of money itself from the impacts of the company operations which deliver it. If we assume that there are no negative impacts of the company, is the act of making money a moral one? A common position is that the worst of the matter is that there is a certain selfishness to focusing only on what matters to oneself – a kind of moral opportunity cost, in economists' terms.

The response is often to turn to philanthropy, which entails giving money away for the good of others. This often appears as a process of purification of the act of making money, making it 'alright'. But this is not the end of the moral difficulties. It has often been asked whether there is a justification for diverting funds from the owners of a company for non-economic philanthropic purposes. In general this is held to be permissible provided there is some benefit to the company in the longer run (Silk, 2004). (Of course this proviso serves to under-mine the perceived morality of such philanthropy.)

The approach of exploring *how* companies deliver their economic role – in particular how they treat their stakeholders – can be used to define 'CSR', as espoused by Michael Hopkins (Hopkins, 2003) amongst others. It can also be used to analyse some aspects of how companies contribute to development (Hopkins 2006). However, the bigger picture of the overall relationship of companies to society is missing from this perspective. Unfortunately, political philosophy which might also be expected to address the issue at a high level, lets us down. It is remarkable that there is almost no systematic philosophical thought on the nature and role of companies. Traditional political philosophy, from writers such as Hobbes and Rousseau, concerns the relationship of the individual to the state. The key issues were how to justify a 'social contract' which limits individuals in some ways in return for protection or enhanced welfare through cooperation. Of course Hobbes and Rousseau wrote centuries ago, well before the modern company had attained the powers it now enjoys. Yet the tradition of Hobbes and Rousseau, with its lack of attention to the role of companies, has persisted to the present day.

One set of clues as to how to approach it can be gleaned from Adam Smith, who considered the relationship of the East India Company (which as we have seen was responsible for literally running India) and the state. He wrote that:

> It is the interest of the East India Company, considered as sover-*eigns*, that the European goods which are carried to their Indian *dominions* should be sold there as cheap as possible; and the Indian goods which are brought from thence should bring there as good a

price, or should be sold there as dear as possible. But the reverse of this is their interest as merchants. As sovereigns, their interest is exactly the same with that of the country which they govern. As merchants their interest is directly opposite to that interest. (Smith, 1999b, p223)

This suggests that the relationship between companies and the state may be antagonistic, aligned, or somewhere in between. Along with Smith, radical social movements can take an 'anti-capitalist' stance, assuming that no good can come of companies. The idea that companies are fully aligned to the state is suggested by companies themselves. It may be beguiling, but if, as companies assume, their primary allegiance is to the shareholder, it is unlikely that their interests often align well to the state. The truth is likely to be in the middle.

A further set of clues can be found in the work of Antonio Gramsci, who originated the term 'civil society'.

What we can do, for the moment, is to fix two superstructural 'levels': the one that can be called 'civil society', that is the ensemble of organisms commonly called 'private', and that of 'political society', or 'the state'. (Gramsci, 1971, p12)

It is necessary to include all of the people and institutions of society in an analysis of how companies impact on them. Including civil society within society makes this more possible. However, the term 'civil society' is used in many, sometimes conflicting, ways. It can refer to institutions such as the family or communities and so encompass the entire population, but most often it is used as a shorthand for organizations, such as NGOs, that are concerned with social or environmental issues. Taking the latter usage would mean that society was composed of three key structural components:

- institutions of the state, or public institutions;
- civil society organizations;
- companies.

This use of 'civil society' is strongly related to the form of an organization (such as a registered charity) and specific legal forms of ownership. Also it does little to convey the *processes* with which public, private or civil society organizations work. As I have written elsewhere in relation to social auditing as a way of assessing the social impact of companies, it is possible to outline another perspective on civil society, which is:

that it comprises the creative matrix from which other forms of organisation may emerge. In this sense, civil society is recognised as the dynamic underpinning all social activity. From this perspective, the formal institutions of the state, or of private enterprise, are borne of civil society. They have, however, in some sense, grown beyond civil society ... what this perspective misses, however is that large NGOs may have grown beyond their civil society roots in much the same sense as their private sector 'cousins' ... I suggest that as organisations grow and develop more formal institutional structures over time, their connection to civil society, and the concerns and issues which actually face people in their day to day lives, weakens. Social auditing is a way to address this problem and to keep organisations alive to the issues with which society as a whole must work. This has benefits for the organisation as well as for society. The role of NGOs in social auditing is therefore interesting, since they are often held to 'be' civil society. While they do seem to be much closer to civil society, it is not obvious how they should therefore relate to social auditing. (Henriques, 2001)

At any rate what is central to understanding the relationship of companies to society, and therefore their social impact, is to include, but to think beyond, other organizations, as the key to understanding social impact. Any useful picture of the relationship of companies to society needs to include them as a significant third force in society, affecting political society as well as civil society. This will mean that any account of companies' social impact will need to include issues such as their tax contributions (or the lack of them) and lobbying, see (Henriques, 2007) for example.

However this picture of the social impact of companies is complicated by two major factors: the 'internationality' of companies and the use by governments of companies. In thinking about the use of companies by governments, the terminology is against us. 'Private companies' are those owned by private individuals; whereas 'public companies' are private companies whose shares are listed on stock exchanges and may be bought by members of the public. There is no appropriate and common term for companies owned by governments, that is where the state is the only (or dominant) shareholder, other than 'state-owned companies'.

One of the consequences of this situation is that the protection provided to companies, as private persons, is extended to the state – *against* which such protections were intended to operate. This can lead to abuses such as taking advantage of privacy rights and commercial confidentiality to hide information from the public. Yet far more significant is the sheer scale of some of these government-owned companies and their consequent impact. The oil companies Exxon and BP are some of the largest companies in the world, yet their turnover is dwarfed by state-owned oil companies. The Saudi Arabian national oil company, Saudi Aramco, for example, has reserves 20 times the size of those of Exxon, the largest private oil company (Euromoney, 2005).

Governments can also invest in companies in the ordinary way, through the stock markets. Some countries have established large funds to do just this – so-called 'sovereign wealth funds'. The response to the financial crisis has also led to a much more widespread state investment in the banking sector. On the one hand, private enterprise relishes the business such large funds can bring

(Willman, 2008). On the other, there are some well-founded fears over lack of transparency. There is also a feeling that governments are somehow not 'proper' shareholders and may destabilize the financial markets. One particular fear is that they will not use their shareholdings simply to maximize profits, but also for 'political' ends – where 'political' means pursuing other interests – and their national interest in particular (Guha, 2007). Yet a responsible shareholder should behave with regard to their own overall interest, not just in the narrow role of profit-seeking shareholder, as economics may require. Even in purely financial terms, it can suit people to lose money at times, for example for tax purposes.

The 'internationality' of companies means that they cannot be considered elements of one society alone. Where should large companies be considered to reside? Most large multinational companies have numerous subsidiaries in many countries in addition to the country in which the group headquarters is located. Such companies are also likely to be listed on several national stock exchanges. There may also be a large private shareholder residing in a country quite different from that of either the corporate listing or headquarters. So in which society should the company be considered to take part? The answer, of course, is 'all of them', although this can lead to conflicts when the legal requirements of different jurisdictions conflict, as has happened over banking transparency for example. At any rate, in trying to assess corporate impact, it is necessary to be inclusive and to consider the full spectrum of impacts across the various countries in which the company is active.

Business, society and CSR

One response to the questioning of the role of business in society has been Corporate Social Responsibility (CSR). Although CSR is usually seen as a phenomenon of only the last 10–15 years and of the West, it also has roots which stretch back much further and more widely. The main influence on CSR has undoubtedly been the environmental and human rights campaigns run by civil society organizations since the mid-1960s, especially in the developed world. This has resulted in sustained pressure on every issue from pollution to the uprooting of indigenous communities. Companies and their role in these issues were some of the main, though by no means the only, targets of such campaigning.

Since the early part of the twentieth century, the movement for socially responsible investment (SRI) in companies has been prominent, driven principally by concern from the organized Christian churches and more recently from Islamic sources. This means that at least one constituency within one of the most significant of company stakeholders, the shareholder, was campaigning for a change in the moral practice of companies. And in many cultures across the world, for far longer, there has been a tradition of philanthropy, whereby private actors (including commercial entities) were expected to return to society some of the gains that commerce had bestowed upon them.

Since the middle of the twentieth century, companies have also achieved far greater prominence than previously. This results from a number of factors:

- The role of the state has contracted due to the insistence on market-based responses to social needs. Many goods and services, such as utilities and social welfare, which were once delivered through the state have come to be the province of the private sector. This has in significant part resulted from privatization, some of which has been imposed upon the developing world through the development process. The collapse of communist regimes has also been a factor.
- Overall, the corporate sector has grown steadily since World War II. Individual transnational companies from all continents have achieved a scale such that some of them are more significant economic actors than some states. The nature and operation of modern transnational companies now routinely spans national borders, making national legal systems and traditional, community systems less significant.
- The development of new information and communications technologies (ICT), especially the internet, has meant both that news of the activities of companies can be communicated far faster and more effectively than previously and also that civil society organizations can organize themselves more effectively across the world, wherever they are based.

This combination of traditions of moral concern together with the vastly greater significance of companies in most of the world has led to a questioning of the role of business in society. This is not only a large topic, but a cause of continuing debate. The debate over what CSR 'really' means is one of the main expressions of this questioning. As a result, CSR today is not only a source of vigorous innovation but also a practice with no universally agreed definition – or even label. Nevertheless, the international standards organization, ISO, is working towards a standard on organizational responsibility (of which CSR is the subset applicable to companies) that may capture a broad consensus. The draft ISO definition (ISO, 2008) is:

> *the responsibility of an organization for the impacts of its decisions and activities on society and the environment, through transparent and ethical behaviour that:*
> - *contributes to sustainable development, health and the welfare of society;*
> - *takes into account the expectations of stakeholders;*
> - *is in compliance with applicable law and consistent with international norms of behaviour; and*
> - *is integrated throughout the organization and practiced in its relationships.*

On the positive side, CSR has led to a growing awareness of social and environmental problems within the corporate community as well as society at large and an acceptance that companies have a significant role to play in the solution of many of them. It has also led to changes and innovation both in business practices as well as in the relationships between companies and many stakeholders, especially civil society organizations. Finally, CSR has led to some improvement in non-financial company performance, particularly in relation to environmental issues.

However, CSR can also have less fortunate outcomes. CSR has been criticized for leading companies to make aspirational commitments to change, without a willingness to declare their progress towards that change. More generally, the charge is that companies focus entirely on the positive reputation which association with CSR may bring. Another issue is that companies can be reluctant to look at the responsibilities of their core business, rather than at the more tractable issues of philanthropy and community investment.

CSR in practice

CSR concerns how a company operates, as well as its philanthropic projects. CSR in practice involves a variety of different activities by companies, typically including:

- addressing major concerns such as climate change, labour conditions in the supply chain and the abuse of human rights;
- engagement with stakeholders over their concerns;
- public reporting on such activities;
- philanthropy.

In addition, a great variety of codes of ethics, behaviour, standards of performance and practical initiatives have been developed, each designed to improve business impact. Worldwide there are perhaps thousands of them although a smaller number have achieved real prominence (Leipziger, 2003). It is not uncommon for a single business to commit to dozens of such codes and standards. There is a great variety in the nature and scope of such codes; some are devoted to a single issue or the impacts of a specific sector, others span the entire spectrum of corporate responsibilities. Many derive their authority from international instruments, particularly the conventions on human and labour rights.

Some of these initiatives have been produced by civil society organizations and others by companies themselves or their trade associations. In addition, some have had international backing. The best known of these is probably the Global Compact (GC, 2008), an initiative of the UN Secretary-General's office. The OECD Guidelines for Multinational Enterprises (OECD, 2000) has also been very significant.

Although ethical codes for companies can sometimes be difficult for smaller companies to use, they do have an important role in setting standards on an international level. This can be particularly important for multinational companies where national laws differ as to the standards of behaviour they require or are enforced in a variable and limited way.

There are a number of overlapping and intrinsically difficult issues which go to the heart of the relationship of business to society. The first such issue concerns the place of legal obligations relative to voluntary commitments within CSR. While most companies, and the European Commission, see CSR as concerned only with voluntary activity, civil society organizations point out that compliance with the law, and support of it, is an obvious foundation for any responsible behaviour. It is also typically expected that a company will implement the highest standard required by law in any of its territories of operation in *all* its operations. The attitude of companies towards their legal obligations and those of their stakeholders is therefore important. In this connection it is significant that there is no legal obligation placed *directly* on companies by the apparatus of international law, including human rights, as the Special Representative of the UN Secretary-General on the issue of human rights and transnational corpor-ations and other business enterprises has concluded (Ruggie, 2008).

Nevertheless, the actions of companies can greatly affect the chances of others' enjoyment of their rights. In relation to the legal risks of complicity, the International Commission of Jurists, the widely respected international human rights NGO whose members include senior figures in the judiciary of several jurisdictions, advises that 'a company would be wise to avoid any conduct that enables, exacerbates or facilitates gross human rights abuses committed by others. A company should avoid not only situations where the gross human rights abuse would not occur in the absence of its involvement, but also where its conduct aggravates the situation by causing a wider range of abuses to be committed by the principal actor or increasing the harm suffered, as well as situations where its contribution changes the way the human rights abuses are carried out, including the methods used, the timing and the efficiency.' (ICJ, 2008)

Whatever their view on the extent of CSR beyond voluntary activity, all companies take compliance with the law seriously. In practice the chief differentiator between companies in relation to CSR and the law concerns where the boundary of moral responsibility is seen to lie. For some, compliance with the law is taken to guarantee social responsibility and any additional proactive initiatives, which may be extensive, are seen through the lens of philanthropy. For others, it is readily admitted that responsibility concerns how core business functions are exercised. In these cases, working with stakeholders to address relevant social issues through modifying business practice is regarded as extending their 'licence to operate' and may also be a source of innovation.

The second issue concerns the role of the business case for good social performance or CSR. While there is no single proof that good social performance is automatically good for financial returns, there is strong support for much good social performance from a business perspective. However the test is what happens when there is no apparent business case for taking responsibility for corporate impacts while there is at the same time a strong moral case for doing so – such as seeking out and removing child labour from a supply chain. This dilemma goes to the heart of the role of business in society. It has not yet been resolved.

Companies and development

What is development and what is the role of companies in producing it? Although very widely used, the term 'development' is not well understood. It is perhaps best grasped through considering its lack. An extreme lack of development implies:

- impoverished lives;
- the absence of money and opportunity;
- the presence of illness and early death.

The Millennium Development Goals (MDGs) (UN, 2008) (see also Chapter 4) encapsulate the practical goals which, by global consensus, development should achieve. As the framework for the MDGs makes clear, the MDGs apply to all parts of the world. It is important to realize that in some respects, therefore, a lack of development is present in the West as much as in the South – that is, the so-called 'undeveloped world'.

> In 2006, 17.4 percent of children in America lived below the poverty line, substantially more than in 1969. And even this measure probably understates the true depth of many children's misery. Living in or near poverty has always been a form of exile, of being cut off from the larger society. But the distance between the poor and the rest of us is much greater than it was 40 years ago, because most American incomes have risen in real terms while the official poverty line has not. To be poor in America today, even more than in the past, is to be an outcast in your own country. (Krugman, 2008)

It follows that development is not the same thing as just reproducing Western patterns of affluence and economic activity in the rest of the world. But the question remains as to what development itself actually is, and what is the role of companies in addressing it. There is no clear, universally accepted definition of what development is. There are, however, three different models, which, together with their implications for companies, are described below. The first conception of development is the simplest: development as money. Here, development is simply the presence of sufficient money. On this conception, development can be directly measured by the level of GDP or GDP per head of population and is the automatic result of this kind of 'quantitative financial easing'. Economic growth, seen as simply an increase in GDP, is another way to think about this understanding of development.

On this measure, the USA will come out amongst the top performers, as its GDP per head is so high. But as we have seen there are large pockets of poverty and lack of development present in the USA. So a key problem with this approach to development is the distribution of resources within economies.

The immediate task of companies on this model is simply to exist and to increase their turnover, which will go to increasing GDP and therefore to promoting development. Yet, of course, if the distribution of wealth is also a problem, then that task is not quite so simple: a finer-grained understanding of corporate impact is needed. How much of a company's spending, for example, is actually linked to the local economy? How much do they simply use a location as a base of operations, but not consider it as somewhere that it is important to nourish? There are ways to measure this local economic impact (discussed in Chapters 10 and 11) which is a part of the social impact of a company.

The second conception of development sees it still as primarily economic, but the quality as well as the quantity of the economic activity is also important. This is also development as growth, but where growth is understood to include the increasing differentiation and sophistication of the economy. In its simplest terms, an economy in which there is a robust industrial sector in addition to an agricultural sector, for example, is one which is more developed than one which only has an agricultural sector.

On this understanding of development, the mere presence of a company and its attendant economic activity is not sufficient to deliver development. The presence of some companies will be more important to development than others. Which kinds of company are most needed will be determined by local economic conditions. Further, to maximize their development contribution, activities such as transferring skills and knowledge will be important. This can be less comfortable for the corporate world, but still entirely possible. Roche, for example has worked in this way in transferring HIV technologies to 'less developed countries' (Roche, 2006).

Unfortunately, all growth-based conceptions of development lead to an ethical dilemma. This centres on the question as to whether making money is good or bad. If making money is good, then development based on that premise will be good – the more the better. Yet at the same time, one of the most common understandings of CSR is that while a company's primary duty is to make money, companies also have an ethical duty to 'give something back' to society. This suggests that they have taken something away from society in the first place; so perhaps making money is not so good after all. The conflict concerns which ethical duty, to shareholders or to society, companies should follow.

The resolution of this dilemma has appeared to be the win-win business case. Where both shareholders and stakeholders benefit, everyone can be satisfied. The most prominent example of this is the 'bottom of the pyramid' approach (Prahalad and Hart, 2001), in which the poor are regarded, apparently without any irony, as a great untapped source of wealth from servicing which companies can grow rich. While CSR can be seen as the enabler of this approach (see Hopkins, 2006 for example), the problem comes when there is no business case, or only one for activity which impoverishes people.

The third understanding of development sees development as freedom. As the economics Nobel laureate Amartya Sen has pointed out (Sen, 2001), economic wealth is simply a means to a greater end. That greater end is not simply bank accounts with larger balances in them, but the freedom to enjoy a richer life. And it requires seeing people as active agents, rather than passive recipients or 'patients'.

> *In terms of the medieval distinction between 'the patient' and 'the agent', this freedom-centered understanding of economics and of the process of development is very much an agent-oriented view. With adequate social opportunities, individuals can effectively shape their own destiny and help each other. They need not be seen primarily as passive recipients of the benefits of cunning development programs. There is indeed a strong rationale for recognizing the positive role of free and sustainable agency – and even of constructive impatience.* (Sen, 2001, p11)

Sen argues that some of the most important freedoms constituting development are:

- political freedoms;
- economic facilities;
- social opportunities;
- transparency guarantees;
- protective security.

This understanding of development may at first actually come as something of a relief to companies. After all, it does not imply that there is an ethical imperative for companies to do things which typically lose them money, such as giving it away. But if they are excused from charitable donations and development gain considerations, the real task set them is actually much more demanding.

Of course, economic facilities are things which companies are good at providing: companies therefore must have a place in delivering development, provided their positive effects do actually reach those who are suffering. On the other hand, there may seem to be little role for companies in enabling political freedom, social opportunities and protective security. And in these areas, companies may have a secondary role to states, but that does not mean they need pay them no attention. A critical responsibility is to ensure that their actions do not impair the realization of these freedoms. In other words, it is vital to ensure that they are not complicit in the obstruction of development through economic actions which support or assume a lack of development. This can happen in states in which there is corruption and where the individuals in government do not have the public welfare at heart. For example, companies may encourage that modern written law with its well-developed protection of property rights be used to override traditional land ownership patterns. More positively, the considerable lobbying powers of companies could be used not to promote the success of one political party over another, but in the promotion of public welfare in many forms.

Corruption also calls for transparency; companies have a critical role to play in overcoming bribery and corruption. But 'transparency guarantees' also has a broader meaning, dealing with 'the need for openness that people can expect: the freedom to deal with one another under guarantees of disclosure and lucidity. When that trust is seriously violated, the lives of many people – both direct parties and third parties – may be adversely affected by the lack of openness. Transparency guarantees (including the right to disclosure) can thus be an important category of instrumental freedom' (Sen, 2001, p40).

Overall, what the concept of development as freedom requires of companies is respect for their stakeholders. This needs to be manifested in many different ways: greater openness to stakeholders does not only mean telling them what is going on and how their lives may be affected, it also means listening to what they want and need and working towards that end.

THE LIMITS OF RESPONSIBILITY

For most companies which have determined to take some responsibility for their social impacts, the practicalities can seem overwhelming. There are many challenges related to techniques of measurement. These will be addressed in later chapters. But there is also a crucial issue as to the boundary of corporate responsibility. For example BT, the UK telecommunications company, provides telephones to a large proportion of the public. That means that almost everyone in the UK is a stakeholder. But what about how their telephones are used – is BT in some way responsible for all the business and other activities that get done over their communications infrastructure? That might seem absurd, but the concerns (AI, 2006) over human rights abuses which the services software and hardware provided by Google, Microsoft and Cisco have facilitated in China suggest otherwise.

The issue concerns the concepts of control, 'sphere of influence' and the associated idea of complicity. There is clearly a spectrum of levels of responsibility for the impacts of the many different actions of companies. For direct impacts, such as the way in which employees are treated, the level of responsibility is obviously high, since such behaviour is under the immediate control of the company. Yet there are many cases in which, while a company may have partial or no control, there would appear to be definite influence. The activities of subsidiaries, joint ventures and agents provide one set of examples. Corporate influence over states, which do have direct responsibility for the implementation of human rights, provides another. One difficulty is where to draw the line between control and influence. Another is how to distinguish between situations of influence in which it should be expected that companies take action to reduce harm and those in which that expectation is unreasonable because corporate influence, though present, is so limited.

In determining the overall social impact of a company, it is therefore important to understand what the limits to its responsibility should be. One temptation is to try to determine a generic boundary which may be applicable to a group of companies – an industry sector for example. This can be very helpful in some respects, particularly in confirming what the principal issues facing all the members of that group of companies may be. The development of the GRI sector supplements (GRI, 2008b) for the automotive, logistics and telecommunications sectors amongst others work in this way. What this approach does not do, however, is to provide anything like a definitive list of issues for a specific company. So the practical problem of scope, and its limits, remains.

Being direct and intentional

It is very helpful, firstly, to separate what companies do deliberately and intentionally from what they do unintentionally. Things done unintentionally are not necessarily less important or of a lesser impact, but they may well need to be addressed in a different way. For example, construction companies set out to build buildings with specific environmental qualities, such as outside wall thermal insulation; this is an intentional result. The same company may be working in a quiet neighbourhood but have no regard for the fact that people don't like to be woken up at 6am when it is not necessary. The fact that people are woken up may not be intentional, but it is still a direct consequence of the company's activities. It is also reasonable to expect them to take responsibility for the fact that they have woken people up.

A much more serious unintentional consequence is provided by tobacco companies. While the production of cigarettes is a deliberate act on the part of these companies, the fact that their products also hasten illness and death is also one of the consequences of their activities. However, it is possible to argue that tobacco companies do not actually deliberately set out to cause ill health – that is, it is not intentional. In this case, in the current climate of knowledge, it does not appear remotely legitimate to deny responsibility for such ill health. The important point for measuring impact is that it does not matter whether or not the impact in question was caused intentionally or not.

Secondly, a distinction is also often made between the direct and indirect impacts of a company's activities. This distinction is similar to and overlaps with, but is not the same as, that between intentional and unintentional. Companies have direct impacts arising from the activities which their staff themselves directly control. Examples include the amount of fuel they purchase, perhaps to heat their offices or to power some industrial manufacturing process. The consequent CO_2 emissions are part of their direct impacts. Companies will usually also have indirect impacts. These arise from the activities which they commission or engender, but which are not directly controlled by the company. An example would be the healthy or harmful impacts of a toy, which may provide a learning opportunity for a child – or may be covered in toxic paint or depend for its production on very poor conditions for workers in the company's supply chain. Again, there is no reason in principle why a company should not be thought responsible for its indirect impacts. However

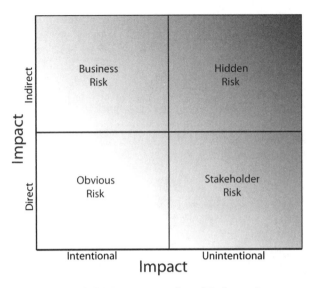

Figure 2.2 *Unintentional and Indirect Impacts*

the more indirect a company's impacts, the less it is likely to be solely responsible for the impacts in question. There are always questions of degree here (see Figure 2.2).

Reporting boundaries

In determining what companies should report on in relation to sustainability, the GRI has a useful approach. The issue for the GRI was which parts of the complex of companies (or entities) with which a reporting organization might deal should be included in its report – and thus for which it was acknowledging some responsibility. Such entities could include subsidiaries, joint venture partners and suppliers and distributors. The GRI protocol is phrased in terms of control, influence and significant impact. As illustrated in the diagram below, an organizational impact need not be reported if it is not significant. If it is significant, however, then the impacts of the entity should be reported by the reporting organization provided they are under the control or influence of the organization.

Control is defined as 'the power to govern the financial and operating policies of an enterprise so as to obtain benefits from its activities' (GRI, 2005, p9); this is intended to include the same entities as would be included by IFRS (international financial reporting standards) guidelines where the reporting organization has at least 50 per cent ownership, thus aligning financial and non-financial reporting to some extent. 'Significant influence' is defined as 'the power to participate in the financial and operating policy decisions of the entity' (GRI, 2005, p10) without controlling them (see Figure 2.3). This includes firstly those cases consistent with IFRS, where the reporting organization has

Source: GRI (2005)

Figure 2.3 *GRI Boundary Protocol*

between 20 per cent and 50 per cent control of the entity. Importantly, it also includes situations such as contractual requirements on the entity relating to sustainability impacts (e.g. operating practices or technologies to be employed) and cases where the reporting organization's business with the entity represents a significant proportion of the entity's business.

Legal responsibilities

Another dimension of responsibility is provided by the law. Of course, because of the power of the law, the legal boundary of responsibility is typically narrow. The result is that while only a limited set of responsibilities is countenanced, those that are acknowledged can be enforced.

One area in which the legal situation is particularly important is that of human rights. Human rights are defined under international law and have been (mostly) translated into law in the national jurisdictions of many countries world-wide. However, as John Ruggie (Ruggie, 2006) and many companies have pointed out, human rights apply to states, not private entities within states, such as companies. Nevertheless, it is clear that companies can have a large influence on how far human rights are observed within particular states. What is not yet clear is how far such an extended responsibility for human rights can usefully be codified outside a formal legal system.

Human rights represent one extreme of the issues which corporate performance can affect, in that where they are abused, the consequences for individuals can be very severe. There are, though, other legal requirements which are also important and may be written in law which is directly applicable to companies. The EC Directive (EC, 2002) on consultations with workers which must be transposed into national law, is an example. An obvious and critical part of corporate responsibility is the extent to which companies are in compliance with such laws.

While the precise scope of the law is important, the law has no monopoly on responsibility. There are many important social issues which are simply not well provided for legally. Examples include many aspects of workforce diversity and the care companies should take of their fenceline communities (that is those living near operational facilities). Responsibility is a moral concept as well as a legal one. Therefore there are issues, such as human rights, whose moral extension is considerably larger than their legal extension. There are situations in which it can be argued that companies may have human rights responsibilities beyond those defined by the law. Consider complicity with human rights abuses: a company may benefit from the national authorities' abuse of their subjects' human rights, while having no direct involvement in the perpetration of the abuse. As I have argued in *Corporate Truth* (Henriques, 2007, pp158–9) and will show in Chapter 3, the moral scope of complicity is considerably wider than the legal one.

Materiality

In common use, to say that something is material means that it is a tangible physical object. On the assumption that what is physical is important, the term 'materiality' has been extended to mean that something is important. For accountants, interested in whether the appropriate matters have been included in financial reports, materiality is defined in this way:

> *Information is material if its omission or misstatement could influence the economic decision of users taken on the basis of the financial statements. Materiality depends on the size of the item or error judged in the particular circumstances of its omission or misstatement. Thus, materiality provides a threshold or cut-off point rather than being a primary qualitative characteristic which information must have if it is to be useful?* (IASC, 2007, p19)

During the lengthy review of UK company law which concluded in 2006 with the new Companies Act, the definition of materiality was hotly debated. At issue was whether companies should be seen as oriented exclusively to share-holder interests and the extent that other stakeholder interests should be formally included. In relation to reporting, the question was how far matters other than financial ones should be covered. It was originally considered (DTI, 1999) an option to talk openly about a 'pluralist approach' which was founded on a stakeholder perspective. This was contrasted with the 'enlightened share-holder value approach'. The enlightened shareholder value approach held that by following the logic of their own interests, especially in the long term, the interests of stakeholders would inevitably be taken into account. The enlight-ened view echoed that of Adam Smith; in any case it won the day and the pluralist perspective was abandoned.

The implications for materiality were that an issue would only be consid-ered material, and so reported, if it affected the decisions of shareholders – or possibly, on the most charitable interpretation, the economic decisions of other stakeholders. There was much effort by those trying to uphold non-shareholder interests to interpret materiality in such a way as to make quite explicit that material issues included matters such as environmental and social impacts which might affect the prospects of the company. What is interesting in how this debate was framed was that shareholders were always contrasted with stake-holders. It was forgotten that shareholders were also stakeholders.

The final outcome, as expressed in the Companies Act (2006), expunged the word 'materiality' in favour of the awkward phrase 'to the extent neces-sary'. That is, matters should be reported 'to the extent necessary' to take account of shareholder interests. Nevertheless, the term 'materiality' is in common use across the world and may be found in sustainability reports to justify the scope of the report. For example, Ford defines the scope of the issues covered in its 2006/7 Sustainability Report according to three criteria, those:

- *Having significant current or potential impact on the Company*
- *Of significant concern to stakeholders*
- *Over which Ford has a reasonable degree of control.*

(Ford 2007)

This sort of analysis is often expressed in a matrix plotting issues on two axes, one being 'the impact on the business' and the other 'concern to stakeholders'. Figure 2.4 shows Ford's version of such a matrix.

The pitfalls of this approach are clear. If, as they assert, an issue must satisfy all three criteria, then it has to have a significant impact on Ford. This means that should the issue not have a significant impact on Ford, it does not have to be reported, however concerned stakeholders might be. For example, if through some quality failure, a car was delivered that was unsafe to drive, that issue would not necessarily be reported, unless perhaps it occurred in such numbers that it began to affect the reputation of the company. Similarly, if it could be argued that Ford had no control over the issue, then it would not need to be

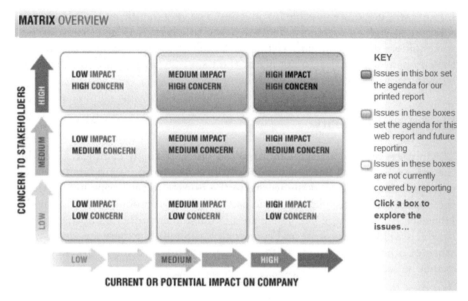

Source: Ford (2007)

Figure 2.4 *The Ford Materiality Matrix*

reported. Interestingly, Ford found that there were no issues in the top left, 'high concern, low impact' category of their matrix.

There is another approach, which has been upheld by AccountAbility in relation to the auditing of reports. AccountAbility in its auditing standard, although not in all its publications (see AccountAbility, 2006b) has universalized the materiality definition to mean the inclusion in a report of:

> *information about its sustainability performance required by its stakeholders for them to be able to make informed judgments, decisions and actions.* (AccountAbility, 2003)

There are two important concepts which are closely related to, and often confused with, materiality: significance and relevance. The significance of an issue is the extent to which it matters to the relevant stakeholder. For example, the abuse of human rights is hugely significant to those abused. Issues may also be more or less relevant to a given company. For example, marine biodiversity is of little relevance to a telecommunications company but may be very relevant to a fishery. In general terms, materiality requires that an issue be both relevant and significant. However, since relevance and significance are both matters of degree, it is also possible for an issue to be both relevant to a company and significant to its stakeholder(s), but not sufficiently so to make it material.

So the fact that whales are endangered is not that relevant to a telecommunications company, but may be very relevant to a retailer selling whale meat.

Importantly, it is quite possible for an issue to be very significant but not actually relevant to a given company, because those to whom it is significant are not stakeholders of the company (which is actually the same thing as saying that the company's activities do not affect the issue). Whales would not therefore be material to a telecommunications company.

Shared responsibility

The impacts of even a single company can be staggeringly complex. Consider the range of effects of Shell, which runs from staff conditions in a London office amongst hundreds around the world, to the impact of gas flaring in Nigeria to the impact on climate change of the use of their core product, oil, worldwide. However, Shell is not alone. There are of course many other companies, some of which will have the scale and complexity of Shell. But there are also a wide range of other organizations and individuals from which the impacts of Shell cannot be separated, for example:

- Actors in its commercial chain, both on the supply and demand side. How much responsibility should the independent companies which transport Shell products bear for the impacts of those products?
- Organizations and others which affect the way in which the impacts of Shell are realized. If legislation requires Shell (assuming Shell has not influenced that legislation) to behave in a particular way which alters the impact the company has, how far should such authorities be responsible?
- Consumers. While clearly Shell will try to influence its consumer customers, how much responsibility should they actually bear for the fact that they purchase petrol from Shell and thus contribute to climate change?

This raises the crucial question: of all the effects of a company's activities in combination with stakeholders, for which is the company responsible? No doubt the way in which such a question might be answered in a practical way by the courts would typically separate the proportion of responsibility for a harm to which the company might have contributed from an assessment of the compensation. Such decisions are also highly specific to a particular situation and deal almost exclusively with negative impacts. They are also, by definition, contested.

It also seems highly unworkable to try to apportion responsibility through legislation as the complexities involved appear to be completely unmanageable. However, if companies are to shoulder their responsibilities, then some kind of accommodation must be reached with their stakeholders. If this is unlikely on a legislative basis, is it possible on a voluntary basis? The alternative is to continue with the current regime of confusion and denial.

There are, fortunately, some grounds for hope. In a few areas, companies have acknowledged shared responsibility for their impacts. One area concerns recycling electronic equipment. In Europe, the WEEE Directive (EC, 2003) requires producing companies to recycle electrical equipment they have sold, after consumers wish to dispose of it. Interestingly, it enjoins that producers share the costs of collection and processing proportionately to their market share.

Another area is in relation to supply chain impacts. It is not now unusual for companies to acknowledge that it is entirely within their sphere of influence and moral responsibility to ensure that the conditions for workers in their supply chains are reasonable. What is interesting is that large companies like Gap, for example, have no legal responsibility for such effects on supply chain workers, who are employed by entirely separate legal entities. Similarly, on large infrastructure projects, most of the workers will be working for subcontractors, and not the well-known company who may be running the project. The management of corporate impacts is therefore mostly dependent upon the terms and conditions agreed with the subcontractors at the beginning of the project. The ability to change these as the project goes on, and the understanding of impacts grows, is limited. The chief reason a number of companies nevertheless do now recognize these responsibilities, however, is that they have been subject to campaigns by NGOs and fear for their reputation.

This also means that there are large numbers of minor brands which are effectively exempt. Only the big brands have been subject in this way to pressure from critical NGOs that have the energy to campaign. Nevertheless, there are grounds to hope that the movement will expand through more of the clothing industry and to agricultural labour conditions. The luxury goods brands, that have so far been exempt, may follow the diamond industry into extensive projects to ensure that the shadow of their supply chain does not fall on their public face.

Parts of the alcohol industry have also looked at apportioning responsibilities among a company and its stakeholders. Part of the purpose of a project to address this (Bent, 2005) was to allocate costs for the adverse social impact of alcohol amongst the various stakeholders in the commercial chain – from producers to transporters, retailers and consumers. This was important as the alcohol company concerned had realized that the cost of the harm alcohol does was very significant in relation to the size of its profits. The process used to reach agreement included a facilitated exchange of views between most of these stakeholder groups. The conclusion was that there was a reasonable way to share responsibility, based on market share.

COMPANY KIND

To this point we have been talking about companies as if they were all of one kind. The default assumption is that all companies exist to make profit and anything else is immoral at best and illegal at worst. But there are different kinds of companies and this relates directly to their purposes.

In the UK, the two principal kinds of company are companies limited by shares and those limited by guarantee. Very similar distinctions operate in the

USA and most other countries. All companies listed on stock exchanges and the large majority of those undertaking commercial trade are companies limited by shares. The phrase 'limited by shares' means that the debts the company's members (i.e. shareholders) are obliged to honour are limited to the nominal value of their shares. For an individual shareholder it is therefore directly proportional to the number of their shares. This is a different matter from the market value of those shares, which are typically worth a great deal more than their nominal value.

Companies limited by guarantee also protect their members, but in this case it is to the value of the guarantee, which is typically a very small amount, and the same for all members. The members of a company limited by guarantee are not usually interested in any financial return. This form of company is typical of NGOs. Such companies are typically used for charitable or explicitly social purposes and frequently also contain a clause limiting the distribution of their assets. However registration with the Charities Commission in the UK, or similar bodies elsewhere, is a separate process, on top of the formation of the company itself. Registration with the Charities Commission is not automatic and entails additional reporting and governance restrictions beyond those required by the basic company form itself.

One of the constraints on charitable registration is the purpose of the company. In the most recent Act (UK, 2006), the permissible purposes must be for the public benefit and also fall within one of the following categories:

- the prevention or relief of poverty;
- the advancement of education;
- the advancement of religion;
- the advancement of health or the saving of lives;
- the advancement of citizenship or community development;
- the advancement of the arts, culture, heritage or science;
- the advancement of amateur sport;
- the advancement of human rights, conflict resolution or reconciliation or the promotion of religious or racial harmony or equality and diversity;
- the advancement of environmental protection or improvement;
- the relief of those in need by reason of youth, age, ill-health, disability, financial hardship or other disadvantage;
- the advancement of animal welfare;
- the promotion of the efficiency of the armed forces of the Crown, or of the efficiency of the police, fire and rescue services or ambulance services.

The reward for charitable registration is the relief from tax for donors to the charity, exemption from corporation tax for trading which is central to the delivery of charitable objectives and in some limited cases, exemption from VAT.

A further distinctive feature of most NGOs in practice is their governance. Beyond the requirement to report to authorities such as the Charity Commission, NGOs will technically be run by a Board consisting of trustees who have no significant financial interest in the organization. On top of this, they may also be membership-based organizations and their members may have a significant level of control over the direction the organization takes. The importance of this for assessing their social impact is indirect, but important. Such governance structures are intended to ensure that the organization's work is appropriately directed to its social aims. Assuming this is indeed so, it means in practice that NGOs enjoy a greater degree of credibility than commercial organizations. One consequence of this in turn is that when such organizations measure and disclose their social impact, their reports enjoy wider confidence than those of commercial organizations, whose governance is intended only to further shareholder ends.

Companies limited by guarantee are therefore typically operating for the public good. Most NGOs are companies limited by guarantee and also charities, as would be expected. But this is not universal. Especially before the 2006 Act in the UK, charities were not permitted to carry out political activities. Since one of the main means to realizing their charitable ends was political campaigning, many charities resolved this by combining two organizations: one for charitable purposes, one for political campaigning. Friends of the Earth (UK) is an example of an NGO with this structure.

There is a further difficulty: trading, which on the face of it appears to be a for-profit or commercial activity, is often a significant part of some charities' activities and sources of income. Yet while selling very cheap food directly to the poor might be a wholly charitable activity, selling expensive watches, for example, to finance cheap food for the poor seems rather different. There are therefore rather complex regulations on what charities may do and may not do and the various related tax consequences.

In addition, purely commercial companies are not *required* to pursue profit. Of course, in practice that is clearly what most of them in fact do. However, there would be no problem with the shareholders of a company agreeing that their company's purpose was to further the public good. Over the course of the twentieth century, the requirements for the description of a company's objects – that is, of its purpose – have become ever more relaxed. With the 2006 Companies Act, companies now no longer need to declare their purpose at all, leaving it entirely to the discretion of their shareholders, and on a day-to-day basis, to their managers.

The implications of all this for the social purpose of companies is that the distinction between for-profit and not for profit activity is blurred. Difficulties such as these have led in the UK to regulation and proposals for other sorts of organization. These are intended to have purposes strictly tied to social benefit, while allowing greater flexibility for their governance and for trading as a normal part of their day-to-day activity. These include the Community Interest Company and the Charitable Incorporated Organization.

As a result, public benefit organizations engage in 'commercial' activity. On the other hand, commercial companies may undertake activities which are for the public benefit. Philanthropy is clearly not the main purpose of most commercial companies, but it is a relatively common part of commercial corporate life. Some companies, such as Shell, have set up charitable foundations which are closely connected to their business. While it is not clear to what extent such initiatives are connected to the tax management or lobbying processes of such large companies, they are also contributions to the public good.

To further complicate the picture, there is a type of organization in between the non-profit and the commercial models: social enterprise. Social enterprises are sometimes defined by the legal form of the enterprise. The Community Interest Company and Charitable Incorporated Organizations legal forms were in some ways designed to recognize this need. Or they may be defined by their purpose, as 'business trading for a social purpose' (SEC, 2008). In either case they are run by 'social entrepreneurs'.

For John Elkington (Elkington and Hartigan, 2008), a social entrepreneur is someone who makes unreasonable, outrageous demands – and proceeds to satisfy them, turning market failure into market opportunity. The range of social enterprises is vast: from the well-known Eden Project and the Grameen Bank to the less well known, such as Ideaas providing cheap electricity in Brazil or the Rural Women Knowing All educational project in China.

Social businesses can be mapped onto a spectrum ranging from the 'leveraged non-profit' organization providing access to markets from which too many are excluded to fully for-profit organizations directed to social or environmental ends. How far can they be the solution to global problems, in some way automatically providing positive social impacts? Two of the principal requirements Elkington identifies for social business to tackle global problems successfully are 'changing the system' and 'scaling up'. His account of changing the system describes the vital work of NGOs which are working directly on the infrastructure needed for social enterprises to succeed.

Given the size of most social enterprises set against that of global problems, scaling up is obviously also critical. This involves mainstream business. It can involve partnering with social enterprises, perhaps buying them up and also encouraging 'unreasonable' behaviour within their own organizations. But why should mainstream businesses concern themselves with social enterprise? For three reasons: future market intelligence, staff retention and because it looks good – in the words of one CEO at Davos 'It is nice to be seen with people who are loved.'

Clearly the vision, determination and persistence – the unreasonableness – of social entrepreneurs is going to be essential for all if the environmental and social challenges we all face are to be overcome. But social enterprises are in a relatively small minority, so it remains of crucial importance to understand and measure the social impact of mainstream business.

3

Complicity and the Sexual Exploitation of Children – A Case Study[1]

Some of the complexities in the nature of a company's social impact are illustrated in this chapter by examining the relationship of companies to the issue of the sexual exploitation of children (SEC). This is a very difficult and emotive issue. As a result it also provides a test case for examining the effectiveness of the management of corporate impacts in dealing with major social issues.

In the last 10 years the idea of companies taking responsibility for their actions has become widespread, triggering a wide spectrum of projects, initiatives and new ways of working by companies. Does all this activity have the potential to involve the private sector in new and constructive ways to address SEC?

There is scope for confusion over the term '*commercial* sexual exploitation of children'. As traditionally used, it means directly making money out of abuse, for example through child prostitution. However, when the link is more indirect, there may be an issue of complicity by mainstream companies with sexual exploitation. How should companies address this? On the one hand, unlike the involvement of organized crime in SEC, the connection with mainstream companies is less overt. On the other hand, the link is plausible and such companies may have the resources to address it.

This chapter does not cover the role of the private sector in child prostitution or informal commercial sectors, such as brothels and organized crime, which may be directly involved in child prostitution. It does discuss circumstances in which mainstream companies may be involved indirectly and unintentionally in SEC. Also, the sexual exploitation of children is taken to include child abuse whether or not it has any financial element attached.

THE PRIVATE SECTOR AND SEC

There are no mainstream businesses whose principal and direct purpose is the commercial sexual exploitation of children. Nevertheless, there are ways in which some industries can be indirectly, but sometimes systematically, involved in contributing to SEC. This section outlines the processes of SEC and how it makes use of companies and their products and services.

There are three important aspects of SEC in which companies can be involved. The first, crime-driven SEC, entails criminality by individual abusers and organized crime. It involves:

- the virtual or contact abuse of children, involving the travel of abusers to places where access to children is easy or the trafficking of children to the countries of abusers or the grooming of children already in the country of the abuser using the internet and other technologies;
- the circulation of images of sexual exploitation, involving the creation of images of abuse and their transfer to others.

Sectors whose products may be involved in this aspect of SEC include the information and computer technologies sectors (ICT) as well as travel-related industries.

The second aspect, socio-economic SEC, is as its name suggests driven by socio-economic factors. It results in the supply of vulnerable children in desperate economic need who may be forced or lured into providing sex for favours or into prostitution. The very low wages paid to many in developing countries is central to this aspect of SEC. It also feeds into the marketplace for sex from children in developing countries used by locals and by regional and western tourists and the demands of international child traffickers. This source of SEC typically occurs in the manufacturing (including garments and electronics) and agricultural sectors. It can therefore involve large multinational companies through their supply chains.

Thirdly, in addition an important role is played by the background legitimation of sexual exploitation, involving the presentation of sexualized images of children in the fashion industry and advertising and also inappropriate editorial and reporting treatments of the subject in the media.

Specific companies may be complicit with SEC through two main mechanisms:

1 they may sell products which are used by abusers in SEC. This can sometimes create new demand for SEC, but typically greatly leverages existing demand;
2 the operation of their business may create circumstances in which SEC can thrive. This increases the supply of children driven towards SEC.

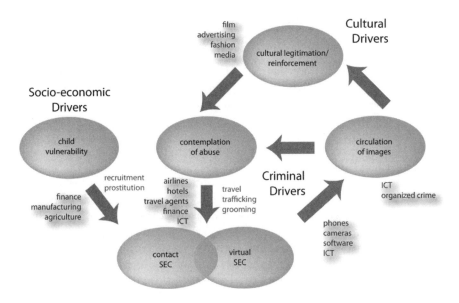

Figure 3.1 *The Sexual Exploitation of Children*

Companies may also produce products tailored to some degree to individual intentions. Where there is already an intention to undertake SEC, the degree of complicity on a company's part can be high. The travel, hotel, fashion, advertising, media and airline industries fall into this category to varying extents. Other companies, such as those in financial services, deliver products which are very little tailored and more in the nature of commodities. The commodity-like products and services produced by companies that are misused for SEC include ICT as well as financial services.

Apart from the impact which their core operations may have on SEC, companies also employ staff. The question therefore arises of whether the way in which companies treat their staff could affect the likelihood that their staff may abuse children. It can be argued that there is a broad sense in which impoverished inter-personal relationships within company workforces, and available outside work as a result of the demands of work, are likely to help to create people who may be more prone to contemplate the abuse of children (Seymour, 1998). This may be compounded by bullying which can lay some of the psychological foundations for the abuse of others (Owen and Sweeting, 2007). These are issues which may affect many modern companies.

CRIME-DRIVEN SEC

The process of crime-driven SEC in the industrial world is complex, involving many different activities and industry sectors. This section will focus on the main cycle of criminal abuse, involving the contemplation of abuse, actual abuse and the creation and circulation of images. The internet and payments systems will be examined in particular as they play a central role in this cycle (CEOP, 2008).

'The internet' in fact consists of a number of different networks and computer systems. In relation to SEC, the software and hardware of the internet facilitates the storage of images on websites, their transfer by e-mail and Usenet (newsgroups) and access to images of children from personal computers. These mechanisms also include the manufacture and use of software for photo-editing and communications and hardware for capturing images, communicating them to others via internet service providers and the extensive communications infrastructure of the internet. The process of luring children into abuse via the internet can involve the use of chat rooms and the deliberate exposure of children to images of child abuse through websites or mobile phones. Finally, access to child abuse images may involve payment which is effected over the internet. Many private sector companies are therefore indirectly involved in SEC. It is therefore reasonable to expect the involvement of the private sector in responses to SEC as part of their efforts to address their social impact.

Tackling SEC is complex since the global factors driving SEC are currently met with fragmented responses. SEC is driven or enabled by international air travel and the global and resilient nature of the internet. This results in the ability of organized crime to work on a global basis and abusers to travel in order to abuse or to access images from all over the world with little difficulty. Moreover the response to this situation is hampered by:

- the variety of different industries from which active participation is needed to tackle SEC;
- the characteristics of multinational companies which, while they may operate globally, may do so with varying national management policies and strategies;
- the overwhelmingly national basis of legal systems together with different legal definitions of, and approaches to, SEC.

Working with voluntary codes and standards on a multi-stakeholder and multi-national basis can be a practical and useful means to cope with this fragmentation. For example the Financial Coalition against Child Pornography (FCACP, 2008) has successfully brought US companies together from a variety of sectors and the projected European Financial Coalition aims to do the same for the more fragmented region of Europe. While there is commitment from the G8 states (G8, 2007) to raise the standards of the law across the world in relation to child protection, this has a considerable way to go before it becomes reality. It is therefore particularly important to involve companies in voluntary standards for child protection when they operate in countries that have not implemented a sufficiently strong legal framework to deal with child abuse.

The voluntary approach to child protection

One aspect to combating SEC concerns controls over access by children to sections of the internet. Individual companies have taken steps to control SEC in this way through:

- developing commercial products to enable parental controls over computer use by children;
- donations of money, time and products to assist public or third sector organizations concerned with SEC.

Viacom and eBay, for example, have supported the National Center for Missing and Exploited Children (NCMEC) in the USA financially. Virgin Media and AOL (UK) are amongst a number of companies which have donated resources, including expertise, to the Child Exploitation and Online Protection Centre (CEOP) in the UK. Microsoft, to assist law enforcement, has developed the CETS (Child Exploitation Tracking System), which enables diverse databases of criminal activity to be integrated. This system is now being used internationally. Microsoft has also altered the design of its instant messaging application, Windows Live Messenger in the UK, so that abuse reporting and advice buttons and associated pages are prominently placed for users.

To achieve safer products for children to use and ones more difficult for adults to use for abuse, more attention should be paid to the consideration of child protection at the earliest stages of internet product design. This principle could be applied to hardware as well as software products. The result would be that child protection measures would be delivered at a far lower cost, by a wider range of organizations, than incurred by retrofitting such measures.

Chat rooms and other online public meeting spaces also represent a risk to children. The origins of this threat lie in the anonymity afforded by the internet. Without very stringent 'know your customer' rules, which are likely to be costly to implement, anonymity is unlikely to be eliminated. Guidelines have been developed by the UK Home Office for a risk-based approach to the moderation of such spaces (Home Office, 2008). Internet Service Providers (ISPs) could adopt such codes on a voluntary basis. Again the question is how far such advice can be promoted and adopted internationally.

Child protection is also relevant to mobile phone companies. In the last few years, it has become far more practical to access the internet on a mobile phone. In addition, a large proportion of children in some parts of the world possess mobile phones. Furthermore, due to the financial pressures on mobile phone companies to recoup their licence costs for the newer internet-capable '3G' networks, many mobile phone companies are exploring the provision of pornography services on mobile phones. This clearly exposes children to risk.

As a result, some mobile phone companies, including Vodafone (Vodafone, 2008) have adopted child protection policies specifically to guard against access by children to general pornographic content; controls are applied by default and will only be removed if proof of age greater than 18 is provided. However, such policies are not universal and are not always applied throughout the range of operation of such companies. Furthermore, the nature of the industry means that numerous joint ventures and commercial partnerships are established and the application of such policies in these circumstances is variable.

Hardware companies are of course also central to the operation of the internet. They manufacture network switches and servers as well as many of the peripherals, such as Xboxes and Wii devices which connect to it. They also develop applications software which has an important role.

Internet blocking

Controlling the content of the internet itself is the other main approach to combating SEC on the internet. This targets adult abusers, particularly those engaged in the circulation of images of abuse. There are two stages to such controls: firstly identification of the abusive material and secondly its technical removal from the internet.

One approach to identification is the reporting of SEC by children and by adults. This may be partly accomplished by hotlines to report suspicious or abusive content. Hotlines of this nature exist in about 26 countries, from Barnaheill in Iceland to the Internet Association in Japan. Many of the hotlines are operated by civil society organizations or by multi-stakeholder groups and receive funding from companies operating in the internet sector. A second approach is to use technology to identify sites containing abuse automatically, either by means of keywords in the site name or on its pages or, more recently, by an analysis of the image content on individual web pages. A number of companies provide such technically-based identification services commercially.

In 2004, BT in association with the UK child protection hotline, the Internet Watch Foundation (IWF), implemented CleanFeed, which blocks access to URLs based on their presence in the IWF database. This system is now widely used in the UK and is also being implemented in the USA. While it is possible deliberately to circumvent the system, it works effectively against accidental access to such material.

Implementation of such measures is dependent in most countries on voluntary adoption by ISPs, that is, it may be regarded as part of their corporate responsibility. In addition the technical means used by those who wish to host child abuse material is continually changing and now includes techniques such as ISP hopping. Furthermore the complex commercial structures of the operation of ISPs, including reselling arrangements, may make the imposition of content control more difficult.

Most ISPs have an acceptable use policy that concerns general commercial and technical issues. Some ISPs also have an acceptable use policy that goes beyond these issues and may specifically make reference to SEC. However, such policies are far from the norm and should include the propagation of such policies through resellers of ISP services.

There is also a need to work on some very practical and technical issues. Peter Robbins, CEO of the IWF has called for:

- a worldwide public–private partnership to investigate, disrupt and remove websites that hop server and region and identification of the distributors of this content;
- increased sharing of good practice between hotlines for reporting abuse and industry to remove content quickly to ensure the longevity of these websites is diminished (Robbins, 2008).

Responsible payments

The financial sector is connected with SEC via the use of its products to support the activities of child sex abusers. This includes banking and payments services. Those activities extend from payments for child sex holidays and associated travel and accommodation, through to the purchase of cameras and other equipment and software which will be used for the circulation of images. However, in the last five years, there has been significant activity in preventing the use of card payments for access to images and to join websites or networks providing such access.

The nature of the card payments business is complex. A card transaction involves not only the card user, who may be seeking to access images of abuse and the merchant which is selling such material, but also the banks servicing each party, one by issuing the card to the user and the other by acquiring the merchant's transactions generated from cards. Similar relationships with different commercial arrangements lead to products such as charge, credit and debit cards.

Child abuse websites will advertise the fact that they are offering card payments by displaying the logos of the payments system on their website. Typically transactions for access to child abuse images are of relatively low value, avoiding the need for authorization by the banks involved. Since the merchants involved will mis-describe their products to their banks, the whole transaction may go unnoticed by normal commercial controls.

The card payments associations, such as MasterCard and Diners Club are membership organizations of the banks involved. Their role is to ensure that all parties are acting within a set of rules which make the transactions viable and trustworthy. This means that complying with the rules becomes a matter for the reputation of the payments systems. While this may be an important motivation, some have recognized the issue of complicity: 'If we did nothing, turning a blind eye to the use of our cards in paying for child pornography, we would be guilty by association' (Visa, 2007).

Within payments systems, the banks involved have to abide by complex operating regulations. Banks acquiring merchant transactions will then themselves impose the relevant regulations on merchants. These regulations usually prohibit illegal transactions through a blanket prohibition on the use of their systems for illegal purposes. However, because child abuse is covered very differently by different legal systems, some payments systems have a specific rule against the use of their systems in relation to child abuse. Visa Europe's Chief Risk and Compliance Officer Valerie Dias has said that 'Irrespective of local laws or customs, we do not allow our cards to be used for any such transactions' (Visa, 2007).

What the payments systems usually do to counteract the use of their cards for child abuse is to identify abusive sites (usually by technological means), identify the merchant involved and finally notify the relevant legal authorities and the ISP. Typically the website will be taken out of action within 24 to 72 hours. However, once the site is taken down or payments systems such as Visa are removed from them, it is no longer possible for the authorities to identify those who are seeking to buy such images. While it would be possible to delay taking the site down for this reason, the payments systems are understandably nervous of the reaction of the media if such a practice became publicized.

Rapid and effective action of this kind by payments systems also leads to another dilemma. The less available the major payments systems are for child abuse, the more abusers will turn to other payments mechanisms which may be more anonymous. With support from Visa Europe, the CEOP is commissioning research into the prevailing types of payment methods and new payment methods exploited in the operation of commercial child abuse image websites. A key factor is that some internet-based systems, such as e-gold, require less authentication than card systems. It is also possible for abusers to make use of informal, trust-based payments systems (such as hawala), or simply cash, to protect their anonymity. A code of practice on these issues would not only help to spread good practice, it should also protect the payments systems from adverse media reaction to the most effective practices in reducing child abuse online.

SOCIO-ECONOMIC SEC

Complex socio-economic conditions in many parts of the world create large communities of children who are very vulnerable (Henschel, 2003). These vulnerabilities, such as the lack of enfranchisement of women and widespread social discrimination on many bases make it far more likely that children will be subject to sexual exploitation. This section describes some of the chief mechanisms involved, particularly that of poverty, and the role which mainstream companies can play in the processes leading to SEC.

Poverty and the vulnerabilities which it creates are one of the principal roots of the processes creating SEC. As World Vision has put it, 'there are ... certain commonalities between [the sexual exploitation of children] in developing, transition and developed countries: crucially, most children become commercially sexually exploited as a survival option. Whether born into poverty or forced into difficult circumstances as a result of abuse, including sexual abuse, their entry into [sexual exploitation] typically occurs as a last resort' (WV, 2002).

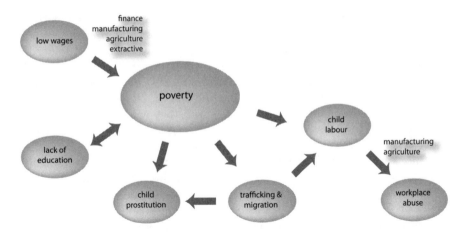

Figure 3.2 *Socio-Economic Factors in the Sexual Exploitation of Children*

Companies have a key role to play in relation to poverty. While the underlying economic origins of poverty have been very widely studied, the immediate cause of poverty for many in the developing world is the level of wages paid. The extractive sector, particularly its informal elements, is one source of low-paying employment. Low wages also characterize the agricultural and manufacturing sectors in the developing world. Large mainstream Western companies may own facilities directly, as happens in the extractive and agricultural sectors. However, in manufacturing sectors, including apparel and footwear, long supply chains are more characteristic. There may be a chain including a number of agents and several companies between a well-known high street brand selling consumer electronics or T-shirts and the worker actually making the goods sold. Low wages are also associated with operations with companies operating in Export Processing Zones (EPZs).

Amongst the many causes of poverty, lack of education is especially significant. This is because not only is the lack of education of parents a principal cause of poverty for children, but poverty results in a lack of education for the children of poor workers. The causes of poverty are thus reinforced. In addition to general education, a lack of awareness of the issues surrounding SEC, particularly amongst women and children, is also a compounding factor in perpetuating it (WV, 2002).

Poverty makes families vulnerable in many ways, including to SEC. One of the responses of a poor family may be to encourage their children, especially girls, who suffer a poor level of social esteem in many cultures, to work as prostitutes. This may occur in rural locations, but more commonly children will move to large towns to engage in prostitution.

A second route to SEC is through seeking work. This is typically driven by poverty. 'Low wage rates for adults have knock-on effects, making it more likely that children will need to work to supplement the family's income' (Traidcraft and Impactt, 2008). Children from poor families may move voluntarily to seek work in centres which provide it, especially towns and EPZs. Alternatively, children may be sold to, or tricked by, child traffickers, who offer the promise of work elsewhere. However, traffickers often simply intend to subject the children to prostitution (Deshingkar, 2006). Sometimes there may actually be work available through migration or traffickers. Yet this, of course, immediately means that the children are involved in child labour. However, if there is no work, or the children manage to leave or escape, they will most likely come to live on the street. At that point, both girls and boys are likely to turn to prostitution as one of a number of survival strategies.

The pattern of child labour, including its worst forms, varies significantly across the world. In Africa, some 30 per cent of children are economically active (and the proportion in HIV/Aids-affected households approaches 95 per cent) (UNICEF, 2008). But the ILO has estimated that the great majority of children (by a factor of about 10) engaged in the worst forms of child labour (including prostitution and pornography, armed conflict and bonded labour) live in the Asia-Pacific region (IPEC, 2003) with over 6 million children involved. Furthermore, the same study suggests the net economic benefit of eliminating the worst forms of child labour from the region to be approaching US$1.5 trillion over 20 years. Those who pay for sex with children in the cities of Asia especially, include local men and both regional and Western travelling sex offenders as well as members of foreign armed forces on shore leave or stationed locally (Grumiau, 2001). In this way the socio-economically driven supply of vulnerable children meet the demands of criminally-driven child abusers.

There is another route to SEC which accompanies child labour. Given the great need for work which children may experience, one reaction from those who are recruiting within companies is to demand sex in exchange for it. This may be continued once they have actually been recruited. 'Persistent harassment drives some women to leave their job, at the risk of not finding another. For Hasina, a former garment worker in Bangalore, India, the only alternative was to turn to sex work. "You are subjected to all kinds of sexual harassment in the factory," she said. "Supervisors, production managers, and watchmen touch you without giving you anything in return. In this job, at least you are paid for the same"' (Oxfam, 2004). Thus, children may not only be subjected to the demands of an adult workplace but exposed also to sexual exploitation.

There are similar reports from the agricultural sector in India. '"The partner of my farm owner used to switch off the lights at night and forcibly carry the girls sleeping on the floor, on to his cot," Hanja said, his eyes on the ground. Many of the young girls ... on the fields there silently acknowledged sexual abuse, but were unaware that formal complaints could be lodged against their landlords' (Prasad, 2007). Where there is awareness of these issues within a company and action is not taken, they can be regarded as complicit with SEC, as has been the case with the issue of child labour more generally.

Corporate impact and the supply chain

Mainstream Western companies are crucial to the economies of the developing world. It is estimated, for example, that EU purchasing of Cambodia's garment exports in 2006 employed 80,000 workers, and indirectly supported approximately 11 per cent of Cambodia's population (Traidcraft and Impactt, 2008). Yet cost pressures can lead to companies paying unacceptable rates (Clay, 2005) and rent seeking can also lead to companies to take advantage and pay less than the market wage (Hopkins, 2006).

The reaction of large companies to the plight of workers in their supply chain can be varied. Human Rights Watch has highlighted poor practice. 'Representatives of Dole, Chiquita, Del Monte, Noboa, and Favorita with whom Human Rights Watch spoke in Ecuador all disclaimed any obligation to demand respect for workers' rights on third-party plantations from which they purchase bananas for export. They explained, in some cases contradicting their own codes of conduct, that supplier plantations are private property over which they have no jurisdiction and that decisions regarding labour matters thereon are ultimately the prerogative of the plantations' administrators' (HRW, 2002). There are also examples of good practice from Gap, L'Oreal, Cadbury and others (Cadbury, 2008; CIPS, 2008).

Supply chain issues have been a constant part of responsible business practice for the last 15 years. Concern about labour conditions in the supply chain began to grow as the trend towards outsourcing of apparel, footwear and manufactured goods began to grow in the 1980s and 1990s, since the main driver for outsourcing was to reduce costs. This has resulted in mainstream consumer goods being produced under conditions which can include very low wages, compulsory overtime and very poor conditions generally. Since the goods produced are often sold under high profile consumer brands, the companies concerned are very sensitive to public opinion and to shareholder pressure (Insight, 2004).

This situation has been successfully leveraged by civil society organizations campaigning on the issue. One of the results of this activity is the formation of projects involving companies, civil society organizations and unions such as the Ethical Trading Initiative (ETI) (ETI, 2008) whose purpose is to promote and improve the implementation of corporate codes of practice which cover supply chain working conditions. Another outcome is the development of SA8000 (SAI, 2008), an auditable code of practice for labour conditions. At the same time the Fair Trade movement has developed, concentrating initially particularly on small scale producers of agricultural and craft products under conditions which include paying a premium to producers as well as reasonable labour conditions. Fair Trade goods are sold under a consumer label which may only be used if the production process has been satisfactorily audited.

In addition, a number of private companies, such as Adidas (Adidas, 2008) amongst many others, in a variety of sectors, have developed their own codes of conduct. These are formulated along similar lines to the CSR codes, although sometimes at a less detailed level. A number of these companies in the apparel sector, together with some civil society organizations and suppliers, work together in the Fair Labor Association (FLA, 2005) which provides another code of practice. The specific issue of trafficking has been addressed by the International Organization for Migration, which in conjunction with businesses has recently developed the Athens Principles designed to combat trafficking (IOM, 2008).

The ETI and SA8000, and other initiatives covering child labour, are based on various human rights and labour conventions. Amongst these are ILO Convention 182 (ILO, 1999), which deals with the elimination of the worst forms of child labour, including prostitution. Yet SEC is not addressed directly. For example, the OECD Guidelines for Multinational Enterprises (OECD, 2000) requires companies to respect freedom of association and to 'contribute to the effective abolition of child labour', but does not directly address SEC.

Moreover the application of such voluntary standards is typically interpreted by companies and the CSR community to apply only to workers directly employed. This would cover the use of sex in exchange for recruitment. However, little consideration is given to the wider consequences of an employer's practices, which, as we have seen, may result in child prostitution.

The various initiatives and private sector codes have also addressed the issue of wages. Civil society organization initiatives have worked towards implementing the concept of a 'living wage', as set out in the ILO Constitution. The private sector codes, on the other hand, tend to make use of the concept of the 'minimum wage', which is sometimes defined in law. As a result there is continuing debate about how a living wage may be set or calculated and about its precise economic effects on the wider economy and on the companies involved. However, there is consistent evidence that poverty rates in developing countries are correlated with the level of the minimum wage (Braun, 1995; Lustig and McLeod, 1997; Saget, 2001).

There is also a danger that the imposition of codes from mainstream purchasing companies may result in inflexible wage levels and weaken the position of the unions. In relation to SEC, the unions should be strengthened as they will be alert to the more direct SEC abuses, especially in relation to recruitment as well as wage levels.

A living wage, of course, is central to the Fair Trade standard. However, to date, while the volume of Fair Trade is growing rapidly, it is very far short of the volumes which mainstream trade achieves. Nevertheless, the profile of Fair Trade is high. It may therefore be helpful for the beneficial consequential effects of an adequate living wage to be spelt out in Fair Trade materials, including the potential for the reduction in SEC.

Companies and their suppliers working in the developing world are likely to have to deal with child labour. The reaction of simply terminating employment of any children employed in their facilities will only lead to the return of such children to the street and the increased vulnerabilities to SEC which that entails. One of the most constructive responses is to provide education until they reach adulthood, followed by a job. Yet such practice is far from universal.

The United Nations Convention on the Rights of the Child defines a child as 'every human being below the age of 18 years unless under the law applicable to the child, majority is attained earlier' (UN, 1989). However, it is important to remember that there is a considerable variability in the legally defined minimum working age throughout the world; the minimum working age in India is 14 years, for example. Under these circumstances, there are grounds for special arrangements for children between the local minimum working age and 18 years.

It is not clear what impact the various CSR-inspired supply-chain initiatives have had, although some civil society organizations are very concerned about their lack of effect (Doane and Holder, 2007). While some level of auditing, whether by the purchasing company or a commercial third party usually takes place, at least on a sample basis, the results of such audits are not typically made public. Also, some studies have found that the audits appear to be inaccurate. One reason for this may be the pressure suppliers can feel to come up with the 'right' answers. The ETI commissioned an independent study (Barrientos and Smith, 2007) of the impact of its code which showed that in the areas of living wage and child labour the code had had mixed impacts.

The purchasing companies at the head of supply chains may have little knowledge of the identity of some parts of the supply chain or of the practices prevalent within it. Nevertheless they have considerable power over their suppliers as exercised through the overall commercial terms of the relationship, including price, order lead times, the regularity of orders and support for unions. A clear understanding of the legislation and a well-defined plan to implement good purchasing practices internally has been suggested as the best approach (Traidcraft, 2006).

The commercial banking and project finance industry also has a role to play in reducing socio-economic SEC. Appraisal of social and environmental risk is already part of the normal lending review process for some major international banks such as Standard Chartered. The Equator Principles (EP, 2006) have been established by a group of financial institutions as a voluntary code governing the treatment of social and environmental impacts of large projects. However while they do not claim to be exhaustive, risks to children are not mentioned at all in the 'illustrative list of potential social and environmental issues' covered by the Principles. However, regional development banks such as the Asian Development Bank and the African Development Bank together with the World Bank also have a critical role to play, since their major financing decisions are powerful influences on the policies and practices of the commercial banks.

It is also important to note that the members of the Equator Principles are largely based in the developed world. There is therefore a question as to the extent to which the social review of risk, including that of SEC, is incorporated into the lending practices of banks and financial institutions based in the developing world, even where such institutions are committed to an existing initiative.

REGULATION AND THE PRIVATE SECTOR

The complexity of outsourcing together with the fragmented nature of the laws relevant to SEC, including the definitions of abuse, the criminalization of possession of images and associated data protection issues, make it difficult for the private sector to operate consistent policies globally. Voluntary codes do represent one valid response from the private sector to this situation. Yet it is also important that these issues are addressed through legislation and the democratic process more generally as well as through the discussion of these matters by the many organizations and agencies involved. However there is also room in this process for the private sector to use its lobbying power constructively to raise these concerns with the various appropriate national and international authorities.

One organization with which this may be possible is the Financial Action Task Force which exists to combat money laundering and terrorist financing. Ordinary financial transactions are deemed to be money laundering when they transfer or store funds derived from criminal activity. While this includes SEC, one of the issues with SEC is the variation in its treatment by the law. However the FATF is mandated to raise the legal standards of states in dealing with money laundering across the world. It should be noted that although the FATF is an intergovernmental body, at its recent plenary meeting chaired by the FATF President, it was agreed that the FATF should 'conduct new joint projects and initiatives with the private sector in relation to the FATF standards' (Swedlove, 2008).

Where companies make use of the voluntary adoption of codes and standards in order to regulate responsible behaviour, it is important to be careful as to the appropriate 'strength' of the resulting code. Such codes may operate at several levels:

- Statements of good practice, which articulate desirable behaviours. These can be useful in generating awareness of SEC.
- Codes of conduct which prescribe how companies should behave. These can not only spread awareness but also help protect the reputation of signatories.
- Codes of conduct which are monitored and for which there may be sanctions for failing to adhere to the code or disclosure of company performance in relation to it. Such codes help change behaviour.

One common criticism is that voluntary codes do not actually change behaviour. This charge is justified for weak codes trying to work with difficult issues. SEC is clearly a difficult issue on many levels. Careful consideration should therefore be given to the strength of proposed new codes for SEC. One example of what is possible is the Virtual Global Taskforce's International Youth Advisory Congress.

Over and above the development of any new codes directly addressing aspects of SEC, maximum use should be made of existing codes and initiatives.

These are invariably of more general application, but working with them will not only raise awareness of the issues, but could also leverage their influence since they are already known and in use.

One such initiative is the Global Reporting Initiative or GRI (GRI, 2008a) which has developed the most widely used set of guidelines for sustainability reporting covering social and economic as well as environmental issues. Reporting and transparency over SEC is likely to be an important driver of public expectations of performance, as it has been for performance in other areas. Moreover, the GRI has often proceeded by the development of approaches to the reporting of specific issues and sectors.

Finally, the UN Global Compact (GC, 2008) requires companies signing up to it to adopt ten principles, three of which are:

- businesses should make sure that they are not complicit in human rights abuses:
- the elimination of all forms of forced and compulsory labour;
- the effective abolition of child labour.

However, there is little formal guidance for the interpretation of these principles. This might take the form of helping to expand the interpretation of the principles in relation to SEC.

GOING BEYOND COMPLICITY

Existing voluntary initiatives have the potential to enlist the private sector in working against the sexual exploitation of children. However, while it can be a positive force, it is far from a panacea; there still remains much to be done in formulating appropriate laws and enforcing them.

Crime-driven SEC relies on the complicity of companies operating in many sectors, including information and communications technology, software as well as travel and tourism. There is already considerable company activity directly related to crime-driven SEC. This must be encouraged. However there are also many companies, particularly in the ICT sector, which have not taken action.

Socio-economically driven SEC involves the exploitation of poor and vulnerable families and children. Companies and their supply chains in the extractive, agricultural, manufacturing and apparel sectors can be involved in the creation of circumstances in which SEC can occur. While there has been considerable activity concerning supply chains, these initiatives have again not directly addressed the issue of SEC.

There are now numerous voluntary codes of conduct and standards – but there are currently very few that even indirectly address SEC. There is therefore much scope for either specifically including SEC within appropriate codes or providing additional guidance on the rationale and importance of working on SEC issues within them. In relation to both crime-driven and socio-economically caused SEC, there are pockets of good corporate practice. The challenge is to extend them greatly.

Finally, a code, standard or initiative which does address SEC is of no use if it makes no difference. There is a real need to upgrade codes and standards so that they are monitored more rigorously and company practices which reduce and eliminate SEC are enforced.

NOTE

1   This chapter has been based on a paper prepared for UNICEF for the Third World Congress against the Sexual Exploitation of Children and Adolescents which took place in Brazil in November 2008.

4

Sustainability's Social Side

A Native American taught me that the division between ecology and human rights was an artificial one, that the environmental and social justice movements addressed two sides of a single larger dilemma. The way we harm the earth affects all people, and how we treat one another is reflected in how we treat the earth. (Hawken, 2007, p2)

What we call Man's power over Nature turns out to be a power exercised by some men over other men with Nature as its instrument. (Lewis, 2001, Ch 3)

Sustainability is important for understanding social impact. It is common to talk about 'the three pillars of sustainability'. The three pillars are usually 'environmental', 'social' and 'economic'. This suggests that any framework for understanding social impact must take some account of sustainability. Unfortunately, the concept of 'sustainability' is very poorly defined, so precisely what its social component or dimension is, is not easy to describe. But in order for companies to gain a full understanding of their social impact, it remains necessary to have some grasp of the social dimension of their sustainability impact.

This chapter will address the problem by looking firstly at the metaphorical structure of the idea of sustainability, suggesting that it has several strands within it that are social in nature. Measurement of these areas is therefore also a part of measuring social impact.

Secondly, this chapter will set out the kinds of connections between social impacts and environmental and economic issues. This will entail looking at the interdependencies between each of the pillars of sustainability.

Thirdly, some ways in which 'social sustainability' can be understood are set out. It is not suggested that this is a definitive account of social sustainability. But it will be helpful in making appropriate use of the various methods for measuring impact.

APPRECIATING SUSTAINABILITY

Whatever the challenge of defining social impact, that of defining sustainability is harder. As important as the concept of sustainability may be, it is notoriously vague and hard to pin down. Sustainability is now usually understood to include social and economic issues as well as environmental issues and to form a natural part of corporate social responsibility (CSR). But just as CSR is hard to define because it questions the role of business in society, defining sustainability itself is even harder, questioning as it does the role of humanity on earth!

Before grappling with definitions of sustainability, it is important to clear up one possible source of confusion. This stems from the use of the term CSR, or corporate social responsibility. The term suggests that CSR is concerned with *social* impacts, perhaps exclusively. However, in practice, CSR has been as concerned with economic and environmental impacts as it has social impacts – indeed attention to environmental impacts predominates in most CSR reports. Although new terms have often been suggested to deal with this, the confusion remains. For the following discussion, it is also important to bear in mind that while significant social issues may have been addressed by companies, the *scope* of what such companies have in fact been addressing and what they choose to call this kind of activity can have little relevance to understanding the nature of social impact. In other words, the nature of social impact cannot simply be identified from what companies happen to have labelled 'social' in their communications.

Sustainability can best be approached as a metaphor. One way to appreciate this is to consider the metaphor that sustainability is replacing. Since the eighteenth-century Enlightenment and until recently, the dominant metaphor for social change was 'progress'. Progress was good, it conveyed movement and getting somewhere. By definition, more progress was better, taking society nearer its goals – although what those goals actually were has, unfortunately, never been very clear.

In the nineteenth century, progress was conflated with evolution and Darwinian competition. This tied in neatly with free market economics, so that a free market became the essential condition of progress. In the twentieth century, social progress became increasingly identified with economic progress. And all of it could be measured by GDP and its rate of growth.

By the close of the twentieth century, it became clear that progress of this kind had many undesirable consequences. Or, in its own terms, progress was not getting anywhere. Not only were there problems for those countries which had managed to increase GDP, but there were also many parts of the world which could not achieve economic growth in the first place. There are, of course, many important explanations – historical, economic and political – as to why progress has become so difficult, but to understand sustainability it is necessary to appreciate that the metaphor of progress was failing.

The appeal of sustainability grew from the soil of progress. It retained the hope of improvement for humankind, but also included potentially the whole planet in its scope. The metaphor of sustainability has many strands. These include:

- Accounting. By extension of the triple bottom line analogy, sustainability is often described in terms of effects on social capital and environmental capital as well as on economic capital.
- Continuing indefinitely. One of the root meanings of 'sustain' is to 'hold up'.
- Social justice. Increasingly, a lack of justice, especially related to economic development, is seen as something which society cannot support or tolerate.
- Acceptable development. Economic development should not override other needs, environmental and social.

The idea of living within limits is another strand to the metaphor, and one which suggests that there may be ways to measure the extent of sustainability. There are limits to the kind of environmental and social outcomes which can be tolerated by natural systems and by societies. From this perspective, sustainability is a property of the global system as a whole, not of any one part of it by itself, such as a country or a company. Of course it might be possible say that a given country is unsustainable in the sense that it is so degrading of the environment, for example, that it breaches global limits as a result of its activity alone.

The remainder of this section addresses some of the implications of these strands of meaning within the sustainability metaphor. In particular, it addresses:

- ideas of time and persistence;
- sustainable development;
- sustainable production and consumption;
- using 'capital' to measure sustainability.

Time for sustainability

The human event horizon is very close. The curvature of our psychological world is very tight. Moving our attention away from ourselves in a straight line in any direction in time or space is hard; our attention soon snaps back to ourselves again somehow. It is hard for us in Western culture to grasp or care about the distant or long-term implications of what we do. It is particularly hard for most people to appreciate the timeless, spiritual and psychological aspects of sustainability. Yet the dictionary meaning of sustainability is about what will last. So in thinking about sustainability the role of time is critical. Can the natural system (including humanity) as we are using it, last? We know the general answer to that question is 'no'. Does this mean that there is no hope for sustainability?

Is time, then, a dimension of sustainability? Trying to see time as a 'dimension' underlines the fact that what is sustainable (or not) is in the end, the world as a whole. The economic, social and environmental dimensions are not dimensions of some independent, abstract thing called 'sustainability'. They are dimensions of events, just as time is. Sustainability is a property of the world as a whole. When events occur under such conditions that social, environmental and economic characteristics are preserved, that system can be called sustainable.

To deal with this in a practical way, some years ago it was fashionable to consider future generations as a stakeholder alongside others, such as the more prosaic customer or supplier, perhaps. This approach has real power when 'future generations' is interpreted to mean not just our immediate children, but seven generations' worth of our descendants. Of course, future generations are by definition not here yet, so some form of proxy must be used, whether in imagination or in a role-playing exercise. Companies still sometimes acknowledge the role of future generations, as in this quote from Toshiba's USA website: 'At Toshiba, we recognize the Earth is an irreplaceable asset and we believe it is the duty of humankind to hand it over to future generations as we found it, if not in better condition' (Toshiba, 2008). But perhaps this owes more to rhetoric than to a systematic examination of the far future consequences of their activities. At any rate, it is difficult to see how Toshiba decides whether it has done its duty or not.

One simple way to make use of time is through the timescales used for assessments of sustainability. The time horizon of Environmental Impact Assessments, for example, is sometimes of the order of a decade, but typically only a few years. From an economic perspective, the key variable which governs the significance of future activity is the discount rate. This is literally the rate at which the future, represented as future cash flows, is discounted. For example, in calculating the current worth of money in future years at a 10 per cent discount rate, £10 earned next year may only be considered to be worth £9 today and £10 from the year after next will only be worth £8.10. Only a discount rate of zero would guarantee future generations' equitable treatment in current decisions. Unfortunately, a large part of the edifice of economic impact assessment is built on using a non-zero discount rate.

One way in which the word sustainability can be misused is to confuse, whether deliberately or otherwise, the social phenomenon of a particular company continuing to operate with the continuation of the world as a whole. Put like that it may seem outrageous; but of course it may indeed seem like the end of the world for those running any given company, should that company have to cease operations. But the absence of secure profits is surely wholly different from sustainability in the larger sense. Of course the word 'sustainability' can be used perfectly legitimately in the sense of corporate continuation; it is just the confusion with the larger sense that is a problem. One way in which this confusion occurs is through a focus on the business case for sustainability. In this way, phrases like 'sustainable profits' come to suggest both that profits can be made continuously and that to be profitable is to be sustainable (in some kind of ethical or environmental sense). Yet for any given company, one or both of these implications may be false.

So can measures of time be used in some practical way as a reliable guide to social aspects of sustainability? Chapter 12 takes this line of thought further through considering it as a resource and measuring the associated 'time burden' of companies on their stakeholders.

It is also worth pointing out that the unsustainability of the modern world seems quite closely connected to the pressure of lack of time, which most people feel. In that respect, one of the most significant impacts of companies is this sense of frenzy which is imparted to many employees, taking us ever further from anything which might be called 'timeless'. But of course, at least in one way, that sense of urgency is entirely justified: time is indeed running out for sustainability.

Sustainable development

During the twentieth century, 'sustainable development' preceded 'sustainability' in the sense we are using it here. The phrase 'sustainable development' emerged from the development community, that is those NGOs, governmental and inter-governmental organizations attempting to promote economic development for countries with high levels of poverty. Among the many factors which obstructed economic development were the environmentally destructive effects of traditional development, such as the sacrifice of rivers and river-based livelihoods for the sake of hydroelectric power schemes. This destroyed local communities, economies and the quality of life without guaranteeing economic advancement. In this way, environmental issues entered the social and economic development dialogue, and have remained an important element of it ever since.

Over time, development has increasingly been phrased in social, rather than solely in technical economic, terms. The Millennium Development Goals (MDGs) (UN, 2008) are the latest expression of this. The MDGs are:

1 Eradicate Extreme Poverty and Hunger
2 Achieve Universal Primary Education
3 Promote Gender Equality and Empower Women
4 Reduce Child Mortality
5 Improve Maternal Health
6 Combat HIV/AIDS, Malaria and other Diseases
7 Ensure Environmental Sustainability
8 Develop a Global Partnership for Development.

Of course, environmental issues are still very important for sustainable development. The seventh MDG directly concerns environmental aspects, while over half of the MDGs will depend to some extent on environmental conditions. The whole idea of sustainable development, then, underscores the necessity of social performance as a critical component of sustainability. This suggests that the measurement of social impact is therefore important to the achievement of environmental sustainability.

67

PRODUCTION, CONSUMPTION AND SUSTAINABILITY

Economic development requires both production and consumption. Sustainability, understood as living within environmental limits, therefore requires both sustainable production and sustainable consumption. Just as there is no universally agreed definition of sustainability, so there is also little agreement on the terms 'sustainable production' and 'sustainable consumption'. However, in comparison to sustainable consumption, sustainable production is much better understood. While the practical implementation of sustainable production is still very much an issue, the analysis of the environmental aspects of sustainable production are much further developed and the corresponding policy portfolio more advanced.

Sustainable consumption, on the other hand, has been treated largely as an accompaniment to sustainable production enjoying much less attention. Sustainable consumption is sometimes seen simply as an extension of health & safety and at other times only as a factor necessary to account for the fall in environmental performance (despite the adoption of sustainable production practices). Yet, at least in the medium term, there is no sustainable production without sustainable consumption. As a result the idea of sustainable consumption is becoming increasingly prominent in the work of the European Commission as well as of national governments and NGOs.

One of the reasons for the relative neglect of sustainable consumption is its complexity. It includes or is affected by a wide range of social issues, for example:

- the overall level of consumption;
- patterns of consumption and individual lifestyles;
- consumer behaviour and psychology;
- the sales and marketing practices of industry.

There are therefore social conditions for sustainability, without which sustainability is unlikely to be achieved. Understanding the social impact of companies is therefore important to achieving sustainability. What is needed is a shared understanding and coordinated action to make not only sustainable production but also sustainable consumption a reality.

Measuring sustainability

As we have seen in trying to understand sustainability and its three aspects, the metaphor of 'capital' is important. The general idea is that sustainability can be conceived as a combination of three capitals: natural capital, social capital and economic capital. Some analyses also add human capital and perhaps use manufactured capital and financial capital instead of economic capital. The idea, however, is the same. On the analogy of economic capital, there is an amount of natural or social resource that is necessary for sustainability, just as a quantity of economic capital is necessary for economic viability. The crucial consequence is that sustainability requires that capital is not depleted continuously, providing environmental and social limits.

While the metaphor of capital is tremendously suggestive, it also brings with it the structure and limitations of economics. In economics, capital is the factor of production produced by human activity. The other two factors of production are land (or the environment, more broadly) and labour (or society, more broadly). One implication of re-framing the other two factors of production is that they are seen as resources which are directly affected by human activity rather than some pre-given – and apparently inexhaustible – resource.

Seeing the environment and society as capital also suggests that they can be accounted for. Chapter 13 will explore exactly how that idea can be followed through. At this point, it is important to see that three major implications of this economic metaphor are that capital can be owned, substituted and accumulated.

The idea of owning natural resources has been with us for some time. Although in many traditional societies the idea of privately owning land is counter-cultural, since the enclosure movement, it has been normal in the West. The consequence is that natural resources are seen as the sole responsibility of individuals, irrespective of their use, and possible depletion, of them. Yet it is still contentious, for example, in the move to privatize the human genome or in patenting plant or animal species for commercial exploitation. As applied to social matters, ownership of capital is counter-intuitive. Discounting slavery, what can it mean to own human capital?

Another implication concerns the substitutability of capitals for each other. For traditional economics, one form of capital can, in principle, be substituted for other forms and still produce the same economic outcome. In this way, natural capital, such as stocks of oil or the composition of the atmosphere for example, can be substituted for educated scientists, who might be of more value to society. But of course there are some hard limits to this kind of substitution: educated scientists may not be able to survive, for all their education, in a world with a shattered climate. The idea of substitutability was behind the distinction between weak and strong sustainability, which was current a few years ago. The following extract from a report about the mining and minerals sector illustrates how it can be used:

> One way to assess the need for minerals is to look at the benefits derived from the use of mineral products – from minerals used directly, such as zinc dietary supplements, to durable uses such as tools, bricks, and aeroplanes or non-mineral products that are made through the use of minerals (such as food produced using tractors, ploughs, and other equipment made with metal). Society today is highly dependent on mineral-related materials for energy genera-

tion and transmission, mobility and transportation, information and communication, food supply, health delivery, and countless other services. Minerals use and production is also essential in terms of the livelihoods provided through employment and income generation ... and to a significant number of national economies ...
(MMSD, 2002, p74)

This train of thought could be used to justify any particular action for the sake of some other gain – usually of an economic kind. Yet this is precisely the perspective which has resulted in the current level of global unsustainability. It may still be decided to sacrifice some aspects of environmental or social well-being for the sake of economic gains, but this must not be presented as sustainable.

However, the main implication for measuring social impact is the quantifiability and possibility of accumulating capital. While financial and manufactured capital is quantifiable, it is much less clear that natural capital can be quantified. Of course, certain aspects of natural capital can be measured, such as the levels of carbon dioxide in the air, but this is an utterly different measure from the level of biodiversity, for example. So there are many different measures of natural capital. It is not at all clear that they can be added together in any meaningful way (Henriques and Richardson, 2004).

When it comes to social capital, the situation is, if anything, worse. As for natural capital, there are many different manifestations of social capital, such as levels of education, the extent of trust, the degree to which human rights are respected, and many more. On top of this, 'the social' is more of a process than a quantity of some measurable kind. And most importantly, what is valuable in social relationships, which must form a crucial part of social capital, is the quality of those relationships. The quality of a relationship is, I believe, inherently unsuited to quantified measurement. It seems even less obvious how it can be accumulated.

It is possible to argue that the demand for human rights in effect specifies a minimum set of conditions for being treated with dignity and respect. I believe it does this. However, respect for human rights is not capable of being measured at all easily. So it does not help in quantifying social capital in the broad sense, even if it does help in defining a threshold of performance. There is also one interpretation of 'social capital' which takes the more restricted view that it is comprised of networks of relationship. This view is explored in Chapter 7. However, the measurement of social capital, even in this relatively well-defined sense, is not easy to achieve, and it is harder still to determine how much is enough.

CAUSES AND CONSEQUENCES
OF SUSTAINABILITY

Some of the confusion about the place of social and economic issues in relation to sustainability arises because of the complex relationships between social, economic and environmental issues. If sustainability is understood in the narrowest sense as simply about environmental issues, then it is possible to be clear about the social and economic causes of environmental unsustainability on the one hand, and the consequences of environmental unsustainability on the other. This section traces out some of these connections, taking sustainability in this narrow, environmental sense.

Society and the environment

Environmental issues concern 'the natural world'. This is usually taken to mean the animals, air, plants, birds, forests, rocks, fish, seas and rivers – everything, in fact, except humanity and its works. However, while the natural world clearly does include all this, it is hard to maintain that it should exclude the human world. After all, the human race is also a natural species and the outcome of natural selection, according to evolutionary theory. So what it does is natural. It follows that sustainability does not mean *returning* to a state of nature – often caricatured by its critics as primitive and uncomfortable – since we are already there!

In fact there is a very strong dependence of social systems on environmental ones. This is often presented in strong terms by saying, for example, that while the world could survive without humanity indefinitely, humans could not survive without insects, to take just one class of animals, for more than a few years. Human society wholly depends on many environmental resources for its continuance. The rate at which we are destroying the environmental resources on which we depend has to make one question the designation of our species as *Homo sapiens*.

At any rate (especially if the natural world is actually everything) it is probably a mistake to look for a single kind of 'thing' which characterizes the natural world. What is possible is to take interdependence itself as the defining characteristic of 'the natural'. That would result in describing social actions which ignore or undermine the dependence of society on the rest of the world as unnatural, or perhaps less moralistically, as simply unsustainable. From this perspective we can define the environment as those factors external to society on which society depends.

The scale and nature of human activity is now such that social activity is having a clear, adverse effect on the environment. It is of course also possible that social activity can have a positive, or at least neutral, effect on environmental conditions. The struggles to establish such activities range from political and environmental campaigning through to initiatives such as CSR. The kind of social factors which are relevant to achieving environmental sustainability include poverty and war, which both drive people to make a living at any cost, and often at the cost of local environment.

Society and the economy

It is important to bear in mind that the economy is a subset of social activity. It is not a different kind of activity from that found elsewhere within the social dimension. Economic activities are carried out as part of normal social activities. As a result the economy is not in any sense independent of society. Indeed, in addition to natural resources, the economy depends on various social resources, such as legal institutions and property rights as well as many other entirely social constructions.

Nevertheless, economic activities can helpfully be separated out in looking at corporate impacts, as it is of particular importance for commercial companies. Unfortunately, in common use, the term 'economic' is ambiguous; it is used in both a narrow and a broad sense. It can refer simply to shareholder finances or it can refer to the wider economy. Consequently, economic unsustainability can simply mean 'unprofitable' or an inability to generate funds. It is therefore quite common to hear that a particular project, for example, is 'unsustainable'. In this narrow sense, this means that it will lose the business money. But this is to reduce the term to an unhelpful minimum. Much more significant for sustainability is the impact of a business on the wider economy. But what does that mean?

The economy can be characterized as that subset of social activities which uses resources to produce things used by society, either for consumption or for further production. An organization's impact on the economy will therefore include the financial flows due to shareholders and other providers of capital and loans. However it will also include the impact on the wider economy, which will usually include, among other factors:

- taxes paid to local and national authorities;
- subsidies received from local and national authorities;
- the nature of investments made, whether as part of its core business or simply as part of cash flow management;
- the economic consequences of employees' wages on the wider economy;
- financial flows to or from all stakeholders as a result of business activity;
- the consequences of payments to suppliers on their businesses;
- the externalities built into the market of its core business products and services;
- the contribution of its core business products and services to the wider economy.

According to traditional economics, one of the perspectives on environmental unsustainability is that it represents distortions of the market called 'externalities'. Externalities arise when transactions do not include the full costs (or benefits) associated with them. As a result these costs (or benefits) will get loaded (or free-loaded) onto other parties. The most systematic treatment of the externalities of climate change is perhaps that of the Stern Review, which contains the following analysis of climate change as an externality:

> *Climate change is a far more complicated negative externality than, for example, pollution (such as smog) or congestion (such as traffic jams). Key features of the greenhouse-gas externality are:*
> - *it is a global externality, as the damage from emissions is broadly the same regardless of where they are emitted, but the impacts are likely to fall very unevenly around the world;*
> - *its impacts are not immediately tangible, but are likely to be felt some way into the future. There are significant differences in the short-run and long-run implications of greenhouse-gas emissions. It is the stock of carbon in the atmosphere that drives climate change, rather than the annual flow of emissions. Once released, carbon dioxide remains in the atmosphere for up to 100 years;*
> - *there is uncertainty around the scale and timing of the impacts and about when irreversible damage from emission concentrations will occur;*
> - *the effects are potentially on a massive scale.*
> (Stern, 2007, p310)

Clearly economies must take account of environmental – and social – issues if they are to function efficiently. It is also true that a proper analysis of sustainability must take account of social and economic issues as well as environmental ones. In the end, many economic issues, and social issues more generally, are simply additional ways of thinking about environmental issues. However, there are also social issues which have relatively little impact on the environment or only do so indirectly, but are important in their own right. Stakeholder engagement, considered as a value in itself, is one of these.

Given the crucial dependencies between environmental, social and economic dimensions, it is easy to fall back on the idea that 'everything depends on everything else' – making priorities seem arbitrary. However, there is a significant causal ordering of these dimensions: the environment is the fundamental dimension, since without it we all die. Second, comes society which is subordinate to the environment. Third, comes the economy. The economy is subordinate to society, as there is no point in economic gains if these do not serve social ends. It follows that the economy is subordinate to the environment. Nevertheless, in understanding and analysing social issues, it remains true that a significant subset of them will hinge on environmental matters. The consequences of global warming, for example, will very likely have colossal social consequences, such as war and famine.

UNDERSTANDING SOCIAL SUSTAINABILITY

There are three ways in which the phrase 'social sustainability' might be understood:

* as a condition for environmental sustainability;
* as the property of a society that does not undermine itself;
* as a set of social goals or values.

The first conception, in which to say society is sustainable means that there are adequate social conditions to support environmental sustainability, has been described very briefly in the last section.

The second conception of social sustainability is as a social system which does not undermine itself. The social unsustainability of an organization – or society – would imply that it is undermining the social conditions on which it rests. Of course the sustainability of human society implies more than just the continued existence of human society in one form or another. What is also meant is to question whether a particular social form which we currently experience will itself last. One answer to this is that it will not – that is, a given society will not be sustainable, in a purely social sense – if it undermines its own resource base. Beyond this, it is also possible to consider whether a particular society will undermine its own social conditions. This, of course is the stuff of history. The view that such contradictions are the essence of historical change is a long-established perspective, raised to a philosophical art form by Hegel.

Returning to the relatively limited horizons of an individual company, it is possible to ask how far the activities of that company undermine its own existence. To that extent they will not be sustainable. Companies are of course quite alert to this issue; a great deal of attention is paid to satisfying customers, for example. It is also possible that corporate activities undermine the conditions supporting other companies. Where the other companies are competitors, this is taken to be normal market activity. Where the activities undermine companies that are not peers, then there may be far more complex questions before a charge of unsustainability can be levied.

For example, if a company changes its manufacturing process and so reduces the demand for some of its inputs to levels which drive suppliers out of business, that will usually be regarded as 'just the way the market works'. If a pharmaceutical company, for example, undermines related but quite different social institutions, perhaps a national health service, then it may not be clear whether the company is sustainable. In these cases, perhaps there should at least be a presumption that such activity is not sustainable until proven otherwise. A further example could be a company deciding to pull out of a community of which it has been an important part. Some may argue that such a course of action would be determined by business decisions and so is 'just business'. However, the confectionary manufacturer Hershey decided in 2002 that their strategy of exiting their local community was unsustainable due to the adverse public reaction. In this vein, it could be argued that an organization which consumed more social resources than it produced could be deemed socially unsustainable. This is precisely the approach that Mark McElroy has elaborated (McElroy, 2008b).

The third conception sees social sustainability as the possession by society of certain social goals or values which imbue social relationships. Precisely what such values might be needs careful definition. If they are defined at too detailed a level, then the attempt to universalize them can be counterproductive and lead to conflict. Much religious conflict seems to stem from resistance to the values which others try to impose. Too detailed an insistence on common social values can either lead to oppression or to a lifelessness borne of submission. Even if conflict is not a problem, another issue with defining common values as a condition of sustainability is that it suggests a certain uniformity of society. This seems to leave little room for diversity or for a dynamic society.

Nevertheless, if values are specified at a high level, then these problems need not arise. Toleration might be one such value. The definition of sustainability used by Forum for the Future incorporates such high-level social aspirations: 'Sustainable development is a dynamic process which enables all people to realize their potential and to improve their quality of life in ways which simultaneously protect and enhance the Earth's life support systems' (Wright and Hooper, 2001).

The collection of human rights also represents an attempt which enjoys global consensus to define a set of social goals. The Millennium Development Goals can be seen in this light. A society in which human rights were respected could therefore be called one which is socially sustainable. Human rights are of course based on the fundamental idea of respecting people. At a more abstract level still, this principle itself could be said to define social sustainability. The principle of respecting other people is more usually stated as the ethical principle of treating people not as means but as ends. This principle is the foundation of one of the most prominent schools of ethical thought. And it is interesting to reflect that an extension of this ethical principle beyond the human world to that of nature would seem very likely to entail environmental sustainability also.

5

Thinking Like a Stakeholder

Stakeholders are absolutely fundamental to the assessment of the social impact of companies. They are fundamental because the impact a company has on society is the impact it has on its stakeholders. It is possible to be so definitive about this simply because of how the term 'stakeholder' is defined. Following Edward Freeman, the term is almost universally defined as 'any person or organization which affects, or is affected by an organization' (Freeman, 1984). But since the social impacts of a company involve people and organizations, those people or organizations must be affected by the organization and so be its stakeholders. In other words companies relate to the rest of society through their stakeholders.

In *Corporate Truth* I argued that it was important to take a radical view of the nature of companies in relation to stakeholders:

> *Companies are to stakeholders as bodies are to cells. It is possible to think of our bodies as 'nothing but' the collection of cells which compose them. Yet it is also possible to describe our bodies as coherent entities with purposes and actions of their own. In the language of complexity theory, our bodies can be said to be emergent entities that cannot be completely described in terms of their cells. Both views are valid. A similar divergence of perspective applies to companies. It is possible to describe them entirely in terms of their stakeholders. In this respect, companies are 'empty' and their activity is simply the co-ordination of stakeholders' activities.*
> (Henriques, 2007, p36)

One of the key implications of this is that shareholders and company management are each stakeholders of their company. They may be psychologically identified with the company, but they are not the same thing as the company. A similar consideration applies to staff in general. While company management is identified with the company, employees are often described as 'internal' stakeholders. This suggests that they are somehow inside the company, but other than the idea – or hope – that they identify with the company, the phrase 'internal' actually makes very little sense.

Stakeholders are stakeholders *of* a company. That is, being a stakeholder is a matter of relationship. It is not possible to be a stakeholder entirely on your own, only in relation to an organization (or possibly also a project of some kind). It is also a matter of fact, rather than decree. Occasionally companies do not recognize stakeholders, and may try to say that one group or another are not *really* stakeholders. But that simply means that they do not *wish* to recognize them.

It is sometimes suggested, for example, that in order to be a stakeholder, the group or individual in question must have a 'stake' in the company. While that appears to make sense, it is necessary to be very careful in practice. The reasoning behind the proposal is that many companies are subjected to campaigns in which those campaigning have no other relationship with the company other than through that campaign. Since they have nothing to lose, the argument runs, why should we bother with them? Animal rights campaigners can be seen in this light. Other than a concern for animal rights, there is no other 'investment' in the company. Unlike shareholders, for example, they have nothing to lose. However the same could be said of human rights campaigners, such as those that campaign on supply chain issues. And to apply that logic to organizations concerned with labour rights in the supply chain seems absurd. In general it would exclude organizations with only a legitimate moral concern from being legitimate stakeholders – including those who campaigned for the abolition of slavery. In addition such stakeholders can have a significant impact on the company's reputation, so to refuse to acknowledge that they have a stake in the company can be dangerous.

The term 'stakeholder' is also used to mean something like 'participant' in connection with government consultations, for example. While such a use makes sense, it is much more difficult to be precise about what it means to relate to a process like a consultation. It is much more straightforward to define a stakeholder in relation to an organization, such as a company.

However that does not make it *easy* to identify the stakeholders of a company! Of course, some appear obvious. For commercial companies, the following list is typically the starting point:

- customers;
- suppliers;
- employees;
- community;
- shareholders.

It is important that shareholders are considered as stakeholders. Shareholders obviously have much power over the company they own, but just as members of the senior management team are distinct from the company they run, shareholders are not the same thing as the company they own.

The term 'community' is often used by companies wanting to explain their 'CSR'. Yet of all possible stakeholders, the community is least well-defined. There are perfectly sensible uses of the term. For example, it can refer to those people who live next to the premises of a company – the 'fenceline community'. This gives it a real meaning. However, the term is also used without any clear designation at all. This often happens when there is an established 'community programme' within a company, whose aim is to make charitable donations, often without a clear logic as to why any particular element of 'the community' (typically a charity) is being granted the largesse of that particular company. So it is important to be precise about exactly which organizations and which people are covered by any use of the term 'community'.

Employees might appear to be more clearly defined. And obviously when companies are employing staff, such people count as stakeholders. Just as with senior management and shareholders, it is again important to differentiate between staff and the company. Although it goes against the grain of much effort to integrate staff into company values and practices, staff are, clearly, entirely separate from the company for which they work. As we have seen, staff are an independent group, not really 'inside' it in any meaningful sense, even though they may fairly often identify with the company they work for.

Yet who counts as an employee is not entirely clear-cut. There is a wide range of employment contracts which at one extreme are the same as supplier contracts. Employment contracts may be part-time, they may be based not on time but on output or they may be effectively entirely casual arrangements. Piece-rate workers or cleaners on zero-hour contracts are examples of stakeholders who can easily be left entirely out of account by large companies keen to showcase how well they look after their 'more important' senior staff.

Suppliers are stakeholders too. Suppliers do not always make it very far into company reports. When they do, they often feature in their role as vehicles for a company to show how it is propagating good environmental practice. This is how Sharp, the electronics company, sees its relationship with suppliers:

> It is necessary for all related suppliers, as well as the Sharp group, in other words the entire supply-chain, to work on the promotion of our CSR efforts, not only in material procurement but also in the entire series of business processes of development, production, sales and service.
>
> Sharp believes that the understanding and cooperation of suppliers is essential for promoting our CSR efforts in the entire supply-chain. We, therefore, have established the Sharp Basic Purchasing Principles, and also the Sharp Supply-Chain CSR Deployment Guidebook, which is in conformity with the Supply-Chain CSR Deployment Guidebook published in August 2006 by the Japan Electronics and Information Technology Industries Association (JEITA). We sincerely request our suppliers to make their own CSR efforts, according to the principles and guidebook.
>
> (Sharp, 2008)

There is of course little wrong with encouraging suppliers to adopt good social and environmental practices. The question is whether suppliers are also treated as stakeholders to whom the company owes some responsibility.

Customers on the other hand *are* more often regarded as stakeholders. Certainly, few companies ignore their customers' needs entirely, for to do so is to fail commercially. Yet very often the relationship with customers is treated as a wholly commercial matter, rather than one for which the company must take responsibility. As a result, customers can feature only indirectly in company reports. Neither the CSR report (Nestlé, 2008a) nor the financial reports (Nestlé, 2008b) for Nestlé for 2007 appear to say even how many customers the company has or what they think of Nestlé.

The rest of this chapter will address:

- the process of identifying stakeholders;
- problems with identifying stakeholders;
- stakeholder engagement in theory and practice;
- the limits of stakeholder dialogue.

IDENTIFYING STAKEHOLDERS

The basic list of a company's stakeholders above is of course far from complete even when shareholders, customers, suppliers, employees, the community and shareholders have been included. There is in fact a significant challenge in identifying a company's stakeholders. This operates on many levels:

- who counts as a stakeholder beyond the basic list?
- will a general category do – or can only specific organizations or individuals count?
- how far is it necessary to go in subdividing a stakeholder category?
- are representative stakeholders really stakeholders?
- is my stakeholder's stakeholder also my stakeholder?

The basic list of stakeholders is incomplete in part because, other than the community, it includes only stakeholders directly concerned with delivering the company's core business. Many companies have a number of stakeholders that are less directly connected with it, such as the following:

- regulators;
- local authorities;
- members of the government;
- opinion formers;
- competition authorities;
- NGOs and campaigning groups;
- religious institutions;

- non-customers and potential customers;
- competitors.

All these organizations and individuals may have an interest in what a company does. Some, such as opinion formers, may affect public perceptions of the company and thus influence its reputation. Others, such as religious institutions, may have a moral interest in what the company does. Still others, such as non-customers, may include people who really need or want the product a company produces, but are excluded from obtaining it for a variety of reasons. This list is of course in no way complete. And it will vary from company to company. For some companies, such as utilities, regulators may be of great significance, while for others they may be of little practical importance (although they must still be counted in the list of stakeholders). The only way to begin to get a complete list is systematically to attempt to understand the variety of relationships the company has with the rest of society.

This may include grouping stakeholders according to whether they are essential to the survival of the business – this is the category of primary stakeholders identified by Freeman. Other possible groupings include whether there is a commercial or legally defined relationship with the group, how frequently the organization interacts with it and, perhaps most significantly, whether the group is particularly vulnerable to the actions of the company. In contrast, another grouping that does not make very much sense is that of internal versus external. We have already seen how there is no inside to a company, so it makes little sense to consider which stakeholders may be inside it.

In considering whether a given organization counts as a stakeholder, there may appear to be a choice between an organization and an individual within that organization who is the actual contact point. For example, a campaigning NGO may have a lead campaigner on an environmental issue. Does that make that person the 'actual' stakeholder – or is it the Director of the NGO – or is it the organization as a whole?

In a sense each of these answers is right. What determines 'stakeholdership' is the relationship with the company. The lead campaigner, the Director and the organization each have a relationship with the company. And in certain circumstances it may be appropriate to deal with each as a stakeholder, but in different ways. As a rule, however, if an organization can be considered as a stakeholder, it is wise to include it in the list. The lead campaigner and the Director may in practice be the way in which the company deals with the NGO; dealing with the organization usually requires dealing with at least some of its staff.

When treating staff as a stakeholder, how far should they be treated as a set of different groups? We have already talked about senior management as a stakeholder group. But senior management are almost always employees of the company. Yet it seems wrong to lump them together with the staff they may be managing. And it is: it is important to divide a stakeholder group according to the relationship it has with the company. The CEO and the cleaner may technically both be employees, but they have such radically different interests in the company that it makes little sense to try to analyse their issues together. That may be obvious. However, senior management rarely features in accounts of employees considered as stakeholders. Beyond seniority, other divisions of staff that merit separate analysis include:

- role;
- gender and sexuality;
- age differences;
- ability and disability;
- ethnicity;
- religious affiliation.

It is becoming more common for companies to analyse their employees' issues in such terms. Of course what is important is whether a particular sub-group of employees has an issue which is not shared with other groups (or the issue may be its relationship to one or more of the other sub-groups). Shop floor workers, for example, may share a stressful relationship with their supervisor. That kind of issue is what makes it useful to consider separate sub-groups.

WILL THE REAL STAKEHOLDER STAND UP?

NGOs

Many companies have a somewhat schizophrenic attitude to NGOs. On the one hand they are given special attention and viewed as a useful source of issues and ideas. On the other they are regarded with some irritation: they are too negative and may seem to lack legitimacy for what they say. This means that they are, on the whole, an important stakeholder for companies in many ways.

But how much truth is there in the charge that they lack legitimacy, or put another way, that 'they are not real stakeholders'? The source of this may well be the fact that their claim to the attention of a company is often based on single issues. It is not usually based on any kind of operational relationship.

Here it is important to differentiate between grass roots consumer organizations which may have grown out of the dissatisfaction with a company's products and services and a campaigning group, perhaps one concerned with animal rights or the operations of a company overseas. While the consumer organization has a more organic relationship with the company, the animal rights group's concern is based entirely on a concern for others.

Although this could lead to dismissing the NGO's concerns, that would be a mistake. Concern for others is fundamental to the ethical outlook. That is not to say that all NGOs are always entirely right in their concern or appropriate in their tactics. But it does mean that to dismiss such organizations as 'not real stakeholders' is an error – and one which could easily backfire on a company taking that attitude.

Supply chain

Supply chains are immensely complex. As Figure 5.1 shows, the relationship of an organization typically involves a number of tiers. There is often no direct commercial relationship between those several tiers down from the purchasing company and the purchasing company itself.

Yet companies often regard members of tiers with which they have no direct relationship as stakeholders. There is no legal obligation to do so. There is however a strong moral obligation, as the whole history of concern with supply chain issues shows. But of course, despite the fact that there is no (direct) commercial relationship, for companies which purchase on a large scale, there is a strong influence by the company on the conditions which obtain throughout the supply chain. They are therefore validly regarded as stakeholders.

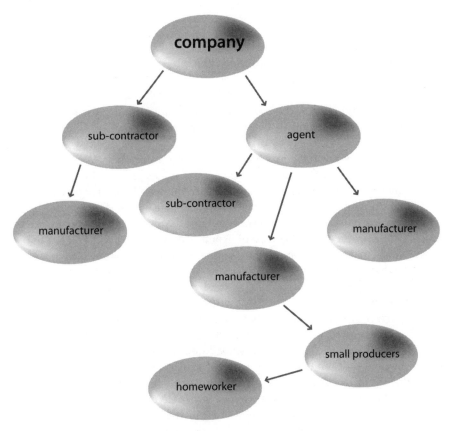

Figure 5.1 *Supply Chain*

Consumers

Stakeholder groups can be complicated. As with a number of stakeholder groups, consumers can present as a complex of different organizations, with some 'real people', the individual consumers, behind all of them. Take the consumers of an electronics company, perhaps purchasers of Sony CDs. A few years ago, Sony included software hidden on its music CDs which infected consumers' computers in the manner of a virus (ConsumerAffairs, 2005).

In relation to such an issue, especially where as in Sony's case, affected consumers number in their tens of thousands or more, there will typically be a range of interested groups, in addition to the individual people who buy the product in question, including:

- consumer NGOs, such as Which? and Consumers International;
- web-based consumer forums;
- ad hoc consumer groups for the company's products;
- policy consumer organizations, such as the NCC;
- hostile websites built by disgruntled consumers;
- potential future customers.

Which of these represents the most valid stakeholder opinion? It is possible to make arguments that can all be discounted and so none of them need be engaged. The NGOs and policy organizations can be disregarded as professional lobbyists that may not have much knowledge of the products in question. The ad hoc groups are clearly reactive to particular issues and the hostile websites are 'obviously biased'. If it is then argued that the web-based forums are solely for the consumers' benefit, that leaves only the consumers themselves. And of course it is costly to address consumers in large numbers, beyond the marketing which is done in the normal course of events. So, for some companies, a tempting answer is that there is no need to engage with their consumers in any way – beyond what the marketing department already does! Fortunately Sony's response was not as negative as this, and the concerns of consumers were ultimately met.

In general, a better answer is to say that all such groups, including the individual consumers, need to be involved. There is a sense in which the individuals who purchased the CDs are the most important – and in a way all the other groups depend on them. It is they who suffer if there is some kind of product issue. But there is a real issue with the numbers involved; it is unlikely to be economic or necessary to engage with every single one. The consumer groups and activities listed above therefore do a lot of the work of the company for it, in filtering out the issues about which the company's consumers care most.

Beyond this, all the consumer organizations are also organizations which have a relationship with Sony. They are therefore among Sony's stakeholders in their own right. They therefore need consideration in this respect – as well as for their relationship and concern for the individual consumers of Sony's products.

Unions

Labour unions are another stakeholder which raises representation issues. Unions were first formed some 200 years ago as a result of workers coming together to protect their interests; they continue today to campaign for workers' rights. They represent a formal way in which the collective voice of workers can be heard. They were founded and are run on democratic principles, with formal procedures for the election of officials and the adoption of policy. Unions now enjoy some legal recognition in some parts of the world, with formal rights to be consulted over issues which affect their members.

One of the central things for which unions have fought is the right to negotiate and discuss on behalf of their members with a company and its management. Are the unions or their members the 'real stakeholder'? Of course to formulate the question in this way is to assume that there is a choice. In much the same way as with consumer groups, there are clearly (at least) two stakeholder groups here. Historically the formation of unions was important as it enabled workers, who may not have had the education or habit of negotiation, to hold their own against a management which was powerful and did not often have the interests of the workers at heart. The representative function was, and is, very real. It is legitimated by their formal procedures for worker consultation as well as the role of union representatives within the workforce of a unionized workplace. The individual consultation of staff which is favoured by management as part of CSR by-passes collective bargaining. While it has a role, the process of individual consultation is usually too close to management to provide, on its own, a complete and reliable source of information on staff issues.

The union movement has only relatively recently acknowledged the significance of the corporate responsibility movement. Since CSR first emerged, a significant proportion of the union movement has been rather sceptical of it. One of the reasons for this may be that it represented both a threat to their relationship with management and at the same time seemed rather distant from the main issues posed by a company's operations. And there is some substance to this: it is quite possible for a company to present 'stakeholder engagement' with its staff – consisting of a few informal discussions or even a staff survey – as sufficient to discharge its moral, if not legal, obligations to consult with their staff. Since the quality of much stakeholder engagement is poor in this sense, unions are right to be sceptical of its significance.

Stakeholder engagement with staff must therefore include unions as the key, representative stakeholder. That is, the discussions and relationship which a company has with its unions is stakeholder engagement. It follows that any reporting of employee engagement in a unionized company which does not reflect the union's view is incomplete.

Accepting the validity of the representative role of unions has a number of consequences. Firstly, recognizing unions in this way does not mean that only union-mediated discussions count as valid engagement. It is entirely possible to engage with staff in addition to maintaining union relationships. This may be desirable in circumstances in which union membership is low. However that does not mean that such consultations should be used to undermine union representation.

Secondly, unions are themselves organizations with a relationship to the company in which they work. This means that there may be issues with how a company treats a union, quite separate from how it treats the union's members. This is particularly applicable to large companies with significant union representation.

Thirdly, while a democratic structure means that their core accountability is discharged to their members, there will usually be more to do to ensure that all the union's stakeholders are properly treated. So accountability for the treatment of their own staff will be an important issue for unions to deal with.

Finally, it is particularly important not to reduce worker consultation to an impoverished stakeholder engagement when extensive supply chains are involved. Some of the worst cases of worker abuse can occur in countries, such as China and North Korea, in which unions are illegal. However it is no substitute for the creation and recognition of unions in such countries to hold discussions with non-union organizations, especially when these are in the West. One reason this may happen is that campaigning for workers' rights may take place in the West, and this may have an impact on public opinion. A natural, but on its own inadequate, response to that is to engage directly with the organizations campaigning in the West. Of course there is nothing in itself wrong with holding such talks; the problem comes when they are held up as stakeholder engagement adequate to address the problem. A better course would be to engage with international union organizations which are fully aware of the problem.

The environment as a stakeholder

The environment is often represented as a stakeholder in stakeholder diagrams. Yet the environment is not a stakeholder – at least in the same sense that unions or consumers are stakeholders. Nevertheless, there is some logic in including the environment amongst stakeholders.

One reason why this makes sense is that it can be hard to identify the actual people who may be affected by an environmental issue. Global warming, for example, affects and will affect a great many people. Yet they may not fall into any group that is easily identifiable or has any other relationship with a company. Despite this, it is known that there is a problem with global warming and that it can and should be addressed. Therefore it makes sense for a company which is not zero-carbon to identify a stakeholder group as 'those who are affected by global warming'. On this logic, the set of environmental issues represents a collection of stakeholders, many of which may have other relationships with the company and all of which will be concerned with environmental issues.

It could be argued that some environmental issues have no corresponding stakeholder. Biodiversity may be cited as an example. Against this it can be argued that biodiversity has many benefits for humanity, such as the discovery of new drugs. And this is not just special pleading for biodiversity, as biodiversity is representative of a number of other environmental issues, such as the preservation of wilderness, which can appear to have no human stakeholder. Careful examination will always show that there is an interested party, which may sometimes be amongst future generations. That group is the stakeholder. In the final resort, the fact that the issue has been identified suggests that there has to be a stakeholder – even if it is only the scientific community which has identified the issue.

However, many elements of the environment, particularly animals, can be regarded as stakeholders in their own right. Of course they will not be forthcoming in stakeholder dialogues, but that does not mean that they should not be treated with respect. Ecuador has followed this through logically and adopted a new constitution which grants rights to the non-human world (Kendall, 2008).

Special groups

The young, the old, the mentally incapacitated and some of the disabled represent another set of people who present particular problems for stakeholder identification, and for engagement. One thing which this diverse set of people all have in common is vulnerability. It can be very easy to ignore them and to misinterpret their needs. The following section will address the difference this can make to engagement strategies; this one will consider the issue of representation.

Since it is not easy to engage with young children, for example, at least using the techniques appropriate to adults, they are very often contacted through representative organizations or NGOs. Groups which represent the interests of these special groups have a crucial role to play, and they often have a deep insight into the issues which such people have. It is therefore very important that they are included in any relevant engagement.

However, this does not mean it is impossible to engage with special groups. It is actually quite possible to work with young children and to find out a great deal about what they need and want. Companies already do this on some issues when they undertake market research into children's products with children. NGOs, such as Save the Children also consult children to develop their understanding of children's needs. There will of course be additional safeguards needed in such engagement, but it is entirely possible as the following extract concerning the way Save the Children (SC UK) consults children on its own activities shows.

> SC UK has tested a variety of mechanisms of engagement with disadvantaged children which includes: information sharing; consultations; focus group discussions; involvement in design, implementation and evaluation of projects and programmes; peer reviews; participation in strategic planning; children advisory's

boards; participation in staff recruitment processes; and, feedback/complaints systems. The organisation also plans to explore in the future e-mail and website links and representation of children on management boards. There is no blueprint about mechanisms to be used in engaging children as stakeholders in the governance of the organisation and there should not be one. Indeed, to be effective, these mechanisms need to be appropriate to the local context, developed in consultation with children and evolve as learning is acquired. (Stefanoni, 2003)

Children can be very articulate. Other vulnerable stakeholders may be much less so, for example the mentally incapacitated. In these circumstances, engagement may well be possible via an intermediary such as a carer. However, using intermediaries alone needs to be undertaken with some care, especially when they are close to the person involved or are family, since there may be difficulties in separating the ill person's needs from that of the carer. Similar issues apply to other kinds of special groups. Children are again relevant here; their carers, normally their parents, have many vested interests connected with their own children.

STAKEHOLDER ENGAGEMENT IN THEORY

The following is a list of stakeholder engagement techniques deemed suitable by the OECD for 'higher level stakeholder involvement' in addressing issues surrounding the disposal of radioactive waste (OECD, 2004):

- public hearings;
- deliberative polling;
- focus groups;
- citizen advisory groups;
- consultative groups;
- nominal group process;
- multi-actor policy workshops;
- charette;
- delphi process;
- round tables;
- citizen task forces;
- study circles;
- scenario workshop;
- referendum;
- consensus conferences;
- citizens' juries;
- citizens' panels;
- participatory site selection;
- local monitoring, oversight and information committees.

The purpose of citing this list is not to begin an exhaustive analysis of the different types of technique available, but to suggest that perhaps such an analysis is unlikely ever to be completed. If there is such a large number of techniques suitable for one sector for one 'level' of engagement, the full, definitive list must be awesome indeed. And yet the list, when examined more closely, includes many techniques which are clearly variants on one another. Beyond this it would be quite possible to extend the list somewhat arbitrarily to produce forms such as a 'study circle charette' or a 'citizen task force study workshop'. This multiplication of practices is one reason stakeholder engagement is regarded as a difficult process.

The more fundamental reason is that, to be successful, stakeholder engagement requires stakeholder participation and involvement. Engagement is not a way to get stakeholders to do what an organization wants or to tell them what it is going to do anyway – although it is used in both those ways quite commonly. True engagement is a joint exercise in which an organization and one or more of its stakeholders interact to find new ways of working together. Partnerships are sometimes regarded as the ideal model of stakeholder engagement. This is misleading, however, since formal partnerships are only suitable for organizations – and for those which are prepared to work on clearly defined projects. While partnerships can be examples of engagement, there are many other ways in which organizations can truly engage with their stakeholders.

If there is a difference between 'consultation' and engagement, then consultation is concerned with discovering what a stakeholder thinks or wants from an organization. This is clearly at a lower level than cooperatively working together, but at least the stakeholder is being treated as a subject with needs and desires, rather than as an object of manipulation.

This is not true of 'stakeholder communications' which usually means simply informing a stakeholder of what the organization intends. Even this may be regarded as better than ignoring a stakeholder, which is clearly not engagement in any sense whatever.

The standard from AccountAbility for stakeholder engagement, AA1000 SES, talks in terms of a commitment by the organization to inclusivity, that is the involvement of the stakeholder with the organization. This is interpreted (AccountAbility, 2006b) in terms of:

- knowing stakeholders' and the organization's material concerns;
- understanding stakeholder concerns, that is, views, needs, and performance expectations and perceptions associated with their material issues;
- coherently responding to stakeholders' and the organization's material concerns.

Above all, best practice stakeholder engagement will include the participation of the stakeholder at every stage. This will mean that stakeholders will be:

- consulted as to how they should best be engaged;

- asked what they want of the organization (not merely what they think of it);
- asked to suggest how what they want of the organization can best be measured;
- given feedback on the outcome of the engagement.

The problem of stakeholder engagement technique is how to do all of that effectively for a particular situation. Many of the techniques listed at the beginning of this section require a significant input of time and effort from the individuals involved to undertake a sophisticated dialogue. This demands a certain level of interest, capability and capacity, which is not found everywhere. Most of the techniques (other than referenda) are also unsuitable, or too expensive, for very wide scale application.

So one way to begin to size the problem is to consider the different kinds of situation which may call for engagement. The dimensions which may be relevant include:

- scale;
- vulnerability;
- language and culture;
- gender;
- the technical complexity of the issues.

I have elsewhere (Henriques and Laerke-Engelschmidt, 2007) given a long and representative list of the variety of techniques which may be suitable, given the considerations just listed. From the point of view of the management, a further question will arise as to what capacity the company has to respond to stakeholders.

STAKEHOLDER ENGAGEMENT IN PRACTICE

Stakeholder dialogue is not easy. This section is about how easy it is for stakeholder dialogue to go wrong, as much as how it can work well.

The first way it can go wrong is to get mislabelled. By stakeholder dialogue, I am not trying to distinguish between 'dialogue', 'consultation' and 'communication'. Of course it is possible to make distinctions, but I would hope that each term is intended to cover meaningful exchanges of information about the issues of concern to the stakeholder and to the organization. Above all it means that the exchange is two-way; it should never only be about an organization telling a stakeholder something.

Stakeholder dialogue or engagement or consultation is the universal mantra of CSR. But what stakeholder dialogue actually *is*, is not so easy to discern. From the majority of social, environmental or sustainability reports it would appear to mean a meeting by a company with NGOs who may be concerned with some of the issues facing a company.

Stakeholder dialogue can simply mean being in touch with stakeholders. This includes the many forms in which an organization may routinely make contact with its stakeholders – through commercial operations, through customer feedback, through shareholder briefings - or even by putting up a sign in the road warning that the road is being dug up. These are all examples, at one level or another, of stakeholder dialogue.

Stakeholder dialogue has also come to mean the set piece consultations which address the topic of CSR or ethical concern itself. In other words the topic of dialogue is not what the organization should be doing about the stakeholder it is talking to, but about what the organization should be doing about some other stakeholder. Unless that is the avowed purpose of the stakeholder in question, as it may be for some NGOs, this approach is not helpful. Even worse is the reduction of the subject of stakeholder dialogue to the process of reporting to stakeholders. Reporting, of course, is a subject of some importance, but can hardly claim to be the centrepiece of stakeholder dialogue.

The many reasons why it is a good idea to talk to stakeholders regularly and often, include:

- establishing, or re-establishing an organization's licence to operate;
- increasing trust between the organization and the stakeholder;
- reducing the costs of transactions;
- alerting the organization to upcoming issues;
- stimulating innovation in dealing with them.

A lot of activity that is labelled stakeholder dialogue goes on. Some of it works quite well. Some of it doesn't really help either the organization or the stakeholders concerned.

The pitfalls include:

- not facing your stakeholder as a result of talking about the right issue to the wrong person, or to the right person about the wrong thing;
- not listening to your stakeholder;
- talking to the right person about the right thing, and listening to them, but doing nothing about it.

The following sections describe some real life instances of stakeholder dialogue. Some of them went right; some of them did not. Most of them have been made anonymous; this makes it easier to talk more directly about the problems as well as the successes.

Supply chain

Large, global scale brands have a lot of stakeholders. An organization of this kind with a big presence on the high street will have even more. A company we can call 'Footsport' was this kind of organization.

To talk to its stakeholders, Footsport had decided to hold a series of three regional consultations, one in the Far East, one in America and one in Europe. This account describes the European consultation. It was attended by several people from Footsport, two trade associations, a near-competitor, an NGO, a union and the facilitators. The ground rules were that:

- the origin of particular views would be treated as confidential, although the comments themselves could be quoted without attribution;
- participants agreed to allow each other a fair hearing.

The first thing to notice is that this was essentially a multi-stakeholder meeting. While it was innovative and helpful to have a near-competitor, it may have been inhibiting for some of the participants. The multi-stakeholder nature of the meeting was deliberate in that Footsport was perhaps hoping to be taken out of the hot seat to some extent – allowing the various stakeholders concerned with the supply chain in particular to talk to each other directly.

However some of the comments from the meeting were that a number of important stakeholders were missing. These included:

- government;
- consumers;
- the press;
- suppliers;
- environmental NGOs;
- challenging or campaigning NGOs.

Just as significantly, it was pointed out that the most important stakeholders operated at a far more local level, and were not likely to attend a meeting such as the regional one.

The main topics of the meeting were firstly for Footsport to set out how it approached supply chain issues, secondly for participants to comment on Footsport's performance and then on its reporting. Finally, there was some comment on the consultation process itself.

In terms of general issues, a number of problems were discussed. One of these was how difficult it would be for Footsport, which was mainly a fashion brand, to build itself into a 'lifecycle brand' which seriously considered all aspects of its products' lifecycles, from raw materials to social impact. There was also discussion of the difficulties of paying a 'living wage'. These centred on how appropriate it would be to pay out of line with prevailing wage rates.

The recommendations of the meeting on improving performance were that:

- there should be more interaction between the various different stakeholders in order to achieve common goals;
- it was important to get workers' feedback – a qualitative perspective – on the supply chain management process and its implementation;

- there was a need to educate staff and workers on the overall lifecycle impacts of Footsport's products;
- a timetable for progress against issues would be very useful.

On reporting, there was considerable discussion as to the purpose of social reporting. It was not felt that the reports were actually read that often, but nevertheless they should include examples of failure and should be verified. It was also pointed out that different stakeholders have very different needs. A single report for all stakeholders would not necessarily meet the needs of any one group properly. A number of technical comments about the presentation of data in the report were also made.

One feature of the meeting was the heavy concentration on feedback on social and environmental reporting. This was of great concern to Footsport, but of only secondary concern to the various stakeholders present. That is partly because the convenors of the meeting were responsible for producing the report, whereas the various participants were only really interested in the underlying issues. A report which was aimed directly at the workers of factories in Asia, for example, would have been a different matter entirely. But then, it would require a wholly different set of participants at the meeting to consider it properly. Even so, it is doubtful whether the workers would have been interested in the minutiae of reporting rather than the conditions in their workplace.

In the closing session, which covered feedback on the meeting itself, an interesting comment was made that the meeting was very interesting, 'but it wasn't really stakeholder engagement, was it?' This comment was made by the union representative who felt that while there had been an interesting intellectual discussion of the issues, it did not get down to the real issues which made workers' lives a misery in the factories run by Footsport's suppliers. That would have required the involvement of the workers themselves first of all and also of local unions.

Shoppers

There are shoppers everywhere, and an NGO we will call 'Shopperforce' wanted to represent them. NGOs, especially membership ones, tend to consult their stakeholders formally less frequently than companies. Indeed this is something that companies often complain about.

Shopperforce, however, set up a consultation exercise with shoppers. The context in which this consultation was developed was one in which Shopperforce was searching for a new, clearer direction for its own work.

The consultation had a number of objectives including:

- Exploration of shoppers' current problems – what were the hot topics?
- How do shoppers perceive and experience these problems: what thoughts and feelings are involved?

- Whom do shoppers perceive to be the 'culprits' and what is the nature of their relationship with them?
- Could Shopperforce be a champion in all of this – and if so, in what kind of role?

A balanced sample of shoppers was independently recruited for this exercise, in the manner common to qualitative market research. There were 16 participants facilitated by a team of three people. A small incentive plus travel expenses were paid to attract people to the meeting. The participants were:

- four aged 18–30, single;
- four aged 25–45 with children living at home;
- four aged 45–55;
- four aged 55+, empty nesters.

Within each of these groups, two people were mid to high income (A/B/C1 socioeconomic group) and two were low income or unemployed (C2/D/E socioeconomic group).

Shopperforce had a number of ideas as to how they might move forward. These were put to the shoppers as well as asking them for their own suggestions.

The consultation lasted most of one day. The first part of the day involved an explanation of Shopperforce, its background and what it wanted to get out of the day. The focus then moved to the participants' experience of the role of shoppers and how they would like to see that change. The afternoon was devoted to a reaction to the ideas Shopperforce had developed and also to participants' own suggestions. Some of the techniques used included working in small groups, exercises to get people to warm up and interact, and sessions in which participants used drawings to express ideas.

In terms of the problems people experienced, it was very striking that for most people, these were to do with poor or inadequate service in general, and from the health service in particular. Another issue was concerned with dishonesty and unfair deals: banks, building societies, 'rip-off tradesmen' and holiday companies were some of the culprits. There was remarkably little overt concern about faulty products.

In terms of internal feelings, it was noticeable that the problem characteristics of the offending organizations were not so much to do with aggression, malice or evildoing but to do with size, power, impenetrability and being impersonal or faceless. Offending organizations were portrayed as being not actively abusive, so much as impassive and unresponsive. People felt they could not make an impact on them. So they ended up feeling small and powerless.

The main request that shoppers had of Shopperforce was to be a kind of powerful superhero who could sort out problems on behalf of shoppers. Clear preferences between the ideas presented to them by Shopperforce emerged and there were also a number of very powerful new ideas suggested by participants.

Was this exercise market research or stakeholder consultation? The methods used were highly influenced by market research techniques. And given Shopperforce's domain of activity, perhaps this was entirely legitimate. But is market research just a kind of consultation? The key difference is perhaps not so much one of technique but of intention: was Shopperforce trying to understand what the participants actually wanted, or were they only testing ideas on them to see which would sell best?

In a sense they did want to 'sell' something: a Shopperforce which better represented what shoppers wanted. It was also open to the participants to suggest what they wanted Shopperforce to be like in relation to their experience of shopping. And they did this quite freely.

The consultation was also very much a one-off exercise, which could tend to make it more of a process of extracting information than anything else. Yet although participants were asked what sort of feedback they would like to see, the main response was to request that something was done – along the lines developed during the day. These were definitely not 'professional stakeholders' such as NGOs, who would have requested a far more systematic response.

For comparison, straightforward market research exercises might have started with an exercise not dissimilar to some aspects of this consultation to find out what issues shoppers were concerned about. This is the qualitative stage of research. Following this, a quantitative stage might be carried out. This would essentially be a questionnaire, whose content would be derived from the qualitative stage. The questionnaire would be administered to a large number of people, so that the responses could be given some statistical significance.

Staff

'Infrapower' is an engineering company. Its products, range from the more traditional to the latest modern technologies. And it had seen the way the wind was blowing: CSR would become ever more important, especially for government contracts. It therefore wanted to review the state of CSR within the company. A key part of this was to discover what its management and staff thought of CSR.

The first challenge was to discuss with a senior management group their view of CSR. This was approached using a workshop session in which ideas of CSR were explored in a fairly open manner. The facilitation tried both to elicit management views but also to challenge them and to present a stakeholder-oriented perspective. It turned out that most of the management held a fairly traditional view of CSR as encompassing environmental housekeeping together with philanthropy, of which they were quite proud. A lot of the discussion turned into reviewing exactly who the stakeholders of Infrapower actually were.

Management, of course, are part of the stakeholder group usually labelled 'staff' or 'employees'. Because of their role they clearly have a significant influence over other members of staff. This was one reason why it was important to work with them to discover their attitudes to CSR. It was important also to discover what aspects of CSR they were aware of. Another reason was to try to bring some clarity to the relationship of staff, including management, with the company. As we have seen, very often staff as a whole, but particularly management, identify with the company quite closely. Typically staff are spoken of as 'internal' to a company, in some inappropriately magical sense. If it is important to analyse what the impacts of a company are, it is important to be able to distinguish between what is 'the company' and what is outside it. Otherwise, thinking can only proceed in very a confused way. Identification with the comany may be helpful to shareholders' interests, but it is not helpful in understanding corporate impact, let alone improving it.

Another type of such confused thinking emerged when the gaps between policy statements and reality was examined. It is not uncommon for management to enthusiastically embrace various aspirational values and policy statements concerning what the organization should do. One such statement, for Infrapower, concerned treating suppliers well. In one meeting, a director of the company was confidently asserting that Infrapower always treated its suppliers well and what was more, this was enshrined in a statement of values. The next obvious step was to probe how relations with suppliers were actually conducted. The question was asked 'how often are suppliers actually paid on time?' (ie on the terms defined in contracts). The response was a very confident assertion that it always happened. As it happened, the Head of Purchasing was also in the meeting. At this point he (somewhat timidly) volunteered that, in fact, there was an operational policy that suppliers were *never* paid on time, deliberately, in order to maximize company cash flow. There followed a period of awkward silence, white faces, and subsequently a rather humbler attitude, which was helpful to the more constructive discussion of the problems which followed.

Following the workshops with management, a series of workshops were held with staff at various levels throughout the organization. Participants ranged from middle management through to skilled professionals of various kinds to technical operatives.

Across these workshops there was a remarkable consensus as to what corporate responsibility actually was. There was almost unanimity that it entailed taking care of the environment, and positive, ethical attitudes and relationships with all other stakeholders. The predominant attitude in these workshops was that ethical responsibility was pretty clear, but that what Infrapower actually achieved sometimes did, and sometimes did not, live up to that ideal. It also became clear that there were a number of CSR projects throughout the company, such as recycling initiatives, of which central management was unaware. In some cases the projects had suffered as a result.

The further away from the centre of the company – geographically as well as in terms of seniority – that the meetings took place, the greater the level of cynicism that was encountered. This expressed itself firstly in an opinion on the worth of the meetings. 'You are the fifth lot of consultants that have come to talk to us. We tell them everything. And nothing has changed. Nothing.' was a fairly typical attitude. Their actual concerns ranged from under-resourcing, following a policy of not recruiting to save costs, to the general lack of attention to suggestions from 'the periphery'. Given the responsibility of some of the jobs which these technical operatives had, such a level of disaffection was alarming. Nevertheless, the basic concept of ethical responsibility was clearly understood.

Was this process 'staff consultation'? The basic aim of this series of workshops was distorted, since, as we have noted, the main purpose was to discover what staff thought CSR was and what CSR activities staff thought were actually going on. But to talk to a stakeholder about responsibilities of an organization without foregrounding what the organization's responsibilities were to that stakeholder, was a dangerous way to approach the subject. This was perhaps the root of the negative reactions that were uncovered. It also risked ghettoizing CSR into an area which could always be someone else's responsibility, but did not necessarily concern them.

Shareholders

It is rare that shareholders are actually included in a stakeholder consultation exercise – at least one labelled as such. One reason for this is that in most companies of any size there is a department already established whose sole function is relating to shareholders. It is often called 'investor relations'. This is evidence that companies treat their shareholders with great care and concern. That is understandable given that shareholders are almost invariably the dominant stakeholder, whose interests most usually prevail. However that does not mean that shareholder consultation run by such investor relations departments is perfect.

The reason for this is that investor relations departments are run by senior management, that is, by another powerful stakeholder. The management of a company is technically the agent of shareholders, yet management has its own agenda; it does not necessarily want shareholders to interfere too closely in 'their own' company or to know too much about the immediate difficulties which the company may be facing. Also, most large companies have a large number of shareholders. However only the large, institutional shareholders are given the particular attention of the investor relations department.

In this context, the organization we will call 'FinancialPush' was unusual. It was unusual for two reasons. First, because its shareholders were few in number and directly represented on the Board. This was the result of its origins as a joint venture. It was also unusual because it agreed to include shareholders within the stakeholder consultation exercise. It is worth pointing out that it agreed to the stakeholder consultation exercise mainly because it was interested in a public contract, and CSR seemed like an important thing on which to have a positive record.

As a result a series of interviews were set up with each shareholder Board member. These people were senior managers of other companies. The subject of the interviews included:

- the role of the shareholder within the company;
- what the shareholder actually wanted and how it wanted to be treated, including information needs;
- their view on the implementation of corporate responsibility.

There were few surprises in terms of the requirements of the shareholders. As you would expect given the direct relationship of the shareholders with the Board of the company, there were few problems getting the information – or the money – they wanted.

The most significant issue which arose in the interviews was concerned with the issue of director's pay. The directors of FinancialPush had recently been in the popular press accused of being 'fat cats', that is, of being paid far too much. This was obviously an important topic of conversation in the context of an interview about ethics.

The view that emerged was interesting. The response of one of the shareholder directors was to point out that within American companies (FinancialPush was not an American company) there were indeed fat cats, whose remuneration beggared belief. In relation to them, they held, the remuneration of the directors of FinanicalPush were far more reasonable. And they were in fact lower. But they did not think that the accusations in the press were reasonable. What was going on here? There was an appreciation of the ethical issue of remuneration being too high, but they could not acknowledge it in relation to themselves, only in relation to others. Perhaps the recent change in public attitudes as a result of the financial crisis may result in a greater level of humility in the future.

Did the series of interviews count as stakeholder engagement? It was certainly representative and touched on the real issue of concern to shareholders and to other stakeholders in relation to shareholders. But of course it was not a process that could be replicated in many other organizations.

Standards

The development of standards can be very variable. Some are essentially private standards made to measure by a relatively small number of organizations for which standardization is in their interest. Others, such as the Forest Stewardship Council or the Global Reporting Initiative are multi-stakeholder in conception and development. ISO 26000 is one of these. But how far do such processes really take account of the needs of stakeholders?

ISO 26000 is a standard for social responsibility of organizations – of any type, from companies to governments to NGOs. The initiative to develop ISO 26000 represented a big departure for the ISO organization. To understand why, it may be helpful to look briefly at the structure of ISO itself. ISO is strictly speaking an NGO devoted to standard setting. It is a membership organization; its members being the national standards-setting bodies around the world. Across the world, there are perhaps less than 10 countries which are not members or do not participate in ISO in some way.

The governance of ISO is complex, reflecting its global membership and reach. One thing that is unusual about ISO 26000 is that its development was initiated by the consumer policy committee, COPOLCO – rather than by any of its members directly, as would have been usual. This probably partly reflects the fact that whereas most standards are developed to follow some established practice, ISO 26000 is a standard for a field which is very much still in development, and far from settled. Indeed much of the debate during the ISO 26000 development process was concerned with trying to pin down exactly what the subject of the standard was!

The process for the development of the standard began in 2002. It is not necessary to go through the variety of committees through which it had to pass, except to point out that the first two years were spent by a specially convened Advisory Group on Social Responsibility to determine whether or not ISO should proceed with the development of the standard. The committee decided that it should, but there was considerable disagreement. One of the committee members was the World Wide Fund for Nature (WWF), the international environmental organization. WWF issued a minority report, which said that ISO should only proceed with the development of the standard if:

- the environment was within the scope of the standard;
- there was broad stakeholder engagement supporting the development of the standard;
- the standard was directed at businesses, rather than other sectors.

Although WWF did not play a very significant part in the subsequent development of the standard and the target of the standard remained a contentious issue for some years, their stance did bear fruit: the environment is covered by the standard and there has been broad stakeholder engagement as part of the development process.

To see just how broad an engagement was built up, we need only to consider that there have been between 300 and 400 participating experts from over 60 countries at the main ISO 26000 Working Group meetings. Moreover the composition of the sub-committees of the Working Group (some of which will be described below) are minutely scrutinized as to the representation of the developed and the developing world. The Chair of the Working Group is from Brazil and the vice Chair is from Sweden. Meetings of the Working Group will have taken place in Brazil, Thailand, Portugal, Australia, Austria, Chile, Canada and Denmark. About 60 per cent of the delegations are from developing countries – although it must be recognized that the size of the delegations from developed countries are usually much larger.

Delegates are also scrutinized as to 'stakeholder composition'. What does that mean in this context? The delegates are appointed mainly through the national standards bodies of the participating countries. Each national standards body which is participating in the ISO 26000 development maintains a mirror committee which should have at least one representative of each of six stakeholder groups. The six groups are: industry, NGOs, government, consumers, labour and something called 'SSRO' which essentially picks up everyone else, from academics to investors. It is possible to criticize the analysis underlying these six groups – for example, why are industry and investors allocated to two different groups? But the thoroughness with which it has been implemented not only for the delegates overall, but in every sub-committee and sub-sub-committee which the Working Group has set up, is impressive. Of course it is not always possible to find a full set of six people who have the time and expertise as well as the right stakeholder credentials – nevertheless, the attention which has been paid to the legitimacy of the process is impressive.

And this is actually very important. Because if ISO 26000 is to have the credibility which it obviously wants, and which it needs to succeed, then it must practise what it preaches. Whatever the final content, if the process is not representative, then ISO will have no authority to lay down guidelines about how organizations should pay attention to their stakeholders in discharging their responsibilities. Working with stakeholders to this extent is something new to ISO, and it is to their credit that they have devoted as much thought as this to the process.

It should also be borne in mind that such attention to stakeholders will have been something new for most of the delegates to the Working Group. One very important outcome of the development process will therefore have been to educate the delegates as to the importance and potential of this kind of process.

As noted above, delegates were drawn from the national standards bodies. However in addition to that, international organizations – representing any of the stakeholder groups – could also apply to the Working Group and send delegations independently. There were typically some 40 such organizations present at Working Group meetings.

The administration to run this large Working Group is also large. So the actual process by means of which things are decided is also complex. Given the size of the full Working Group, it is clear that a great deal of discussion must go on in smaller groups. One set of such sub-groups is derived from stakeholders. Another set is drawn from the specific tasks for which groups are formed. For example, the 'TG4 committee' was responsible for the development and drafting of the introductory sections of the standard. Even TG4 was several hundred delegates strong. So smaller groups were formed for some of the active work involved. As a result, politics was very much at the fore – especially considering the fact that opinion within stakeholder groups was routinely divided.

Among the many other aspects of the process, two are important, reflecting the sustained attention to stakeholder needs. The first is that of the plight of NGOs. It is noteworthy, following WWF's public statement of dissent, that few large NGOs have been involved in the process. Smaller NGOs have been involved, but these smaller organizations do not usually have the funds to support their involvement. (All costs of attending meetings have to be met by national standards bodies or delegates' organizations themselves.)

In response, the Working Group has provided some support and is actively seeking further resources to support NGO input – and balanced stakeholder representation overall – into the process. Funds have been received from some companies and from the government of the Netherlands.

Another source of disadvantage was quickly acknowledged to be language. The language of the Working Group is English. In response, groups have been set up to provide translations into Spanish, French, Arabic and Russian. There were already official translations of the draft standard into some of these languages at an early stage.

To complete this overview of the governance of the Working Group, there are two more points to be made. The first is that ISO has made special arrangements for two of the organizations which were represented on the Working Group. The first of these is the ILO – the International Labour Organization. The labour movement in general has been particularly active in the ISO 26000 development process. ISO and the ILO have signed a Memorandum of Understanding which gives the ILO a more privileged position, granting them the right to contribute to the process for longer than might otherwise be the case and committing that the final standard will not contravene any ILO Conventions. ISO has also signed a similar Memorandum with the Global Compact, which is a United Nations initiative on responsible business practice. While these Memoranda also give the ILO and Global Compact veto rights, it is important to remember that in all ISO Working Groups, including ISO 26000, all the main delegates to the Working Group (or the national standards bodies at a later stage in the process) have the right to veto any proposal. This is a strong constraint on progress – but it does mean that there is real agreement on what finally emerges.

Secondly, the standard and the development process behind it is open to the public. In contrast to most ISO standards, the drafts and all working papers are freely available on the internet.

This account of the work of ISO 26000 has deliberately concentrated on the stakeholder consultation which has attached to the development process of the standard. Of course it is important to remember that the actual subject of the standard was itself social responsibility. There is therefore another set of questions to ask about whether the recommendations within the standard actually promote proper stakeholder consultation itself.

THE LIMITS OF STAKEHOLDER ENGAGEMENT

At this point it would be understandable to think that there is very little that stakeholder engagement cannot do. And it is true that working with stakeholders is the principal approach to understanding the social impact of any company. However there are limits to what stakeholder engagement can deliver and to when it should be employed. These arise from the practicalities of implementing engagement, from the potential for conflicts with absolute values (especially human rights) and from the democratic process.

Practical limits

As we have seen, there are some stakeholders with whom it is very difficult or impossible to engage directly, such as those who cannot speak (eg future generations or animals). But in other situations also there may be practical difficulties in the way of engagement. The most obvious of these occurs within multi-stakeholder engagements. Particularly when several different stakeholder groups are present in the same room, the weaker stakeholder may simply remain silent. Even if this does not happen, the more powerful stakeholder may be more articulate than others, or may be able to hire professional representation unavailable to the more vulnerable group. As a result, multi-stakeholder consultations need to be handled with great care if they are to be successful.

Even if different stakeholder groups are not interacting face to face, some will always be more powerful than others. Also, the organization itself, or rather its management, is a stakeholder too, and usually they are one of the more powerful groups. This too affects the engagement process. In practice the way all these power relationships manifest themselves varies a great deal. So if stakeholder engagement is to deliver a legitimate result, the relationships between the different stakeholder groups must be carefully factored into the process. As a result, one of the key measures of the quality of an engagement process is the way in which such power imbalances are handled.

There may also be social conditions which make stakeholder engagement impossible. One of these is conflict and war. The subject of an engagement exercise may be unrelated to the causes of conflict. In such cases, the problem is that it is unlikely that engagement is going to be a priority. But it can happen that the content of the engagement is directly related to the causes of the conflict. For example, the search for oil may have resulted in people being thrown off their land, which in turn can lead to continuing conflict. In such cases, the oil company may wish to consult local people to understand their reaction to oil industry activities. However it is unlikely that an ordinary consultation process conducted by the company at the root of the problem can be productive or legitimate, since the pressures of war are likely to override any but the most carefully thought through consultation exercise. It is quite possible, for example, that people may endanger their lives through taking part in a consultation.

Democracy

There is a danger that the use of stakeholder dialogue by companies can undermine the democratic process. National laws should not be 'adjusted' in the light of stakeholder dialogue. Again, dialogue can be used to supplement compliance with the law, and to make clear how such compliance might best be achieved.

It is interesting to note that, especially for voluntary and some public sector organizations, stakeholder dialogue is seen as a way of remedying a 'democratic deficit'. The problem is that the granularity of the decision-making of democracy – that is, a two or three way decision every four or five years – cannot begin to address the practical complexity of all the decisions that affect people's lives.

Finally, governments are increasingly making use of 'stakeholder dialogue' in the process of making law. As pointed out above, the concept of stakeholder is not well-defined in this context. While in practice such consultations are open to the public, in reality the selection and recognition of different stakeholders by the government is critical to the legitimacy of the outcome. All this means that the power relationships between existing stakeholder groups will immediately come to the fore in any such consultation. Large companies obviously have more resources to defend their interests than do vulnerable groups (Henriques, 2007). If the duty of a government is to implement law in the interests of society as a whole, then the content of a particular law cannot be read off from even the most statistically refined analysis of stakeholder consultation.

Absolute values

Human rights and other international norms of behaviour might seem to override stakeholder engagement. Do they represent an absolute consensus which makes stakeholder engagement unnecessary?

It should first be pointed out that human rights, as enshrined in the UDHR, have been derived from international stakeholder dialogue conducted at the highest level. As a result, human rights represent a broad consensus on minimum acceptable levels of behaviour. While human rights are not formally binding on companies, from a moral perspective, they are fundamental. This means that there is no role for stakeholder dialogue to justify any weaker standard in specific circumstances. In particular, stakeholder dialogue should never be used to ask stakeholders to give up their human rights. Any attempt to do so should be regarded with great suspicion.

However, human rights do not cover every area of concern to stakeholders, or much of the detail of acceptable performance in the areas they do cover. The following section provides a case study of the issues which can arise.

On some occasions, stakeholders may actually be more interested in cash compensation from a company than in preserving their human rights. While there can be a role for stakeholder dialogue to help a company consider how to extend its performance in relation to human rights, stakeholder input should never be used to justify reducing people's rights.

THE DILEMMAS OF CONFLICT AND HUMAN RIGHTS – A CASE STUDY

Conflict provides a fertile ground for some of the most serious human rights abuses. The number of conflicts at all intensities in the world has increased fairly steadily since 1945. Companies are therefore increasingly likely to need to confront the issues resulting from operation in zones of conflict.

International companies may readily avoid zones of open warfare in relation to new investments. Yet today the majority of conflicts world-wide are of low intensity (i.e. non-violent) and occur within states, rather than between them (HIIK, 2008). However, where violence is latent, and particularly where the issues concern continuing operations, there is a danger that companies operate without a full appreciation of the fragility of their situation, presuming that the state will discharge its duty to protect human rights.

In fact, at all stages of the investment life-cycle, conflicts present dilemmas concerning how best a company should in practice respect human rights. Some of these dilemmas are illustrated below. Most such dilemmas can be addressed through developing appropriate, practical and context-sensitive responses, rather than opting for one or other of the apparent alternatives that their framing would suggest.

Planning and initial investment

Good practice suggests that companies should assess the human rights risks arising from a projected investment; where there is low intensity conflict this may identify appreciable, but not severe, risks connected with the investment. In these circumstances, how can an appropriate threshold be identified such that decisions to invest can legitimately be justified?

Natural resource extraction has often in the past led to conflict in host countries. This is not usually the result of company activities directly, but can arise through corruption, struggles over the distribution of wealth or as a result of the clearance of the land. This means that even where conflict does not currently exist, the arrival of a company can precipitate it. If such companies are to continue to make investments, how can this be justified?

Continuing operation

Once companies have established valuable assets in a country in which conflict arises and over which the government is not seen as independent by all parties, to what extent is it permissible to cooperate with the government in the protection of these assets? For example, is it justified to provide logistical support, such as vehicles, to a host government for security purposes when this support could be used directly in the conflict, or could enable the government to commit additional vehicles of its own to the conflict?

Good commercial practice requires maintaining positive relations with host governments. Part of a company's human rights obligation is often seen to be working to persuade a government to take its human rights responsibilities more seriously. If in a conflict situation the host government is resistant to their responsibilities and resents the company's suggestions, is there still an obligation on the company to lobby in this way?

In order to protect its property, the most effective route may be to negotiate with (non-government) armed groups. This may reduce the short term risk, but is also likely to increase the confidence and power of such groups. Is it permissible to negotiate with armed groups?

Withdrawal

As a result of conflict a company may decide to evacuate all expatriate staff. The company may also have local staff that are at risk because of the conflict. What responsibilities does the company have to the local staff it employs? Should it evacuate them or provide for them in some other way?

End of life

At the end of the natural life of a project, a company may wish to withdraw from the host country. This may severely damage the local economy. Where there is low intensity conflict, the consequences of such withdrawal may escalate the intensity of the conflict. Should the company continue to operate the project (uneconomically) for this reason?

6

The Voice of the Stakeholder

What do stakeholders typically say about their issues and their relationship with companies?

This chapter concerns techniques for discovering stakeholder concerns *without* engaging them in a systematic way. One of the most important ways to understand a stakeholder is through talking to them and treating them as equal subjects in their own right. It is crucial simply to listen to them. Listening is the main subject of this chapter.

It is possible to study what stakeholders say under controlled conditions: this is what surveys of stakeholders, for example, are concerned with (see Appendix I). More generally, stakeholder engagement is centrally concerned with opening and maintaining a dialogue and exchange with stakeholders, as we have seen in the last chapter. But what do stakeholders say freely and on their own account? This is an important way to discover what their concerns may be. Yet it also raises the question of how what they say can be analysed intelligently to ensure that their principal concerns have been identified correctly.

So this chapter will firstly examine the sources of stakeholder opinion, including the way the web and the media can be used – and misused – to identify stakeholder opinion, the use that can be made of academic publications and the use of case studies by companies on the web and in sustainability reports. Secondly, it will look at the techniques which can be useful in the analysis of such sources.

SOURCES

The internet

What can the web tell anyone? If you are trying to discover the views of particular stakeholders of a company, how much reliance can be placed on what can be discovered on the web? This is a complex question, as the internet is such a large collection of sources of information that judging reliability is critical. And it is an important question, as ever-greater reliance is placed on it.

One way in which the web is used is to simply quote the number of returns to a search with Google, on a particular topic – especially to emphasize its importance. For example, at the time of writing, about 14.9 million results were returned to the Google query 'concern global warming'. The first thing to note is that the word 'about' which Google inserts into the response pages to queries with numerous results. The second point is that the scale of results is a very poor indication of the strength of concern. If the order of words of the search is changed to 'global warming concern' only about 3.34 million results are returned; if it is changed to 'warming global concern' the number of results drops to about 426,000. So it is quite possible to make a difference of a factor of 100 in the magnitude of results just by changing their order. Of course, what this really points to is the peculiarities of the Google search algorithm, rather than real differences in people's level of concern.

This experiment also raises the question of who – or rather which stake-holders – are putting pages on the web which will be found by searches. The answer is partly individuals, who might contribute their thoughts on global warming via their blogs or social networking sites. But it is also the organizations, including governments, NGOs and companies concerned with the issue. There are over 1 million NGOs and similar groups worldwide, many of which have a web presence (Hawken, 2007). The internet is an obvious and very widely used campaigning tool by all parties. Within the internet as a whole, attention should also be paid to chat rooms, newsgroups, user forums and the various forms in which the internet is used.

From the corporate point of view of course, the internet is principally a resource to be used for marketing and PR. This may not always be done transparently, so that it is possible that the contributions of a 'member of the public' may in fact be those of a corporate employee directed to make such contributions.

More important than this 'misuse' of the internet is the extent of its unavailability. Even in the UK a few years ago, only 61 per cent of households had direct access to the internet (ONS, 2007). In other parts of the world the figure is much lower. Globally, only 1 in 6 people have internet access (Wray, 2007). Yet the use of the internet is a valuable campaigning tool and resource. And, for that reason, those who are most vulnerable are in that position partly because of their lack of internet access.

The media

News is now delivered by the internet as much as through any other medium. Nevertheless, the media may be regarded as another, or at least particular type of source of information about stakeholders. A great deal of news coverage of the more serious issues concerning corporate stakeholders may be found in the media. However, therein lies one of the main problems with news media as a source of stakeholder information: the topic has to be newsworthy.

This means, as I have written in more detail elsewhere (Henriques, 2007, pp101–111), that news stories, in order to become sellable, are often laced with bias, suffering from inaccuracies, sensationalism and poor context. Journalism becomes, as Andrew Marr has put it, simply 'the industrialisation of gossip' (Marr, 2005). To this catalogue of failures, Nick Davies has added a penetrating analysis of the impossible pressures which news editors, and therefore the whole journalistic machine, are under and how this constrains the production of news. The old-fashioned pictures of the reporter-at-large covering events as they emerge, or the intrepid investigative reporter uncovering social woes, are now rarities. As a result, the most serious danger of relying on the news is that of the lack of coverage of important issues.

> *Omission is the most powerful source of distortion. The fact that ...*
> *non-stories achieve only the most marginal coverage in global media*
> *is just as important as the falsehoods embedded in those stories*
> *which are covered.* (Davies, 2008)

Another important source of distortion arises from the Public Relations (PR) industry. The PR industry now works for government as well as the private sector. Its function is to alter to order the perceptions of its clients' stakeholders and of the public at large. This matters because as one PR firm puts it, PR can 'Move minds. Influence decisions. Alter beliefs. Create relationships. Initiate dialogue. Provoke a smile. This is what perception can do ... Is perception truly reality? ... we say yes' (DPA, 2008). Furthermore, the use of PR is widespread – and effective. Nick Davies commissioned research from Cardiff University which found that PR material typically penetrates over half of news stories in mainstream UK newspapers (Davies, 2008).

> *So the picture emerges. Journalists who no longer have the time to*
> *go and find their own stories and to check the material which they*
> *are handling, are constantly vulnerable to ingesting and reprodu-*
> *cing the packages of information which are provided for them by*
> *the PR industry. At the very least this involves their being directed*
> *into accepting stories and angles which have been chosen for them*
> *in order to satisfy somebody else's commercial or political interests.*
> *At the worst, this embroils them in the dissemination of serious*
> *distortion and falsehood.*
>
> *This is inherently irrational. The news factory selects its stories*
> *and it angles and its facts under the pressure of the rules of its*
> *production, which may or may not deliver what is important and*
> *what is true. The PR industry aggravates this irrationality. It uses*
> *the most sophisticated mechanisms to monitor the emotions and*
> *beliefs of its target audiences and then consciously fabricates news*
> *to appeal to those emotions and beliefs, recycling whatever false-*
> *hoods and misunderstandings it finds.* (Davies, 2008, p203)

So if you want to use newspapers and the media to discover facts about stakeholders, then you have a problem. The source of information is unreliable, in part because it is itself being used in order to try to change stakeholder attitudes. Nevertheless, the media is an important source of information on stakeholder attitudes. But it clearly has to be used with great caution. It should never be assumed that because an issue has not appeared in the media that it is not a real concern; and just because an issue has appeared, it should not be assumed that it is of real significance.

Academic publications

Academic publications include journal articles, books and conference proceedings. Of course, stakeholders do not often speak directly through academic journals, but these sources may nevertheless provide a fairly direct conduit for stakeholder concerns. There is, for example, a large academic literature concerning development issues in which the plight of vulnerable stakeholders is prominent. The same is true for environmental issues.

This literature provides a good evidential basis for more sensitive approaches to these matters. However, there are also drawbacks. One of these is that the focus is often not on the role of companies in the genesis or alleviation of such problems, but may be on the wider economy or on associated social problems. Thus the actual impact which a particular company may be contributing is often only tangentially explored. This makes it hard for companies to use the academic literature to assess their impacts.

A second problem is that such material, unsurprisingly, is presented in an academic context. This can make it fairly inaccessible to those not grounded in the various theoretical debates concerned. Finally, and most importantly from a practical point of view, the academic process is not quick. It can take several years from the time an article is submitted to a publication to the time it is published. And that of course starts after the empirical work has finished, which may itself have taken a year or more to deliver. As a result, the timeliness and applicability of such material can be fairly limited in practice.

Nevertheless, particularly for long standing corporate impacts, such as biodiversity loss, academic sources provide a valuable contribution.

Case studies

Case studies do not really constitute a separate category from the other kinds of source material. It is possible to find case studies on the internet, in the media and in academic material. Yet it is important to consider them separately since they are not only widely used, but also have a powerful appeal. As a result they are often used by companies themselves to attempt to demonstrate the impact which they have.

There is no uniform format for a case study, which may extend from a paragraph or two up to perhaps 30 or more pages. There is little uniformity in any of the other aspects of case studies, either. The crucial variables are

---

Box 6.1 BP and Climate Change – Business Developments

In 2007, we continued to build BP Alternative Energy, our business that invests in new, low-carbon energy options for power and transport. We began the expansion of solar plants in the US, India and Spain. With our partners Babcock & Brown, we built the 300MW Cedar Creek wind farm in the US and inaugurated our first wind farm in Asia in Dhule, Northern Maharashtra, India. We created a joint venture, Hydrogen Energy, with Rio Tinto, to develop hydrogen-fuelled power projects with carbon capture and storage. We formed several biofuels joint ventures, including a partnership with Associated British Foods and DuPont to develop a major commercial bioethanol plant, a business with D1 Oils, to plant Jatropha curcas, a biodiesel feedstock. We also selected academic partners in the US for the Energy Biosciences Institute, which we are supporting with $500 million over 10 years. We supported initiatives to promote responsible biofuels production, such as the Round Table for Sustainable Biofuels. Our targetneutral™ programme received contributions from customers and BP sufficient to offset around 52,500 tonnes of CO_2 equivalent emissions.

---

probably format and authorship. 'Format' includes the choices made regarding how far an attempt is made to present a whole and complete picture, rather than presenting a specific feature of a situation only.

The 'case study' in Box 6.1 is taken from a Sustainability Review which BP produced in 2008. It paints a picture of the work BP is doing in renewable energy. It leaves the reader with the impression that BP is energetically pursuing this important agenda. But it does not provide a systematic picture or convey the larger context. For example, what is not clear includes the answers to questions such as:

- What is the scale of this investment, particularly in relation to the larger mainstream fossil fuel businesses?
- How does it compare to what other companies are doing in this area?
- How does it compare to the scale of what needs to be done?
- How much carbon has been 'saved' as a result of such projects?

In order to see the issues which authorship raises, consider the case study in Box 6.2 from Exxon.

The Exxon case study describes a project which seems undoubtedly beneficial, although largely unconnected with Exxon's core business. The reader is left with the impression that Exxon is clearly using some of its profits to fund worthy projects. As with the BP case study, there are a number of facts and figures which would be very helpful in evaluating such a programme. Also what is not so clear is the extent to which the quotations actually represent the views of Bassey Abraham. What is the full extent of her comments on the programme? Did she have any reservations about its nature or the way it was conducted? Did she see ways in which it could have been improved?

Box 6.2 Global Women in Management Programme

Exxonmobil Foundation provided scholarships to 25 women leaders working for non-governmental organizations in 18 countries to participate in CEDPA's Global Women in Management Programme. While their backgrounds were diverse, these women were all united around one objective: educating other women and girls to help move their countries and the world forward.

'I want girls to go to school and have better jobs,' said Nne Bassey Abraham of Nigeria. 'If they do, they won't have the problems we are having.'

The course participants also joined a network of non-governmental leaders working to advance the causes of girls and women worldwide.

'If each woman here changes something in her country, the world will change.'

Source: (ExxonMobil, 2008)

The purpose of asking these questions is not to devalue the Exxon programme, but to illustrate that the interpretation of stakeholder views should be left, as far as possible, in the hands of the stakeholders themselves. The case study from Exxon was obviously written by Exxon. Bassey Abraham may have been asked to say something appreciative of the programme. Alternatively, she may have been asked, and given, a balanced evaluation of the programme, but all we have to go on in the case study are these few quotes. And whatever the background, there will have been pressures from the designers of the brochure from which this case study was taken to keep any comments short and simple. So who is really speaking here: Exxon or Bassey Abraham?

On the whole, then, case studies are not good ways to give a balanced view of a given project or company. It is possible to address the challenges of format and authorship, but this is likely to result in a case study rather longer than the average. In general, case studies can illustrate points made, but should rarely be the sole source of information about stakeholder views.

PRACTICAL ANALYSIS

Initial assessment

There is, then, a mass of material from 'free sources' which is available; one question is how can it be analysed and made useful. And the most crucial question is perhaps: how reliable is it?

It is first of all important to conduct a conceptual analysis to arrive at a basic understanding of what stakeholders might be saying in any of these free source materials. This has to be a thoughtful process. After there is a basic understanding of the material, it is important to assess how it should be regarded and what status the 'evidence' should be given. This process will involve three main stages:

1   assessing the origin of the material;
2   understanding the circumstances which produced it;
3   assessing its representativeness.

The first step in analysing free source material is to be clear as to its origin. That is, who produced it? Was it produced by the stakeholders themselves, by someone acting on their behalf or by someone who had some other interest in the stakeholder's situation (such as a company)? On the whole, the more directly it is connected with the stakeholder in question, the more reliable it may be taken to be as a valid representation of their view. Of course, as was noted in Chapter 5, there may be situations in which the stakeholder in question cannot have produced it and another stakeholder will have to have been involved; this is the case with very young children, for example, but need not be the case with most children.

The second step is to understand the circumstances of the production of the material. This firstly requires that there is a clear separation of the event – good or bad – which is of concern to stakeholders from the way it is conveyed (e.g. by a news story). In relation to the production of the material, it is important to be able to answer a number of questions:

- *Who produced it?* This may of course have been partially answered in the first step. But it is important to be able to trace the material back to its original source, if possible ascertaining the name and identities of the authors. Of course if the author is a whistleblower, this may well not be possible.
- *What happened?* It is important to try to get corroborating evidence of the events in question and to compare alternative versions of the events. This can be more difficult than at first appears, since as soon as one news service carries an event, all the other news services will copy it, usually without any further verification.
- *When was it produced?* A story which was crucial 10 years ago may have lost significance. On the other hand, issues such as the Bhopal disaster which happened in 1984, still have great significance and relevance to companies today, including the former Dow Chemicals and its current owners.
- *Why was it produced?* The answer to this question may simply be that the stakeholder was so concerned or pleased about the event that they wanted to communicate their feelings widely. However, if the stakeholders themselves were not the producers of the account, then why was someone else sufficiently interested in it to describe it? Were they paid to do so, and

if so by whom? The actual producers may have had only a moral interest in the situation, but other interests should be considered.

- *Where was it produced?* This question may have less relevance in the days of the global production of media. It may nevertheless be important to understand that the process of communication may have taken place in a different country to that of the event. This may mean that there are issues of translation, culture or language involved, which could affect understanding of the event. Of course in some situations and for some issues, the location may give less cause for concern through language difficulties, such as the reporting on the state of the ice at the North Pole.

The third step is to ascertain how representative the author of the account (or its subject, if it is a news story) is of a wider set of stakeholders. This must of course be explored with some sensitivity. It is entirely possible for a stakeholder to be gravely and justifiably concerned about an issue, even if they are the only one to be affected, if their grievance is sufficiently serious. Fatalities occurring at work, for example, may be very rare but still merit concern from all connected to the organization in question. The representativeness of the author also raises the challenges of formal representation discussed in Chapter 5.

There are also more formal techniques which can be used for analysing stakeholder narratives. These have a long history, pre-dating the analysis of the social impact of companies by many centuries. The various techniques do not form a unified whole, but the principal strands are:

- hermeneutic analysis;
- narrative analysis;
- content analysis.

Taking meaning seriously

Hermeneutic analysis arose as a result of the problem of the possibility of the differing interpretations of religious texts. For thousands of years in the Jewish oral tradition and for perhaps 1,500 years within Christianity, the problem has been how to understand sacred texts of great significance for which it is not possible to appeal to the author. The key issue was how to reconcile the variety of interpretations of which almost any text is capable and to identify the 'true' interpretation. At least in the Western tradition, this search for the true interpretation can be dated back to Aristotle, who in 'De interpretatione', wrote that: 'Spoken words are the symbols of mental experience and written words are the symbols of spoken words. Just as all men have not the same writing, so all men have not the same speech sounds, but the mental experiences, which these directly symbolize, are the same for all, as also are those things of which our experiences are the images' (Aristotle, 1968, p40). The irony of such an approach is that a close attention to texts tends to multiply, rather than to reduce, the number of meanings. New interpretations of the Bible which arose during the Reformation of the Catholic church in the sixteenth century, for example, appealed to hermeneutics as part of their justification.

The relevance of hermeneutics to stakeholder discourse is considerable. If great weight is to be placed on stakeholder perspectives, as I argue, how should they be interpreted? Within hermeneutics, two traditions have emerged, following Schleiermacher (Schleiermacher, 1998). One is concerned with the technical aspects of grammar and wording, the other with the context and psychology of interpretation. The technical examination of texts has been used to prove that a text cannot be genuine. This is a useful technique which can be directly applied to stakeholder texts, for example in the process of auditing them or the company reports using them. But the process of understanding the context and psychology of written material has been applied very widely, giving rise to historical and cultural analyses of a wide variety of 'texts'. This aspect of hermeneutic technique has in fact been used for the analysis of everything from books to oral traditions and films.

In relation to understanding stakeholder narratives, it is of course important to emphasize the context in which a particular account was produced. But the crucial difference in the analysis of stakeholder dialogue is that, very often, the original author of the narrative is available – in principle. Nevertheless, in practice, access to the author is frequently difficult, so the interpretation of stakeholder accounts remains important. This emphasizes the key dilemma in interpreting the stakeholder voice. On the one hand it is vital to recognize that the interpretation of a stakeholder narrative must be accomplished with sensitivity to the context in which it was produced. On the other hand, primacy in interpretation must be given to the stakeholders themselves; to do otherwise is to disempower them.

In practice the techniques of hermeneutics are used to present a coherent story to the advantage, often, of the presenting company. An example is provided by the Exxon Case Study quoted above in Box 6.2. Here, before each direct quotation, a short piece of context is provided. This crucially affects our interpretation of the women's quotes. In this example, what we do not actually know is what the women made of Exxon's project, although their remarks are presented as if they were endorsements of it.

While it does not derive from quite the same philosophical tradition, anthropology also makes use of hermeneutic techniques. Deriving particularly from Malinowski's practice (Malinowski, 1929) of participant observation of others' cultures, anthropology has developed a set of techniques which are based on an observer immersing themselves within the culture or practices to be observed together with the insistence on a deep accumulation of such empirical data.

Anthropological techniques (also called 'ethnographic' techniques) have been employed by companies in a number of contexts. One, perhaps quite close to the context in which they were developed, is for mining companies to employ anthropologists to study the communities whose activities will be affected by mining. Several large companies, including RioTinto have employed anthropologists on their staff for this purpose. Another use, and possibly the most common one, is to use anthropological techniques to understand consumers. Here the purpose is quite clearly for the direct benefit of the company, rather than the stakeholder in question. Nevertheless, it is significant that in order to get inside the minds of their stakeholders, there is no route but to take on board in full, and to share, their subjectivity.

Beyond this, organizations sometimes recognize the importance of the narratives which they (their staff) seek to understand themselves through the stories they tell. One example of this is the attention paid to 'watercooler culture' in change management practices. It is also used in organizational development techniques which explicitly use storytelling and in participatory action research. Participatory action research is a technique which combines the methods of participation, which involve the researcher in the experiences under study, together with an experimental approach to change.

Overall, hermeneutics recognizes a crucial aspect of the experience of being a stakeholder: that what stakeholders say expresses their meaning and intention in the richest way possible. To acknowledge that fact is to acknowledge the stakeholder's subjectivity and accord them a fundamental respect. But as we have seen, the insights of hermeneutics can also be used to distort, or perhaps cloud, what stakeholders mean to say. Furthermore, although it is integral to the expression of subjectivity, the idea of a single author and a single meaning of a text are perhaps not in the end sustainable.

Narrative analysis

Narratives are not only meanings, they are also words. The syntactic or grammatical branch of hermeneutics has been developed in what has come to be called 'narrative analysis'. Narrative analysis is based not on an attempt to get inside the storyteller's head, but on an attempt to pay close attention to their words. The great advantage of this approach is that the texts or accounts can be studied in isolation and processed far more systematically, which appeals to a sense of rigour.

Writing in the 1920s, Vladimir Propp (Propp, 1977) looked at the structure of fairytales. He analysed the basic units of stories, concluding that there were a relatively small range of elements from which all stories are built. He also identified a small set of characters (such as villain and hero) which populate the stories. Following Propp, work by Labov and others (Labov and Waletzky, 1967; Labov, 1997) the techniques of narrative analysis were developed so as to apply to a much wider range of narratives.

Still later writers have applied derivative techniques to every kind of narrative, including films, newspapers and television. Since stakeholder 'stories' will also share these structures, a knowledge of them can help to elucidate the key thrust of stakeholder accounts, by making their underlying structure clear. Narrative analysis has also been used to analyse company news releases (Gilpin, 2008). In Gilpin's study, news releases relating to company disasters formed 'the story' which was subjected to analysis.

Content analysis

Content analysis is a technique which analyses the words, and to the extent possible purely through verbal analysis, the concepts which are employed by texts. However, the essential preliminary to this still has to be a basic analysis of the key themes and messages – and of the words to which they might correspond if content analysis is to be used.

The principal approach of content analysis is to count the frequency of words used. It is thus eminently suitable for computer-assisted analysis, and it may be found quite widely used by websites to give viewers an idea of the site's significant ideas. This kind of software essentially counts the occurrence of pre-specified terms in a mass of material. This may be augmented by refinements such as taking account of the local word-context within which a given word is used.

Content analysis can be used for a number of purposes. According to Berelson (1952), one of the pioneers of content analysis, it can be used to:

- describe trends in content over time;
- describe the relative focus of attention for a set of topics;
- compare international differences in content;
- compare group differences in content;
- compare individual differences in communication style;
- trace conceptual development in intellectual history;
- compare actual content with intended content;
- expose use of biased terms in propaganda research;
- test hypotheses about cultural and symbolic use of terms;
- code open-ended survey items.

Content analysis has been used to analyse company reports (Deumes, 2008). It has also been used to analyse communications from stakeholders as for example with the aid of software (Dearne, 2008).

Content analysis is at the opposite end of the spectrum from hermeneutic approaches. There is no recourse to the originator of the text, or the stakeholder. So stakeholders (or their stories) are treated as objects to be analysed. There is clearly a significant loss of power by the stakeholder through the use of content analysis.

7

Sociological Impacts

This chapter describes two techniques which borrow much from sociology: social impact analysis and social capital. To varying degrees they both look at society as the primary context or object of analysis, rather than the company or its stakeholders. Nevertheless, they are both important representations of sociologically informed techniques useful to understanding some aspects of corporate impact.

SOCIAL IMPACT ASSESSMENT

History

The idea of systematically assessing the full range of consequences of actual and potential policy has a long heritage in public policy and decision making. The phrase 'Social Impact Assessment (SIA)' was born in the late 1960s and 1970s. It emerged as a result of concern over the impact of large public sector projects such as oil pipeline construction. The idea of using social science as a tool to assess the impact of such projects was enshrined in the US National Environmental Policy Act of 1969, which in section 102 requires all agencies of the Federal Government to 'utilize a systematic, interdisciplinary approach which will insure the integrated use of the natural and social sciences and the environmental design arts in planning and in decision making which may have an impact on man's environment' (USA, 1969). Also, from as early as 1980 the United Nations Environment Programme (UNEP) has in practice been assessing the social as well as environmental consequences of development projects. Today in the UK, for example, through the New Approach to Transport (NATA) Guidelines, as well as in the USA, a relatively integrated assessment of the environmental and social impacts of major projects is normal. In addition, drafts of UK Bills are required to be accompanied by suitable impact assessments, which typically include economic, environmental and social issues in some form.

Another driver of social impact assessment has been the foreign aid and development policies of many governments. Overseas development was originally primarily economic in intent. However, the somewhat over-simplified early prescriptions for economic development met with very limited success. As a result, the social consequences of such interventions became ever more central to international development efforts. Today most international development agencies, including international organizations such as the World Bank, routinely require project assessments. It is therefore commonplace for social impact assessments to be made of international development initiatives – giving rise, as we have seen, to the idea of sustainable development.

In this respect, social impact assessment techniques have evolved hand in hand with those for environmental assessment. In the remarks that follow, the focus is on SIA, although much of what follows is applicable to both social and to environmental impact assessments. The characteristics of such requirements and frameworks are usually that they are forward looking, attempting to predict future consequences of policies or projects – and of course that they are linked to the public domain.

SIA and the private sector

While originally, social impact assessment was very largely a tool of the public sector, a number of factors have led to the use of SIAs by private companies. One is the implementation of aid and development policies through private companies, rather than by direct government effort. As a result, the evaluation of the results of such projects has been applied to the work of private companies.

Other factors have been the increasing scale of private sector projects coupled with increasingly vocal criticism of projects by NGOs. This has meant that private companies have been challenged to justify their activities – and given the scale of such ventures the resources have been available to do so. However the results of such studies are rarely put in the public domain. Rio Tinto's assessment of the impact of its major ilmenite (titanium ore) mine in Madagascar is an example. Friends of the Earth commissioned an independent review of the impacts of the ilmenite mine (Harbinson, 2007), which was highly critical. While the company has published an impressive list of its positive social contribution (RTZ, 2007) there appears to be no public overall assessment, including adverse impacts. Today most large projects which rely on financing from international financial institutions will have to undergo some form of SIA, and the results may be published in some form. The International Finance Corporation (part of the World Bank Group), for example, publishes summaries of its SIA results.

Techniques

The techniques used for SIAs are many and varied. As a consequence there is no universally agreed definition of what an SIA involves. There are however some 'principles' for impact assessments. These define SIA in these terms: 'social impact assessment includes the processes of analysing, monitoring and managing the intended and unintended social consequences, both positive and negative, of planned interventions (policies, programs, plans, projects) and any social change processes invoked by those interventions. Its primary purpose is to bring about a more sustainable and equitable biophysical and human environment' (IAIA, 2003).

The process the principles describe is one in which SIA:

- participates in the environmental design of the planned intervention;
- identifies interested and affected peoples;
- facilitates and coordinates the participation of stakeholders;
- documents and analyses the local historical setting of the planned intervention so as to be able to interpret responses to the intervention, and to assess cumulative impacts;
- collects baseline data (social profiling) to allow evaluation and audit of the impact assessment process and the planned intervention itself;
- gives a rich picture of the local cultural context, and develops an understanding of local community values, particularly how they relate to the planned intervention;
- identifies and describes the activities which are likely to cause impacts (scoping);
- predicts (or analyses) likely impacts and how different stakeholders are likely to respond;
- assists evaluating and selecting alternatives (including a no development option);
- assists in site selection;
- recommends mitigation measures;
- assists in the valuation process and provides suggestions about compensation (non-financial as well as financial);
- describes potential conflicts between stakeholders and advises on resolution processes;
- develops coping strategies for dealing with residual or non-mitigatable impacts;
- contributes to skill development and capacity building in the community;
- advises on appropriate institutional and coordination arrangements for all parties;
- assists in devising and implementing monitoring and management programs. (IAIA, 2003)

In practice techniques to understand stakeholder impact include:

- researching the history of an area;
- conducting interviews and surveys with local communities;
- economic and financial analysis.

One important variant on SIAs are human rights impact assessments (HRIAs). John Ruggie has documented (Ruggie, 2007) the differences between human rights and more general SIAs. While there are of course significant similarities in general terms, the key differences are that HRIAs will work within a human rights framework and might make use of the Human Rights Based Approach used by development agencies.

> *HRIAs should deviate from the ESIA approach of examining a project's direct impacts, and instead force consideration of how the project could possibly interact with each and every right. For example, the ESIA approach might not result in any discussion of freedom of expression, whereas an HRIA could envision a community protest against the project being suppressed by state forces.*
> (Ruggie, 2007, p6)

Issues

SIA does enable some understanding of a project to be gained. Other than the lack of precise definition, the main difficulty with it is its openness to manipulation. It is quite possible to massage the results in a particular direction to favour the views of those who commission the study, be they in government or the private sector. One indication of this is the rarity with which projects are abandoned as a result of such studies.

A further issue with SIA, for the purposes of measuring corporate impact, is that it is applicable to projects, rather than organizations. Insofar as it is a method to assess a project or initiative it does not provide a technique for assessing the impact of an organization as a whole. There is perhaps further scope to develop a 'Strategic SIA' method which would cover the whole company through analysing its policies, plans and procedures. This has been successfully done for EIAs, especially in relation to public sector projects (Therivel, 2004).

SOCIAL CAPITAL

Social capital is an alluring term with a long history, an unfortunate wealth of definitions and an under-explored relationship to business. The term 'social capital' immediately suggests something vital to society, a valuable resource and at the same time, borrowing from economics, something which can be counted, built up and should be preserved. This idea of an important social resource which is integral to society can be traced back to the earliest social science writers. De Tocqueville, for example, writing in the nineteenth century, stressed the importance to the United States of its citizens' participation in associations. The first use of the term itself seems to have been by Lyda Judson in 1916:

The tangible substances [that] count for most in the daily lives of people: namely good will, fellowship, sympathy, and social intercourse among the individuals and families who make up a social unit ... The individual is helpless socially, if left to himself. If he comes into contact with his neighbor, and they with other neighbors, there will be an accumulation of social capital, which may immediately satisfy his social needs and which may bear a social potentiality sufficient to the substantial improvement of living conditions in the whole community. The community as a whole will benefit by the cooperation of all its parts, while the individual will find in his associations the advantages of the help, the sympathy, and the fellowship of his neighbors. (Quoted in Putnam, 2000, p19)

However current writings on social capital stem mainly from Pierre Bourdieu (Bourdieu and Wacquant, 1992), James Coleman (Coleman, 1988) and Robert Putnam (Putnam, 1993; Putnam, 1995). Today, a typical definition of social capital is that provided by Assist, a social enterprise devoted to promoting good practice in relation to social capital:

Social Capital can be defined as the norms, networks and trust that facilitate collective action and oil the economic and social wheels of society; the glue and the grease of community life. It is growing in importance daily with governments and economic regeneration specialists becoming much more interested in the impact of social capital on policy and practice. (Assist, 2008)

Businesses clearly make use of social capital, as James Coleman has so vividly described in relation to diamond merchants' apparently extreme trust of each other and in the way a traditional market in Cairo functions:

In the Kahn El Khalili market of Cairo, the boundaries between merchants are difficult for an outsider to discover. The owner of a shop that specializes in leather will, when queried about where one can find a certain kind of jewellery, turn out to sell that as well – or, what appears to be nearly the same thing, to have a close associate who sells it, to whom he will immediately take the customer. Or he will instantly become a money changer, although he is not a money changer, merely by turning to his colleague a few shops down. For some activities, such as bringing a customer to a friend's store, there are commissions; for others, such as money changing, merely the creation of obligations. Family relations are important in the market, as is the stability of proprietorship. The whole market is so infused with relations of the sort I have described that it can be seen as an organization, no less so than a department store.

> *Alternatively, one can see the market as consisting of a set of individual merchants, each having an extensive body of social capital on which to draw, through the relationships of the market.*
> (Coleman, 1988, pS100)

Within larger businesses, much work has been done on the importance of internal relationships which facilitate work (e.g. a 'watercooler culture') and on the importance of goodwill and brand value. Businesses of all kinds clearly make use of social capital; the question for this chapter is how do they affect it? And how can that be measured?

The remainder of this chapter will cover:

- how social capital is now conceptualized;
- how social capital is typically applied;
- what 'corporate social capital' might mean;
- how social capital can be measured.

The concept of social capital

If physical capital is made of plant and machinery and financial capital is denominated in pounds or dollars, what is social capital made of? Social capital is fundamentally different to economic capital; it is a social process composed of networks, norms and sanctions. Networks are connections between individual people, or groups of people, or between institutions. For example, it has often been pointed out that the more 'contacts' or acquaintances someone has, the more straightforward their working life is likely to be. Contacts provide opportunities and access to resources. And of course, networks exist between companies and other organizations – more or less independently of the particular individuals within them who may know one another.

Norms describe how networks behave, or what 'normal behaviour' within that network is. At a local community level, norms may be established of consideration for one's neighbours, or may sometimes include the terrorizing of elderly inhabitants by its younger members. Sanctions are those 'policing' activities which maintain the norms. Sanctions may be positive and include praise for good behaviour. The common practice amongst companies of holding awards ceremonies for the best marketing campaign or the best social report is an example. Negative sanctions are punishments designed to deter; these may be formal, as embodied in laws, or informal, and include reputation damage.

One immediate consequence of this analysis is that attempts to change behaviour, such as reducing anti-social behaviour on housing estates, may not work if they are introduced through (negative) sanctions. Sanctions are effective at maintaining existing norms; other means may need to be used to change them. Similarly if it is desired to make companies behave more environmentally responsibly, simply punishing the offenders is not likely to be an efficient way to establish a new norm of behaviour, although it may be a necessary part of the long term solution.

The examples of social capital given so far have been mainly micro-level and concerned with the behaviour of individuals in small groups. Social capital is also useful for analysis at larger scales. Macro-level analysis encompasses nations and international structures. There is also a third, meso-level analysis that concerns institutions at an intermediate level. Companies are typically at this intermediate or meso level. While some companies are large enough to be operative at international scales, many more work at the meso-scale, rather closer to the micro scale characteristic of family businesses or market traders.

The most widely used categorization of social capital in the literature concerns how it functions. A distinction is made between bonding social capital, which as its name suggests, binds people or groups together, and bridging social capital which creates connections between such social groups. Companies may make great efforts to get close to their customers. To the extent that this is successful, this is an example of bridging social capital. However companies are often consistently antagonistic towards their competitors. Indeed, it is illegal in many cases for companies to work too closely together with their peers. This is an example of a lack of bridging capital. So from the point of view of traditional economics, too much social capital can be a bad thing.

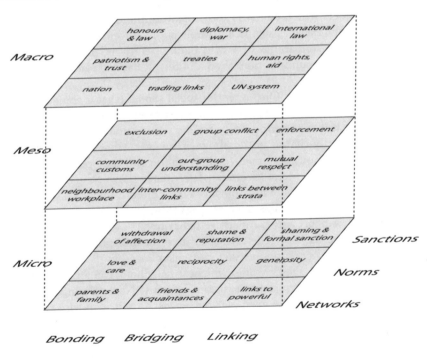

Source: (Halpern, 2005)

Figure 7.1 *Examples of Social Capital*

Finally, a third function of social capital, which can be considered a particular kind of bridging capital, is that which *links* different groups that have different levels of power or access to resources. Utility companies are usually regulated in various ways; the relationships they have with their regulators are an example of linking social capital.

Figure 7.1 above illustrates the relationships which each of these different aspects of social capital have to each other.

Applying capital

The majority of studies on social capital consider it a property of society. They usually focus on the relationship between social capital and major features of society, such as the incidence and distribution of crime, education or health.

For example, it is now accepted that close relationships, particularly with partners, reduce the risk of and shorten the length of depression (Brown and Harris, 1978; Sherbourne, Hayes et al. 1995). On the whole, an increase in social capital has a positive effect. It is generally associated not only with better health outcomes but also higher educational attainment, better careers, lower crime and so on.

In terms of development, the World Bank has recognized and strongly emphasizes projects which contribute to social capital, declaring that 'Social Capital is a concept that has significant implications for enhancing the quality, effectiveness and sustainability of World Bank operations, particularly those that are based on community action' (WB, 2008b). It has been labelled a 'public good' as a result.

Yet it is not all one-way. One aspect of social capital (that is sometimes also included in definition) is its capacity to support or enhance collective action. One example of this is the propensity to join associations and to strengthen civil society generally that as noted above. However, what if the purpose of such associations is not conducive to the public good, but perhaps towards crime? As studies of the Mafia (Servadio, 1976) have shown, the close bonding of such family-oriented groups also enhances *their* effectiveness. This is also the case for less formal organizations, such as gangs (Liu, 1999). And as noted above, social capital can support anti-competitive behaviour.

Indeed Liu has suggested the term 'negative social capital' to capture this effect. Of course this presupposes that consensus social goals are always good and their opposites bad, which while it might usually hold, cannot account satisfactorily for a positive attitude to resistance against Nazi rule in Europe, for example. Nevertheless, these examples do suggest that it is unwise to assume that all social capital is actually working for the public good.

Roger Leenders and Shaul Gabbay (Leenders and Gabbay, 1999) describe social capital in this way: '[social capital] represents the resources that accrue to an actor [including companies] through the actor's social relationships, facilitating the attainment of goals. When social structure hinders the attainment of goals, it yields social liability' (Leenders and Gabbay, 1999, p10). They provide an entertaining example of what happens when social capital fails to deliver in the following example:

> *In February 1996, Ben van Schaik, the CEO of Dutch aircraft builder Fokker, gave a presentation to a potential alliance partner. 'We are the second largest aircraft builder in the world,' he said, supporting his claim with a colourful bar graph – the bars represented various aircraft manufacturers; their length represented the number of the manufacturer's clients. With this graph, van Schaik showed the audience that Boeing/McDonnell Douglas had 846 clients, Fokker had 225 and the rest trailed behind at a large distance. Unfortunately, the number of ties did not represent the number of aircraft sold, nor did it represent the credit rating of the customers. Fokker's clients were primarily small companies, leasing one or two airplanes (rather than buying them), and many of them 'forgot' to pay their bills. Fokker declared bankruptcy only a few months later and was liquidated. Its 'much smaller' competition is still alive and kicking.*

Company capital

> *It can be argued – rather convincingly – that one of the most common and important forms of social capital is the company.*
>
> (Halpern, 2005, p53)

How does the idea of social capital apply to companies? Is there a coherent sense to the term 'corporate social capital'?

In applying social capital to companies, it is important to remember the distinction between a company and its stakeholders. A company is not the same thing as its stakeholders, and in particular it is separate from its management. Individual senior managers, of course, may identify closely with the company and their success may depend on that psychological stance – but that does not make them the same as the company. A company is an organization which is a wholly different kind of entity from a person. Managers are stakeholders of a company. While motivation is important, if that distinction were borne more carefully in mind the result might be better management and would certainly be better governance.

It is also important to remember that 'a company's capital', of any kind, including share capital, does not actually belong to the company concerned, see (Henriques, 2007, pp130–132) for more detail. It is an entry on the liability side of the balance sheet, representing the shareholders interest in the company. And of course, the shareholder, like any other stakeholder, is different from the company in which they own shares. Social capital is therefore also separate from a company, however much that company might benefit from it.

But how far can the metaphor of 'capital' be extended to *social* capital? From an economic perspective, social capital has its problems. One of these is that it is hard to measure in any definitive way (the following section will deal with the issue of its measurement). Also, unlike the more traditional forms of capital, it cannot be privately owned and therefore it cannot be transferred to others. As a consequence it is not capable of being sold, cannot have a price and therefore, the reasoning goes, it is not really a form of capital at all.

On the other hand, like traditional forms of capital, it can probably substitute for other forms of capital. Hiring someone with extensive social contacts, for example, under some circumstances might be an alternative to investing in a software sales system or purchasing mailing lists. It is also something in which companies and individuals may invest: companies do spend time and money arranging 'social events' at which their staff may get to know each other or clients, better. The OECD has produced a major report highlighting the concept and its advantages (OECD, 2001).

These examples suggest the real nature of corporate social capital. It consists of the networks, norms and sanctions between a company and its stakeholders and between a company's stakeholders. One example, and perhaps the one most studied, is the relationships between employees. This provides an example of bonding social capital. In a well-functioning company there are many networks of social relationships between different members of staff. These make it easier to get business done; for example, if you know the person in accounts you need to talk to, it can make the process of requesting a new account code take a few minutes rather than a few days. From the shareholder point of view, there are real advantages to this: it lowers the cost of doing business. And it must be more pleasant for the staff concerned than the frosty caricature of formality we associate with staff relationships in Victorian companies.

However, where staff work in different departments, with each adopting a 'silo mentality', bonding social capital can be harmful in that it accentuates a 'them and us' mentality. In these circumstances, it is important to develop bridging social capital to ensure organizational effectiveness. But this is simply a re-statement of common organizational development theory insights.

Another example of corporate social capital is provided by relationships between clients or customers. If customers are happy to recommend a company to other potential customers, then more business is more likely. What matters in each of these cases is that there is trust between the people involved. The network of relationships therefore produces the norm of trust. There are also obvious examples of sanctions in such networks. On the internet trading portal eBay, for example, buyers and sellers are each encouraged to rate each other. If a trader receives a series of bad ratings, it can be a real disincentive for people to trade with them.

A third example is provided by the series of interlocking directorships which bind many public companies to each other. Quite apart from the social relationships enjoyed by the individuals in question, it is of definite value to the Board of one company to have some access to the concerns and interests of other companies, especially where their businesses are related – an example of bridging social capital. Diversity in directorships can only enrich the potential of such non-executive directors.

This last example, however, can also show the dark side of social capital. Such networks of interlocking directorships tend to be self-perpetuating, in the sense that a small number of individuals will recommend each other for such posts and the total pool of individuals filling these positions is smaller than it might be. As a result, the talent and knowledge available to any one company is smaller than it might be and poor decisions will be made. Perhaps the most serious example of where this has been a problem is the culture of remuneration committees staffed by 'insiders' which insisted that very big rewards, even in the case of failure, were necessary 'to attract the right talent'. This seems to have been one of the contributory factors in the recent financial crisis.

Other shareholder benefits of access to social capital can be just as important. When suppliers work together with a company to deliver supplies under 'just-in-time' arrangements, this requires excellent communication and networking within the supply chain.

Uzzi and Gillespie have documented the benefits in terms of the reduced cost of financial capital which social capital can deliver. They showed that small businesses with good relationships with their banks enjoyed lower loan rates (Uzzi and Gillespie, 1999). Other work has been done to show that those biotechnology companies collaborating with other companies tend to produce more patents, and if patents are a measure of creativity, this suggests that they are also more creative (Smith-Doerr, Owen-Smith et al., 1999). Indeed the connection between social capital and creativity led Alex Macgillivray to make it a central feature of the concept and its measurement (Macgillivray, 2004).

The way mining companies work with communities close to their mines provides another example. In these situations, good relations with the local community are essential, otherwise the disruption caused by mining operations could well cause sustained opposition to the company, which can be a real difficulty. Of course good social capital, from a shareholder perspective, may also be bad for society at large. When companies get too close to their regulators, it is possible that regulatory decision-making can be impaired, favouring that company at the expense of the consumer.

NGO relationships provide yet another example. Although they may at times compete for funding, many campaigning NGOs collaborate with each other on campaigns. This is not only because their campaigns will benefit from additional views, but also, on a deeper level, because the individuals involved generally share a world-view in which the various campaigns they may be involved in are complementary.

NGOs also collaborate with companies. Such company–NGO partnerships have been given a high profile recently and much has been expected from them. It is not the place here to discuss the details which make partnerships succeed or fail. But it is important to point out that the specific projects on which they depend, however important, do not substitute for a rounded or complete relationship. They are specific projects whose success may well be influenced by the nature of the relationship (i.e. social capital) which preceded it, as well as by other (apparently unconnected) actions of the company which can prejudice the partnership.

Measuring capital

If social capital is so pervasive and important, how can it be measured? While considerable attention has been devoted to measuring social capital in relation to broad social issues, (see, for example, ONS, 2008; WB 2008a) little attention has been paid to the concept in relation to companies.

The importance of measurement can be seen from the share price of many companies: the total value the share price places on the company exceeds – sometimes by a factor of 20 – the value of the physical assets they own. Shareholders, then, feel that their companies benefit from something beyond traditional capital. These assets are often called goodwill, but the valuation of goodwill, independently from the share price, has been notoriously difficult. And goodwill appears to be closely connected to social capital.

From one point of view, then, the way to value the total of social capital available to the shareholder is to treat it as goodwill writ large and simply to take that portion of the share price which is not represented by tangible assets. One objection to this approach is that investors do not always get it right; with respect to those who believe that we already live in a perfect free market, the share price may simply be wrong. There are in any case so many things that affect the share price, as it changes minute by minute, that it is very difficult to extract the part of the share price that is due to fundamentals. The extreme volatility of world stock markets during 2008 and 2009 bears this out. Still, it is all we have in most cases.

An apparently more serious objection is that part of that goodwill may be represented by assets such as rights, leases and contracts. While these are not tangible, they are generally based on legal agreements. However, this is not a good argument that such things are not social capital, merely that they are items of social capital which have been created or underpinned by the legal infrastructure – the legal infrastructure being a particularly good example of well-defined social networks, norms and sanctions.

In any case, the principal problem with the share price method of valuation is that it provides no detail or analysis of the nature of the social capital it may measure. And the underlying problem is that social capital is not an asset of the business, but a liability; the corresponding asset is 'owned' and maintained largely by the company's stakeholders. It is therefore not surprising that it is not readily captured by a measure appropriate to assets which must be closely managed by companies.

The more everyday interpretation of goodwill as reputation however provides one way to measure something of social capital. In recent years, companies have become ever keener on measuring their reputation. One of the principal ways in which stakeholder relations are captured in many social reports is through this measure. Of course reputation is an outcome of social capital, not a measure of the networks involved directly (although it should be argued that the pressure to maintain reputation is part of a system of norms and sanctions).

One way to measure the networks in which a company is involved is to measure the contacts which people make. This is a relatively intensive exercise, but it has nevertheless been carried out by academics and occasionally by companies. Companies usually record the contacts they have had with customers and sometimes extend this to NGOs, suppliers and other stakeholders. Han and Breiger have measured the number of ties between pairs of contacts amongst investment banking companies (Han and Breiger, 1999), establishing that networks can be measured directly. But there are few obvious lessons from these studies as to how to develop the most fruitful links between stakeholders.

However, what can be concluded, as David Halpern points out (Halpern, 2005, p33), is that the principal result of social capital is trust. It has proved possible to measure trust fairly consistently using survey techniques. In relation to employees' trust of customers, a typical question might be the following:

> *Generally speaking, would you say that most customers can be trusted or that you need to be very careful in dealing with them? (Code one answer):*
> 1 *Most customers can be trusted.*
> 2 *Need to be very careful.*
>
> (Adapted from WVS, 2005)

Of course, market survey techniques (see Appendix I) are something of a blunt instrument. At the other end of the scale are the techniques of anthropological study, described in Chapter 6. These involve living among the people being studied – in this case it might be employees or other stakeholders. Anthropologists work like this for up to several years, before reporting on their findings. As a result, far greater insight is obtained into the actual networks and relationships involved, and therefore of the social capital being maintained.

A crucial part of their method is to gain the trust of the people under study; this requires learning their language and living as they do for extended periods of time. While anthropologists have been used to study both customers and employees, it is clearly an expensive process and perhaps not suitable for the continuing monitoring of social capital. On the other hand the quality of the results is likely to be far more reliable.

If the hallmark of social capital is trust, then the lack of trust betrays its absence. One of the areas in which a lack of trust is most obvious is corruption. Corruption and its associated lack of transparency stifles business activity. It follows that countries, or industries, in which corruption is widespread will suffer low rates of social capital. The lack of social capital is perhaps the underlying reason why business is so much more difficult amidst corruption.

Social capital is a useful indicator of an important aspect of corporate impact. Although not easy to measure, it does capture an essential aspect of the relationship of a company to society – and therefore of corporate impact.

8

Signs of Impact

The problem of measuring the social impact of companies is often seen as one of indicators. It is not clear what social issues should be measured with which indicators. Also, social indicators seem to be in some way 'weak' compared to environmental indicators. As a result, the social sections of company reports are usually shorter and less developed than other sections.

What is the problem with social indicators? To answer that it is necessary to understand how indicators in general work. That will be the main subject of this chapter. Yet before embarking on that analysis, it is important to remember that social impact is a matter of relationship, rather than a relatively well-defined quantity, such as profit. As a result, the way indicators work in relation to social issues is complex.

WHAT IS AN INDICATOR?

An indicator is something that 'points out' something else. The height of mercury in a thermometer indicates the temperature. It can do this because the height of the column is fairly directly proportional to the temperature: a longer column indicates a hotter temperature than a shorter one. The length of the column is directly connected to its temperature and this is in turn directly connected to the temperature of the environment in which the thermometer finds itself. Indicators are therefore ways of leveraging information. They provide insight into something other than themselves.

One of the problems with social indicators is that all indicators are assumed to work on the same model as thermometers. This is true of many environmental indicators, such as tonnes of CO_2 or waste paper. As a result, environmental issues are often said to be more 'measurable' or quantifiable. Unfortunately this is not so true of social issues. There is no thermometer for relationships, even if there are qualities of that relationship, such as trust, which (if they were measured) could give a reliable insight into the relationship.

The following sections will set out a number of ways in which indicators can be classified. This helps with choosing indicators and understanding how they can function in relation to social issues.

TYPES OF INDICATOR

The importance of being connected

Indicators such as the height of mercury in a thermometer are directly connected to what they indicate. This type of indicator is seen as the ideal type of indicator – that is, what all indicators should *really* be like. If an indicator is not like this, the temptation is to see it as somehow not really an indicator in 'the true sense'. Unfortunately many indicators of social issues (and therefore of social impact) are not and cannot be like this.

Other indicators which are less directly connected can still provide useful insights. Such an indirect indicator of temperature might be the number of layers of clothes which someone is wearing. In general, you would expect that the more clothes someone wore, the lower the temperature. There is a general causal connection between the indicator and what is indicated. Of course the relationship is somewhat statistical: it is quite possible that there are good reasons that a given person is not wearing very many layers of clothes even though it is cold, such as that they are engaged in heavy exercise. So while there are good reasons to connect layers of clothing with temperature, it is not as connected as the height of the column of mercury.

An indicator which is perhaps even more indirectly connected with temperature, but which is definitely meaningfully related, is the nature of clothing which is displayed in clothes shops. Such seasonal displays are obviously meaningfully related to the outside temperature, because the temperature varies with the seasons. However, it would be unwise to rely too heavily on the predictions of clothes shops, as they only give an approximate indication of the temperature, since this varies widely during the day, let alone during a given season. In fact for some reason in many countries, the relationship is further distanced, as the actual type of clothing which is sold in a given season is more closely related to the expected temperature of the next season, rather than to that of the current one. Furthermore because of the vagaries of the weather, it is quite possible to experience high (or low) temperatures accompanied by any kind of seasonal clothing display.

The table below gives examples of these three types of indicator relevant to both environmental and social issues. This is based on an analysis of indicators developed by C. S. Peirce (Peirce, 1868) which distinguishes three levels of complexity in the relationship between an indicator and what it indicates.

One consequence of this analysis of indicators is that it makes clear that the indicator itself (the signifier) can usefully be distinguished from what is being indicated (the signified). In turn this means that the nature of an indicator does not have to be the same as what is being indicated; it is possible for an indicator of one type to be (indirectly) connected to factors of another type. In Table 8.1, the social indicator '% supplier bills paid on time' may in some contexts also function as an economic indicator. This is why 'hours of training', for example, can be an indicator both of economic investment and also of social

Table 8.1 *Levels of Indicator*

Indicator type	Environmental	Dimension Social	Economic
Direct or substantive Level 1	Tonnes of CO_2 emitted	% supplier bills paid on time	Profitability
Indirect Level 2	Energy utility bills	% supplier invoices queried	Productivity
Level 3	Commitment to dealing with climate change	Level of trust of suppliers in company	Quality of management

impact. Training of employees affects not only the employees themselves but also the prospects of the company doing the training; it is indirectly connected to both issues.

This is reflected in the classifications of some of the Global Reporting Initiative (GRI) indicators. For example, the GRI indicator measuring anti-competitive behaviour is classified as a social indicator, not an economic one. Similarly, indicator EC6 in the GRI Guidelines is 'Policy, practices, and proportion of spending on locally-based suppliers at significant locations of operation' (GRI, 2006). Although it is concerned with relationship to suppliers, it is classified as an economic indicator.

So the general expectation for social indicators, as for other indicators, is that they should all be direct and thus of the same nature as that which they indicate. But since social impact is a matter of relationship, it is hard to find very many direct social indicators.

Different kinds of measure

It is also important to realize that indicators, whether direct or indirect, may be of several different kinds. The prototypical indicator (such as tonnes of CO_2) is quantitative. But other sorts of indicator are possible and can also be very revealing. Possible different kinds of indicator include:

- **quantitative** – e.g. the number of prosecutions there were under relevant equal opportunity law;
- **binary** – e.g. was an equal opportunity policy in place or not?
- **qualitative** – e.g. how many staff knew of the equal opportunity policy? Note that many qualitative indicators relate to perceptions and are expressed as the quantity of people that hold a given view and may be useful to gauge awareness of an issue internally or externally;
- **anecdotal** – e.g. 'I think our company policy towards ethnic minorities is excellent!' This type of indicator is by definition 'unrepresentative'. However, such indicators not only bring life to a report, they also may in

fact be most directly related to what the indicator is trying to measure (i.e. outcomes), in this case perhaps company–staff relations.

Measuring different kinds of things

Turning to the sorts of things which indicators measure, two main classes of indicator are often distinguished: *process indicators* and *substantive indicators*. Our prototypical indicator (tonnes of CO_2) is substantive. It measures a particular level of performance which is directly related to climate change potential.

Process indicators

Process indicators do not measure the result which is sought, but what is being done about achieving that result. One use of process indicators is to describe the (management) processes put in place in order to lead to a substantive result. For example, a measure of the roll-out of an environmental management system, perhaps capturing the number of sites which have introduced it, would be of this kind.

In relation to environmental issues, process indicators seem not only indirect, in the sense we have been defining it above, but perhaps rather ineffectual. It is all too possible to have a management system in place which entirely fails to achieve acceptable substantive performance. On the other hand the desired result is unlikely to be achieved without an appropriate management system – so such indicators clearly have their place.

However, process indicators are particularly important in the measurement of social issues for several reasons. Firstly, the relationship of a stakeholder to a company is itself a social process. Some process indicators can therefore give an important insight into the quality of that relationship. The arrangements established by a company to talk, on a regular basis, to an NGO concerned with some aspect of the company's performance would be a case in point. The process of engagement is regarded as valuable in its own right. Without any process indicators, it is therefore unlikely that the social performance of a company could accurately be captured.

The second reason that process indicators are important to the measurement of social issues is that it can be hard to develop or use appropriate substantive indicators. As a result, process indicators are substituted. In the G3 version of the GRI Guidelines, that often takes the form of reporting on risk. For example, indicator HR7 reads 'Operations identified as having significant risk for incidents of forced or compulsory labor, and measures to contribute to the elimination of forced or compulsory labor' (GRI, 2006). What it does not require is reporting on the number of incidents in which children were employed. This is partly because there are difficulties in evaluating how many children might be employed by suppliers, since suppliers can see it as in their interest to disguise the fact. Another cause, which is hardly justified, is that the company can be very sensitive to the effects of such disclosures on its reputation, and therefore would prefer not to report on such indicators. Similar arguments apply to a number of other human rights indicators and to those for corruption.

Process indicators are also closely linked to the question of governance. This is because process indicators can measure not only whether there is a management system in place, and how effective it is, but also how decisions are made and how the indicators themselves are chosen.

Process indicators can capture, for example:

- the existence of policies for stakeholder engagement;
- the existence of social and environmental policies;
- how dialogue processes address the issue of power;
- the involvement of stakeholders in identifying indicators;
- the practice of setting targets for improving social performance.

Substantive indicators

Substantive indicators measure specific levels of achievement that have been attained. They are commonly categorized as *input*, *output* and *outcome* indicators (defined in Table 8.2 below). Input and output indicators can often be quantified and may refer to physical quantities and/or financial values. Outcomes, on the other hand, are often best approximated through perceptions (which can also of course also be represented quantitatively).

This classification of indicators is most directly applicable to clearly defined project-based work – such as contribution to the local community. Table 8.2 defines and compares these different types of indicator.

Table 8.2 *Input, Output and Outcome Indicators Compared*

	Input	Output	Outcome
Definition	• resources expended (e.g. money, effort used to construct a building)	• deliverables produced (e.g. number of buildings erected)	• the reason or purpose the project was undertaken (e.g. improve health or community well-being)
Advantages	• easy to measure • can be measured early in project life	• easy to measure	• most directly related to project objectives
Disadvantages	• less meaningful • may create perverse incentives (e.g. to spend more)	• can usually only be measured later in project life	• hard to measure (often qualitative) • may take years to materialize • may be affected by wide variety of factors • may be local or anecdotal in nature and not readily aggregated

The London Benchmarking Group (LBG, 2009) model, which is a standard for analysing and reporting community involvement, makes good use of input and output indicators. Its stakeholder focus is communities, staff of the company, suppliers and customers. So input indicators might include staff time and money donated and outputs can include projects delivered. Outcome measures, as might be expected are less well-defined and reported.

THE PURPOSE OF INDICATORS

Indicators serve a number of different purposes. They:

- provide enterprises with a management tool to enhance the quality of their operations through continuous improvement;
- guide policies and decision-making at all levels of the organization;
- aid priority setting by providing early warning of adverse trends;
- strengthen public accountability by addressing the needs and expectations of external stakeholders.

Social indicators are also intended to enable a change in a company's social performance. To achieve that they must be appropriately connected to what they are measuring. In this vein, Halpern has suggested (Halpern, 2005, p32) these technical criteria of a good indicator:

- reliability, giving consistent results under consistent conditions;
- surface validity, appearing a reasonable thing to be measuring;
- criterion related, that is connected with the subject matter;
- predictive of underlying performance. This is the strongest criterion, and also the hardest to verify in practice.

A good indicator must also communicate well. It is therefore one which simplifies complex events or trends and is:

- practical;
- clearly defined and communicates well;
- reproducible and can be monitored;
- action-orientated.

Very few indicators, however, are intended to give a comprehensive picture of a situation, and will therefore be a complement to, rather than a replacement for, more detailed analytical techniques. This is particularly important to avoid the danger of perverse incentives. If an indicator is not well aligned to the underlying outcome to which it is supposed to relate, and if at the same time management are rewarded on the basis of the indicator, then the results can be disastrous.

The implementation of waiting list indicators in the UK National Health Service (NHS) is an example. To a background of general complaint about the NHS, it was determined that patients were on waiting lists for entry into hospital for far too long. Because NHS managers were targeted with reducing waiting lists and rewarded accordingly, they did reduce them. However this also had perverse and unintended results. One method of reducing waiting lists was to discharge patients somewhat before they were ready so that new patients could be admitted from the waiting lists. This indeed reduced some waiting lists, but it also clearly endangered the quality of care which patients received. The overriding goal was the provision of high quality of care, not waiting list times. So the wrong indicator was targeted.

DEVELOPING INDICATORS

Since social indicators measure a company-stakeholder relationship and how the company affects stakeholders, in one sense there is only one way to develop indicators: with stakeholders. While that is true at one level, it is rarely necessary to start with a blank sheet of paper. There are several sources of ready-made (or perhaps 'nearly-made') indicators, such as the GRI indicators, discussed in the next chapter. These may be useful without modification or they may form a useful basis for stakeholder dialogue.

An ideal indicator is then one which:

- has been developed in a participatory way with stakeholders;
- is meaningful to stakeholders, that is, it should measure something believed by stakeholders to be important or significant in its own right;
- is accepted as meaningful and 'owned' by the company.

In contrast to this approach, there is usually a great temptation to select indicators because it is immediately possible to gather information on them from readily available datasets. While this may seem more practical it is the wrong way round, and should really only be used as an interim measure. Of course it is cheaper to measure those things for which the data already exists. But this is to put too low a value on the principal purpose of indicators, which is to satisfy stakeholder needs.

Fortunately, there are several sources of pre-existing indicators which may be appropriate to a company. The first of these is existing company values, objectives, Key Performance Indicators and policies. All of these will capture what the company is trying to achieve as part of its overall mission. Such values and policies should also be, and sometimes are, articulated in relation to each stakeholder. For example, the goals of the company in relation to consumers may be spelled out in such statements in such a way as to lead to a workable indicator.

A second source of indicators is social norms. An example might be expectations in relation to labour conditions in the supply chain. There is undoubted consensus in Western societies (and emerging consensus among global business), for example, that companies are responsible for the labour practices on which they rely, whether or not the workers concerned are directly employed by the company.

A third source, which draws in some respects on the first two set out above, is that of voluntary standards, such as SA8000 which is a site-based standard for labour conditions . There is a large body of standards on many issues relevant to corporate responsibility. Such standards typically suggest indicators which should be used to evaluate company performance. The body of human rights conventions is in many respects a source of sources, since human rights underlie many such standards.

In deriving practical indicators from all these sources, care should be taken to ensure that the indicators derived from them are relevant to the issues the company faces. Many standards for example are quite generic and intended to apply to any company. As a result, in some situations the indicators suggested may not be suitable, however significant the issue to which they relate. Conversely, if they are relevant, they may not exhaust stakeholder concern for the issue.

While company management may be able to make very educated guesses as to how the indicators could be developed, it is important to include stakeholders in that process. This is not only in order to ensure that the process of indicator development is, and is seen to be, participative, but also because there are issues which only interaction with stakeholders will expose.

Indicators of CO_2 production and health and safety will be applicable to virtually all companies. However, an indicator of product labelling appears to have little relevance to a mining company, for example. But at another level, the specification of ore quality is a critical feature for their customers. Furthermore, with increasing consumer concern for the ethical aspects of their purchases, there are a growing number of sectors for which consumer labelling is becoming significant. The sectors affected currently include forestry, fisheries and diamonds as well as garments and footwear: all of these are now under some pressure to adopt product labelling which would have been thought very unlikely only a few years ago.

In terms of the different types of indicator distinguished earlier in this chapter, there is in general no goal for a particular distribution of binary versus anecdotal, or substantive versus process indicators. The expectation should be that a range of such indicators will be needed to convey a credible picture. A set of social indicators must be judged as a whole.

However, there always remains a strong bias for direct (substantive) indicators. While these are indeed powerful and helpful to providing corporate accountability, they are not always achievable. More distantly related indicators can give a very meaningful and occasionally much more practical insight into a situation. It may be very helpful to have a direct indicator of water quality of a local stream, for instance. But this would be very technical in nature, involving measuring chemicals with difficult names and expressed in units of 'parts per million'. This is hard to understand and may be expensive to actually measure.

As an alternative, counting the number of fish in the river, which is more distantly related to water quality, is a very practical indicator – and one to which far more people can relate and even enjoy measuring!

At a fundamental level the indicators selected reflect values held and what a company and its stakeholders are each seeking to achieve. Indicators are also, therefore, not chosen just once, but are subject to challenge and change as relationships change, and understanding deepens. Indicators need to reflect an evolving set of differences in views and priorities among those involved and affected.

In one sense, developing indicators is only the beginning. The hard work begins when it is known what indicators to use. This is because to be actually useful, data needs to be collected for it, that is, the indicator needs to be evaluated.

USING INDICATORS

The first main way in which indicators should be used is to track and manage the performance of a company over time. To do this, the indicator must be evaluated not only for the current period, but also for past periods so that trends can be seen. Furthermore the same indicator can be used to define appropriate and measurable targets for future performance.

In addition to comparisons between the same organization at different times, indicators should be used to compare or benchmark the performance of the company against other companies. These other companies may or may not be direct competitors. Clearly information about competitors can be difficult to obtain. However it is possible to use some creativity in obtaining such benchmarks, such as choosing an organization for which information is available and which is similar in useful respects. Information about one office-based company may be comparable with others, perhaps in regard to carbon emissions. It is also possible to use industry associations or other organizations to gather and pool data, making it available in a useful but non-competitive form.

9

Reporting Social Impact

How companies *report* their social impact is itself an important indicator of how well they understand it. The first part of this chapter sets out the general features of much corporate reporting of social impact through a case study. The second part reviews the key standard for reporting, the GRI, in relation to reporting of social indicators, which is an important part of reporting though far from the whole of it.

COMPANY SOCIAL REPORTING

In general, corporate reporting of social issues is considerably less well developed than that of environmental issues. Other than for specific industry sectors with well-known social impacts, such as clothing manufacture, social issues are treated lightly. One exception is reporting on employees, which is common and in some companies, fairly well developed. The reasons for this general situation include:

- companies do not know how to analyse and appraise their social impact or social issues more generally;
- it can be hard to do as suitable social indicators may not be available – although this is exacerbated by the lack of understanding of social impact;
- it is perceived to be 'too revealing'. The issues concerned are seen as too sensitive for full public reporting and are often labelled 'commercially confidential'.

There is now a trend to acknowledge major issues, such as climate change and human rights abuse. However in practice, much reporting of social issues is based on process indicators, that is, an account of what the company is doing about its social impact and how it is managing it, rather than an actual assessment of the impact itself.

The case study in the following section is taken from a review of a real corporate report written by a financial institution '1FI'. It represents the middle of the road in terms of practice: it is neither an especially outstanding example, nor is it particularly bad. It should therefore give a picture of what the issues often are with the reporting of social impact.

A case study in reporting social impact

The 1FI report contained a short profile of the group and of each of its main divisions. This was followed by sections devoted to customers, employees, investors, suppliers, regulators, the environment and community investment. It also provided a clear summary of progress in the reporting year and of its targets for the following year. One of the mainstream accounting-based firms provided independent assurance.

The 1FI report says that it provides 'an insight into the policies and practices which ensure that our business is sustainable in the long term'. While this is one valuable objective, it also raises the following issues:

- Is sustainability (or 'corporate responsibility' or 'CSR') also understood to mean the ability for 1FI to continue its social, environmental and (wider) economic impacts at current levels?
- Many stakeholders would appreciate a report which also provided a systematic and quantitative analysis of sustainability performance.

In fact the report provides a discussion of policy, supported by case studies, for some stakeholders, but also provides considerably more, quantitative, detail for others (e.g. staff, investors and for the environment). This additional information is welcome. But the setting of more quantitative targets would help considerably.

The stakeholder structure of the report is helpful; and the report also recognizes the significance of trust from stakeholders for the business. However, an organization the size of 1FI will have a much richer and more complex stakeholder structure than the report conveys. It would be particularly helpful to analyse the composition of all stakeholder groups, as has been done for employees. This in itself can highlight significant issues, particularly for more vulnerable stakeholder groups.

Stakeholders' response to a report of this nature can be affected by assurance. However, the Independent Assurance provided has been directed at 1FI itself, rather than at its stakeholders (or even its shareholders). In addition, the assurance opinion provides very little feedback on how well the report fulfils its own objectives or the needs of 1FI's stakeholders.

Responsibility for indirect impacts, that is those impacts caused not by an organization itself but by its stakeholders, is perhaps the single biggest issue for the financial sector as a whole. The report does begin to acknowledge at least the environmental aspects of this issue and discusses a major pipeline project 1FI had supported as an example. But in assessing the overall impacts for which 1FI is responsible, a much fuller treatment is needed.

All large companies, and particularly international ones, can generate significant tax contributions. The report says that 1FI makes significant corporate tax contributions; further details on what is presumably already public knowledge would help put this claim in context. In addition, an understanding of what 1FI's tax policies are would be invaluable.

The report declares the company's support for the Global Compact which includes human rights amongst its commitments. However, the report does not explicitly include a commitment to the Universal Declaration of Human Rights, which is becoming increasingly common, and certainly more widely expected, from major companies. Also, the description of the pipeline project refers very largely to the environmental impacts of that project; however the human rights implications were regarded as at least as significant for most of the campaigning groups concerned with it.

The section on the Equator Principles describes how 1FI is gearing up to address these systematically in its financing projects. It would be extremely helpful to have further details on the extent and plans for training of lending officers and also on the numbers and types of loans which have been assessed against the principles.

It is very welcome that the performances of different national operations can be compared and that actual figures are given; however, the presentation of the data could be considerably improved. It would also be useful to have some kind of commentary on the factors which have caused the various trends in performance that the figures describe.

There are two major groups of 1FI customers (retail and commercial) which are not clearly separated in the report. On the whole, they have different interests and concerns which should be set out accordingly. On the consumer side particularly, it would have been of great benefit to list the various brands clearly, rather than as an illustration. For example, it is not clear whether the pictures of brands near the start of the report represent a complete set.

The report mentions several means by which the treatment of customers and their views and are assessed, including surveys, complaints processes and a Mystery Shopper exercise. It also describes some initiatives which have been undertaken that relate to customers. However, there is no real account of what the customer views or experience might actually be, or what views (positive and negative) they have expressed.

The length of time it takes to clear a cheque is acknowledged in the report; this is an issue that has antagonized many customers. Clearly this is not a responsibility of 1FI alone, but it would be helpful to have an account of what 1FI's policies are and the nature of any representations to the regulators or politicians on the matter might have been.

Some other issues which must be of concern to customers include:

- The adequacy of pension and (endowment) mortgages performance and related mis-selling. The report covers the policies 1FI has in place, however it would be greatly strengthened by providing some analysis of the performance of 1FI products in this regard.

- What do 1FI bad debts look like?
- How fast are claims actually settled?

The employee section provides a useful analysis of the stakeholder group. However, the basic facts on employee pay should be reported. It may be possible to report the ratio of the highest paid member of staff to that of the lowest. The objective of reporting the employee opinion survey is welcome. However, it is quite hard to understand exactly what the percentages depicted actually mean. The Health and Safety data should include the fact that there were no fatalities. In a previous year, some staff had been so concerned about their remuneration that they staged protests. This is not reported.

It is very helpful (and still relatively unusual) to treat investors as stakeholders and further to differentiate shareholders from other kinds of investor. In addition, the data this section contains measures hard performance. However one omission, which uses data very readily available, is that of benchmark performance to support an understanding of performance relative to the sector. This is definitely of concern to shareholders.

The supplier section mainly concerns the sustainability performance of suppliers. This is of course an important issue. It would therefore be helpful to understand how well suppliers are actually adhering to 1FI's policies for them. However it is also important how 1FI performs towards suppliers as stakeholders of 1FI in their own right. For example, how quickly are invoices settled? Finally it would also be useful to present an analysis of the different kinds of suppliers to 1FI. How many are small and dependent on 1FI? How many are located in the UK and elsewhere?

As with investors, the regulator is a stakeholder for which company performance is rarely reported. The report principally identifies areas in which 1FI has been active. However, other than money laundering, a critical omission is the lack of an account of what lobbying or other consultation positions are actually taken on the various issues identified.

The environment section suggests that indirect environmental impacts are discussed under the customers and suppliers sections. This is partly true for suppliers, but as noted above, the major environmental impacts of customers have not been reported. One place to start may be the environmental impact of the investment property portfolio.

A consultation exercise on 1FI's environmental impact is described and two high-level findings set out. A much fuller account of the consultation would have considerably added to the report. This would then allow a proper discussion of how 1FI reacted to their suggestions.

The community section is entitled 'community investment', not 'community'. This accurately reflects what it covers, but does not do justice to 'the community' as a stakeholder. What the report suggests is that their 'strength' is important; but in what that strength consists is not specified. The consequence is perhaps that the objectives and rationales of the community programmes are not as well-defined as they might be. A key, and commonly reported, statistic which would help put the Community Programme into context, and permit clear targets and benchmarks, is the percentage of community investment as a proportion of profits.

So on the whole, the 1FI report clearly acknowledges its major stakeholders and some of their real issues of concern. It also presents the information it does cover in an accessible way. However, the social picture is incomplete and a more thorough, stakeholder-informed understanding of some of the principal issues would be necessary if 1FI were to provide a proper picture of its social impacts.

SOCIAL INDICATORS IN THE GRI

Many of the best reporters make use of the Global Reporting Initiative (GRI) Framework for sustainability reporting. Others may refer to the GRI, without actually using the Guidelines in any systematic way (as did the 1FI organization whose report was described in the last section). The GRI is important because it was developed through a genuine multi-stakeholder process – and also because it represents the only general standard for sustainability reporting. It contains much guidance for reporting on each dimension of sustainability, including a series of indicators on social impacts.

A review of the social indicators within the GRI is therefore important to understanding how social impact is commonly understood. GRI indicators are arranged in a format consistent with that for the other dimensions of sustainability and which has been taken from the practice for classifying environmental indicators. The classification is organized in three levels:

- **Category** – the general class or grouping of issues of concern to stakeholders (e.g. labour practices; market presence).
- **Aspect** – a specific issue about which information is to be reported (e.g. occupational health & safety; diversity).
- **Indicator** – the most precise (and often quantitative) measures of performance during a reporting period (e.g. percentage of total workforce represented in formal joint management–worker health and safety committees that help monitor and advise on occupational health and safety programs; rates of injury, occupational diseases, lost days, and absenteeism, and number of work-related fatalities by region).

Historically, the development of the social indicators within the GRI process was amongst its most challenging elements. One factor was the difficulty of selecting the most important indicators for social impact. As a result the number of social indicators in the most recent release ('G3') is still more than the number of economic and environmental indicators added together.

The most basic question must be 'has the GRI captured all facets of social impact?' At one level the answer to this question must be 'no', since the Guidelines are intended to be of sufficient generality that they can be applied by any organization. It follows that the specificity of social impact for many organizations will not be entirely described. To some extent the additional Guidelines designed for particular industry or organizational sectors address that. Nevertheless, it is easy enough to identify important social issues which are missing from the list of social indicators, such as the (maximum) hours of work for employees.

To an important extent, the GRI has provided for this by giving stakeholders and stakeholder engagement a significant role in determining report content. It would be quite within the spirit of the GRI to report on indicators which have not been specified in the Guidelines, should stakeholders request it. It would be expected, for example, that a Western organization in the clothing industry which outsourced its main production to countries in the South would report on the maximum hours of work that are expected of their suppliers' workers.

It has been particularly hard to identify substantive indicators for social impact – not only because it is difficult to define them, but also because, even where reasonable definitions can be found it may be hard for companies to reveal their social performance against the indicators. As a result there had been a particular emphasis on process indicators, rather than substantive indicators, in the first two generations of the GRI Guidelines. This was widely regarded as unsatisfactory, and it is significant that the proportion of substantive social indicators significantly increased in the G3, compared to the previous version.

The GRI also differentiates between 'core' and 'additional' indicators, in this way: 'those designated as Core are generally applicable Indicators and are assumed to be material for most organizations. An organization should report on these unless they are deemed not material on the basis of the Reporting Principles. Additional Indicators may also be determined to be material' (GRI, 2006, p7).

An analysis of core and additional social indicators showing those which may be considered process and substantive (as described in Chapter 8) is given in Table 9.1. The full list of GRI social indicators may be found in Appendix I.

Table 9.1 *GRI Social Indicators*

GRI Social Indicators	Core	Additional
Substantive	10	7
Process	15	8

10

Measuring Economic Impact

As has been suggested in earlier chapters, the sphere of the economic is really a part of the sphere of the social. Nevertheless, in most discussions they are treated separately. The GRI Guidelines, which contains economic indicators, is no exception. The economic indicators within the GRI cover financial performance (including financial relationships with stakeholders), the scale of market presence, and impact on the wider economy. Yet a full economic analysis would provide a different and much more detailed picture. This chapter and the next will explore what a more detailed economic analysis of a company can look like. This chapter describes techniques to analyse overall economic impact; the next chapter focuses on the financial impact on stakeholders.

ECONOMIC ANALYSIS

There have been a few attempts to use traditional economic analysis to analyse the impact of an individual company. These have typically looked the local or national impact of a large multinational. The companies that have been (partially) studied in this way include Unilever (Clay, 2005; Kapstein, 2008), Honda (Honda, 2004) and Toyota and BMW (Honda, 2004; Phillips, Hamden et al., 2004).

The study of Unilever (Clay, 2005) was interesting because it looked at the impact of a company, Unilever Indonesia (UI), on an entire country – although it did not cover all aspects of the company's operations to the same level of detail. It was also interesting because it focused on the extent to which the company contributed to the alleviation of poverty – not simply on the generation of economic activity.

The process, which involved the active participation of Oxfam and local UI staff and a considerable number of other stakeholders, included four components:

- an assessment of the beneficial economic impacts of UI and the extent to which these benefits extended to the poor. This covered employment impacts, trade flows, foreign exchange and tax payments;

- an analysis of the policies and practices of UI and the extent to which these are effective in maintaining standards;
- an analysis of UI's supply chain, looking at the opportunities for the participation of the poor in the supply chain;
- an analysis of the way the poor could participate in the distribution process and have access to UI products.

The findings included the following:

- the majority of revenues generated by the company remained in Indonesia;
- UI (with some 3,000 employees) contributes to the support of some 300,000 jobs in Indonesia.

There are a number of issues arising from this study. Firstly, the production of this study involved a considerable effort from a wide range of people. And it is still not a complete analysis of even one subsidiary of one major company. Is it reasonable to expect an analysis of economic impact from every company done in this way?

Secondly, the study only looked for positive impacts. It measured part of the gross impact of UI on Indonesia; it did not attempt to assess effects such as local manufacturers which might have been put out of business by UI's activities. Any full analysis of economic impact must measure both positive and negative impacts.

From an economic perspective – if not from a stakeholder participation perspective – Unilever's study of its economic impact on South Africa (Kapstein, 2008) was somewhat more rigorous. This exercise was based on the standard macro-economic tools of input–output modelling and the social accounting matrix. Input–output models and social accounting matrices are standard macro-economic tools designed to show the connections, through monetary flows, between different parts of the economy. The virtue of using them is that the techniques are fairly widely used to analyse national accounts and sometimes regional accounts and so at least some of the data is readily available. These techniques firstly capture the company's investments, taxes and purchases. But they also capture the 'multiplier effect' deriving from the fact that a company's suppliers will themselves make purchases and create employment as a result of their supplies to the company; furthermore this effect continues down the supply chain. As a result, £1 spent by a company results in more than £1 of total economic activity. The study also used Economic Rate of Return (ERR) analysis to understand the opportunity cost of Unilever withdrawing from South Africa, and so the corresponding economic benefit of staying there.

The principal findings of the study were that Unilever South Africa contributed about 0.9 per cent to the country's GDP and that for every £1 (or Rand) received in sales, £1.45 was added to GDP. The study also acknowledged that:

- the study was extremely complex and data-intensive. By implication such an approach would not be suitable for widespread and regular use;
- the fundamental technique rests on analysing activity at a single point in time. This means that it is not likely to capture the effects of technological change over time;
- the input–output and social accounting matrix (SAM) analysis assumes that the technical characteristics (such as labour–capital coefficients) of companies in the same sector are the same. This makes it inappropriate to use for comparing companies for which these characteristics are likely to vary, such as in comparisons between local and multi-national companies.

One of the lessons of economics is that private economic activity has public benefits – or at least benefits to other private actors. Adam Smith (Smith, 1999b) characterized it as like the work of an invisible, and benevolent, hand. In the twentieth century, Keynes (Keynes, 2007) made the idea rather more concrete with the idea of the economic multiplier.

It is now accepted that in the course of ordinary economic activities, the result of everyday purchases cascades through the economy. The result of one purchase represents income to another organization or person; they will then spend at least part of that, which in turn represents yet further economic activity. Purchases beget more purchases and so spending £1 will result in a net gain to the economy of more than £1. Since, according to orthodox economics, economic activity measures social welfare, that will result in a net gain to society – a social benefit.

Of course, everything depends on the pattern of economic activity. Precisely who benefits from any given economic transaction will depend on how and where the various consequent transactions take place. This has become particularly obvious in assessing the effectiveness of aid to poorer countries. The rationale of aid is that it will help those countries which receive it. Yet when aid money is spent in donor countries, i.e. outside the ostensible recipient country, the recipient country cannot benefit from multiplier effects, even though they may receive the corresponding output, which may be training or some other form of 'technical assistance'.

Action Aid notes that 'eighty-six cents in every dollar of American aid is phantom aid, largely because it is so heavily tied to the purchase of US goods and services, and because it is so badly targeted at poor countries.' (Greenhill and Watts, 2005). Furthermore some 25% of aid worldwide is in the form of technical assistance which is largely purchased from donor countries (Greenhill, 2006).

The UN has also acknowledged the problem in relation to Foreign Direct Investment (FDI), which is now more significant than aid flows. In practice, investment of all kinds can be realized in a number of ways, some of which are of more benefit to the recipient country than others. The World Investment Report of 2001 emphasized the importance of 'linkages' in relation to the effect of investment. In essence, when investment expenditure is spent locally, more of the benefit is retained: 'A dense network of linkages can promote production efficiency, productivity growth, technological and managerial capabilities and market diversification for the firms involved' (UNCTAD, 2001).

Individual companies can also calculate their economic impact through assessing the consequences of their purchasing activities together with their wages. Yet few companies have done this. One of these few is BT, the telecommunications company. They have made use of government economic statistics, particularly Global Value Added tables and input–output tables, to calculate their regional impact within the UK as well as their overall economic impact. This is illustrated in Figure 10.1.

> *The economic impact of BT's activities on national income and employment can be estimated in terms of the following:*
> - *Direct impact: persons employed directly by BT (including contractor staff) who receive wages and salaries*
> - *Output impact: Income and employment created in businesses which supply the goods and services used by BT in its day to day activities; and further income and employment generated as incomes created directly and indirectly are spent within the economy.*
>
> (BT, 2007, p7)

BT has concluded that for the year to April 2006, they spent £8.8 billion, of which £0.96 billion was capital investment. As a result, this generated some £10 billion, representing a multiplier of about 10 per cent. They also point out

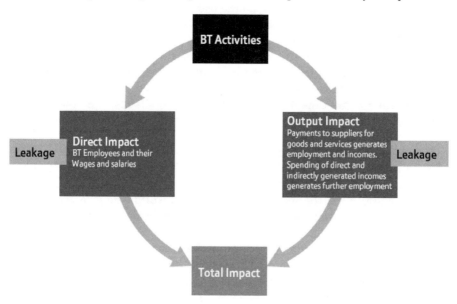

Source: (BT, 2007)

Figure 10.1 *BT Economic Impact*

that this activity 'supported' 173,000 jobs. BT also gave regional breakdowns throughout the UK, showing that the total economic activity generated by their spend in Scotland, for example, was £0.6 billion (BT, 2007).

PRACTICAL LOCALIZATION

It is possible to make estimates for similar effects for much smaller companies or other organizations or departments of larger ones, which may not have access to the resources necessary to work with official economic statistics. The New Economics Foundation (NEF) has developed a method called 'LM3', which stands for 'local multiplier 3' for this purpose. Some academic work has also been done subsequently on this topic (Stoeckl, 2007). In essence, the process involved is one of surveying suppliers and employees to see how they spend their payments and wages in relation to a boundary of concern. The boundary of concern is the boundary of the 'local' economy for the purpose of the exercise.

The New Economics Foundation has shown (Sacks, 2002) that it is possible for small organizations to calculate their local economic impact through surveying their employees, their suppliers and their suppliers' suppliers in turn. This can be done on a sample basis also, so that the largest 3 suppliers – or those typically representing over 60 per cent of purchases, are included.

As part of their work, NEF has estimated the proportion of spend which is retained locally by different types of retail outlet based on publicly available data and based primarily on the proportion of labour involved. This is reproduced below as Table 10.1. In addition they estimate the proportion of local spend by specific companies. As you might expect, the larger and more international the company, the less is spent locally. By sector the least local kind of company tends to come from the financial sector, although Shell comes bottom of this table, spending 0.2 per cent of its income locally according to their calculations. Oil companies and banks are also heavily infrastructure dependent,

Table 10.1 *Local Spend by Store Type*

Store type	Average % spent locally
Supermarkets (e.g. Tesco, Iceland)	10.2
Department stores (e.g. Marks & Spencer)	12.1
Clothing (includes footwear and accessories)	12.9
Electronics (e.g. Dixons)	9.6
DIY/Household goods (e.g. B&Q, MFI)	12.7
Convenience stores (e.g. Kwik Save)	10.5
Pubs and restaurants	20.6
Health and beauty (e.g. Boots)	19.3
Fuel/petrol (e.g. BP, Shell)	2.1
Banks	1.0
Overall Average	11.0

From (Sacks, 2002)

which means that major expenditure tends to be concentrated and therefore not very local.

Some recent examples (Sacks, 2009) of private companies in the UK using LM3 include Rio Tinto Alcan (mining), Egger (wood panels), and Sheffield Forgemasters International (steel and engineering). Rio Tinto Alcan used LM3 to support their discussions with European policymakers. Egger used LM3 to bolster a local planning application to expand their premises. Sheffield Forgemasters used LM3 Online, a web-based version of LM3 developed by LM3's inventors in 2007, to underpin their bid for regional and national economic incentives for a major physical expansion. A notable theme in these three examples is the microeconomic (i.e. local) and practical motivation behind their application. None of these companies labelled their use of LM3 as 'CSR' – there was a direct commercial reason to use it.

11

Investing in Impact

A History of SROI

This chapter centres on Social Return on Investment (SROI), a technique for measuring social impact based on financial measures. Before examining the techniques of SROI in detail, it will be helpful to look at an economic tool which is likely to have been the inspiration of the SROI technique. In the development community since the 1970s, the social impacts of projects funded by the World Bank and the International Finance Corporation as well as by national governments, have been assessed using the technique of 'economic rate of return' based on social cost benefit analyses. From the perspective of traditional economics, a perfect market system ensures that the market rate of private return to an investor is always at a level such as to maximize the overall social return.

Of course, for many reasons, we do not live in a perfect market system. Economic theory suggests that the actual social return can be calculated by taking careful account of opportunity costs, as reflected in so called 'shadow prices'. In general, shadow prices are those that would have obtained for the same factors of production, in the absence of the project. For example, labour costs might have been significantly less for the same workers prior to the project start. The factors which cause a shadow cost to vary from the actual cost include taxes and subsidies, transaction costs, externalities and the consequences of imperfect markets.

The calculation of such shadow prices is not straightforward, but as Lysy and others have shown (Lysy, 1999; Esty, Lysy et al., 2003), there is a simpler route to the same formal economic result. This relies on breaking down the actual and opportunity costs to each stakeholder and summing these separately. So, for example, one component of the social return will be the additional wages that workers on the project receive, compared to their previous employment. The idea of considering the financial flows of each stakeholder of an organization is the kernel of Social Return on Investment or SROI.

'SROI' is a term which has been interpreted rather differently by its various practitioners. But what SROI is meant to capture always includes the impact of a project or organization on society – measured in financial terms. The term SROI was coined by REDF in the 1990s. REDF (originally the Roberts Enterprise Development Fund) is a Californian philanthropic organization working through social enterprises in which it invests. As discussed in Chapter 2, social enterprise is yet another term with a wide range of interpretations. What most of the definitions of social enterprise have in common though is a dedication to the achievement of social goals through business activities. A typical social enterprise might offer disadvantaged people work making something which is sold on the open market. The income of social enterprises is sometimes subsidized to some extent by grants from philanthropic or government sources.

REDF's own objective is to adopt an approach to social problems that 'combines the best of private, market-based initiative and public spirit, maximizing the value of investments by delivering outcomes efficiently' (REDF, 2008). In order to understand its own success in investing, REDF needed to understand how successful the organizations it was helping were in terms of generating positive social outcomes. SROI was developed in order to clarify this.

The original version of SROI that REDF developed (REDF, 2001) is based on separating the social value creation from the market value creation aspects of a social enterprise, that is the purely economic from the purely social elements. Thus a dual accounting system is proposed in which all purely market elements are completely separated from subsidies and additional expenses incurred as a result of the social nature of the enterprise. Suppose, for example, that the social enterprise receives grants and subsidies to employ and train long term unemployed people to make clothes which are sold on the open market. In this case the revenues received from selling items of clothing would count as business revenue, while the grants and subsidies would compose an entirely separate income stream, with a similar separation for costs. The rationale for this 'True Cost Accounting' is that the opportunity cost of operating within a market system should be separated from the philanthropic element, so that the specific contribution of the social investment (e.g. grants) can be identified separately from that of the market.

Subsequent applications of SROI have not always maintained such a separation. One factor which has led to this breakdown is that the SROI technique has also been applied to organizations with an entirely social purpose and very little if any, market component, which would make the separation unnecessary even to meet REDF's criteria. Also it can be argued that for a social enterprise, neither the market side nor the social side could actually exist or function without the other. In the example set out earlier, it may be very unlikely that the social enterprise would receive any grant funding if the clothes it made could not be sold on the open market. This point is crucial when considering how far SROI techniques can be applicable to pure market-based organizations, which may have no social activity aspect to them at all.

REDF today is trying to move beyond SROI. In particular, they have identified a number of challenges for the technique, including:

- the reliance on public sector costs;
- the difficulty of attributing costs;
- the cost of undertaking the analysis.

There are several aspects of the issue of relying on public sector costs. What REDF was referring to was that a more 'positive' SROI result will often depend on a reduction in the use of the health or justice systems. This is undoubtedly a good thing, but even where there is a reduction in health or justice spending, this does not capture the full extent of the benefit either to society or to the individuals involved. There is a sense in which a financial, quantitative technique cannot capture the subjective essence of what has happened to a person's life, for example if the impact of the project supported by REDF meant they become capable of staying out of jail. One aspect of that might be an enhanced sense of self-esteem, for example.

The attribution problem is common to many assessments of social issues. Just because a person is no longer a burden on the justice system, it does not follow that this is entirely the result of the social initiative which has been working to get the person away from crime. There may well have been other influences, such as a change in family circumstances that will have been very important to their welfare and their likelihood of committing a crime.

The cost of undertaking the analysis results from the detailed investigation and skilled work which is necessary in order to complete an SROI analysis. There is little getting away from this, particularly for the first analysis, whether it is undertaken using internal or external resources. However, there may be a number of mitigating factors for subsequent analyses. One of these is that the learning curve the first time it is employed should be absent on subsequent attempts. Also, on subsequent applications, systems should have been established which will make the collection of data easier. Finally, it would be possible for government and organizations to share the unit costs for impacts such as a reduction in crime. At the moment it is hard to discover such data in the first place and difficult for an organization undertaking SROI to make use of the prior discoveries of other organizations.

These issues are recurring themes for the subsequent development of SROI elsewhere. The approach to SROI has been described in a number of places. The best known are perhaps the approach of the New Economics Foundation (Lawlor, Neitzert et al., 2008), the Forth Sector (Durie, Hutton et al., 2008) and that of Scholten and others (Scholten, Nicholls et al., 2006). Some useful guidelines may also be found in the earlier work of Sara Olsen and Alison Lingane (Olsen and Lingane, 2003). However all these approaches share the same fundamentals, even if the terminology employed is slightly different.

THE BASIC SROI CALCULATION

What is at the heart of SROI? It is simply a cost-benefit calculation, albeit one which looks at financial flows for all stakeholders consequent on an investment.

It uses the traditional means to calculate the net present value (NPV) of financial flows due to a stakeholder and compares this to the value of the investment. For one stakeholder, it is typically presented something like this:

$$SROI = \frac{NPV(stakeholder\ value)}{NPV(investment)}$$

So suppose, in a simple case, the stakeholder in question is the beneficiary of a training programme and as a result is no longer unemployed but finds employment. The financial flows due to the trainee are both positive and negative – because while they will gain wages, they will lose benefits. As these flows continue for some time, the future flows are discounted to obtain the net present value. The investment in this case is the cost of putting on the training programme. An illustration of this formula in relation to different stakeholders is given in Figure 11.1

However, this formulation is oriented to mission-oriented social (or environmental) organizations in the sense that the investment is derived from a grant. For private companies, the investment is just that: shareholder investment. So the formula would look like this:

$$SROI = \frac{NPV(stakeholder\ value)}{NPV(shareholder\ investment)}$$

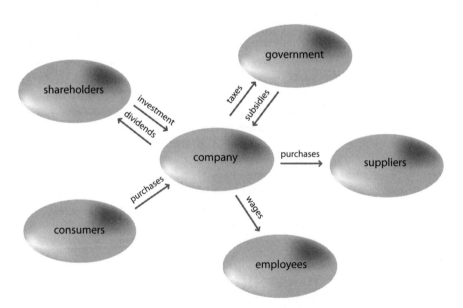

Figure 11.1 *SROI Cashflows*

But this of course puts the shareholder in a privileged position. They are not the only stakeholder to 'invest' money. The employee in the simple example considered above is also investing in the sense that they are giving up their unemployment benefit. It would therefore be possible to calculate the SROI for each stakeholder, which might give a more rounded perspective. However, the 'investor' is usually considered to be that stakeholder providing the capital for a project.

Staying with the traditional formula, there are two points to note, concerning the quantifiability of the financial flows and the calculation of net present value. The fundamental critique of SROI is that it captures only what is monetized. SROI as a technique does not capture the more qualitative benefits or problems, such as changes in self esteem, unless these are quantified in some way through a 'proxy'. One response to this might be that SROI should capture only those flows that actually take place. This approach would have the virtue of maximum credibility, but it is not tenable for several reasons:

- In most cases the relevant financial flows extend into the future. They are therefore estimates, not actual financial flows, although these flows are expected to take place and become actual flows of money.
- The impact on stakeholders may not be priced by the market even though it clearly has a financial impact. Illness caused by pollution is an example. More generally market externalities, both positive and negative, will by definition not turn up in actual financial flows.

Market externalities themselves may be of two types, those which could be priced by the market but which are not, and those which seem inherently unpriceable (or 'invaluable'). An example of the former, priceable, kind would be the training that an employee receives while on a job; an example of the latter might be the increase in self-esteem which goes with promotion and career advancement. Taking all these different types together leads to a matrix of types of financial flow, as illustrated in Figure 11.2 below.

The other point about the basic SROI formula relates to the calculation of net present value. In line with traditional financial and economic analysis, SROI discounts future cash flows (of whatever kind). The traditional reasoning is that £1 tomorrow is worth less than £1 today. The reason is that there is risk and uncertainty about what tomorrow may bring and moreover it is possible to find alternative uses for money which would bring an identifiable return. The formula for calculating this is shown below.

$$NPV = current\ year\ (0)\ value + \frac{year\ (1)\ value}{1 + discount\ rate}$$

$$+ \frac{year(2)\ value}{(1 + discount\ rate)^2} + ...\frac{year(n)\ value}{(1 + discount\ rate)^n}$$

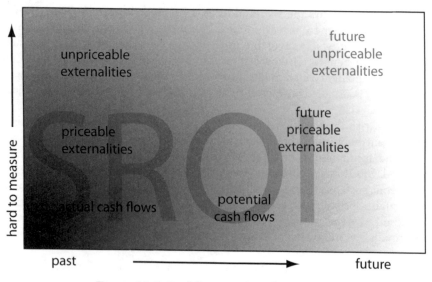

Figure 11.2 *Cashflows, Externalities & SROI*

This discount calculation is typically applied to all the different stakeholder flows which have been identified and included in the calculation. So the formula above for SROI, could be expanded to show that it is summed across all relevant stakeholders.

The discount rate is usually chosen to represent the cost of capital. It usually reflects current interest rates and may also allow for inflation. In practice this means that government projects usually work with a rate of around 4 per cent representing the cost of long-term capital, whereas venture capitalists may use a much higher rate of up to 20 per cent reflecting their relatively risky business. Which discount rate is used matters a great deal. The higher the discount rate, the less future benefits (and costs) are valued and the lower the SROI value.

This suggests that it may be appropriate to use different discount rates for different investors. But it may also be suggested that different stakeholders use the different discount rates appropriate to their circumstances *within the same SROI calculation*. As a result, a government, as social investor, might use a discount rate of 4 per cent to calculate the present value of savings to the Treasury from lower welfare payments, whereas a private company may apply a higher rate to the expenditures they may be making in relation to the same project.

However, it is possible to go one step further and to query the necessity of the use of discount rates at all. Discount rates are somewhat antithetical to the concept of sustainability as sustainability requires a long term view of the future – it sees the future as just as valuable as the present. But the value of some social benefit or some environmental cost will be just as real when it is experienced as it might be now, which suggests that discounting it is miscounting it. Zero-discounting makes particular sense for cash flows which represent a change to a capital amount. The production of carbon dioxide, for example, actively destroys the capacity of the environment to maintain an equable temperature. This is a permanent loss in any foreseeable future. Therefore the costs which are meant to represent it should not be discounted. In the same way, any monetizable gains in social capital should perhaps also be treated to a zero discount rate.

While this may be accepted in theory, it does bring with it a practical problem in deriving a figure for SROI. The problem arises because the formula for NPV is a convergent series and can be summed to a finite figure – but only if the discount rate is greater than zero. When the discount rate is zero (or less) the formula becomes infinitely great, which however consonant with sustainability would be of little practical value.

Yet there are a number of reasonable responses to this issue. One is simply to limit the number of years of the future that are counted towards SROI. In practice such calculations rarely go beyond 5 years anyway. Another option which may be available in some cases is to pick a year which is representative of a steady state which may be obtained after a year or two and to work out the SROI using the financial flows for that year alone. For example if a training course is run every year, then it may be appropriate to take the cash flows for the second or third years as representative of the effect of the training course.

SROI IN THE REAL WORLD

As was noted in Chapter 2, it is hard to identify exactly what any organization is actually responsible for. Most companies produce carbon dioxide and this is damaging. Yet we know, according to the Stern Review, that the collective outcome could well be a reduction of global GDP by up to 20 per cent (Stern, 2007). But clearly no single company is responsible for all of this. If it is reasonable to apportion this outcome in some way to an individual company, how may this be done? One way would be to compare the turnover of the company in question to global GDP. This immediately suggests a measure of 20 per cent of company turnover as the eventual cost of carbon dioxide emissions attributable to that company.

Just as immediately, it raises several objections, principally in relation to the justice of assuming that all companies are equivalent in terms of their carbon emissions, which is clearly not the case. However it should be pointed out that this figure is an average; if some companies will be responsible for less than 20 per cent, others are going to be responsible for more. Nevertheless, this illustrates a recurring problem in trying to estimate figures for SROI calculations: for any given effect, how much can be attributed to the company in question?

The formula which NEF use (Lawlor, Neitzert et al. 2008, p21) to capture the impacts for which the organization is responsible is this:

$$impact = outcome - (attribution + deadweight + displacement)$$

The example of carbon responsibility just given is an example of how the proportion of an outcome which can be attributed elsewhere may be approached. Often, however, it is very hard to determine this figure.

The third term in the formula, 'displacement' is meant to ensure that negative outcomes of a particular activity are captured. The displacement in question occurs when a benefit to one person is at the expense of that to another – perhaps one person gets a job as a result of a training course, but this means that another person does not. This is one instance of the general effect of any project or organization, which will have negative as well as positive effects. These should of course all be taken into account.

This particular formulation of the issue results mainly from the heritage of SROI which as we have seen was developed in a context of organizations devoted to producing positive social outcomes. In this case, the tendency is to over-estimate positive effects and to set the boundaries of the SROI analysis where it will give the most positive results. When the organization in question is in the private sector, there may also be a temptation to ignore the negative impacts. But in both cases, the problem may be the result of basing the SROI calculation on a project, rather than the whole organization, and as a result, selecting which stakeholders are included in the calculation. If all the organization's stakeholders are included, then so will those who suffer from it.

The middle term in the formula, 'deadweight', is perhaps the most difficult to deal with. It refers to the fact that in the absence of the activity in question, something would have happened anyway. If the activity is trying to ensure trainees get employment as a result of the training, then if there were no training, some would have got employment anyway. For what, in that case, is the organization actually responsible?

The normal practice of SROI is to calculate the outcomes for the counterfactual case and subtract these from the otherwise calculated outcomes. This does do justice to one sense of the word 'responsible' – particularly when the issue is to discover what difference, or 'added value' the activity in question has actually made. After all, why should an organization take credit for what would have happened anyway? It also has the advantage that it is exactly what economists try to take into account with the use of shadow pricing and opportunity cost in calculating an economic rate of return.

Yet it assumes that the market in which an organization operates is deep and highly liquid. If that is not the case, then it cannot be assumed that some other organization would have stepped in. In the very specific, local micro-circumstances of a particular project, this may not be so. In that case, relying on national or perhaps regional figures for re-employment rates may give a misleadingly depressed SROI result.

However, even if there is no such problem with the counterfactual case, it is possible to argue that there is another sense of 'responsibility' under which it makes sense to know what the absolute contribution to a problem or positive outcome an organization has made. If we want to know the answer to the question 'what overall difference has this organization made to the world?' a response which does *not* adjust for deadweight is a reasonable one. If we want to know what difference an organization has made which others would not have done, then it is necessary to adjust for deadweight. But in that case, how is the overall impact of the organization to be judged?

GETTING THE NUMBERS

In the literature and the discussion of SROI so far, much use has been made of the terms 'proxy' and 'monetization'. Since SROI is about quantifying social impact, they are important and must be understood. Unfortunately, they have not been used with much clarity or consistency in the literature of SROI. The term 'proxy' appears to have several separate meanings:

- an approximate or low-accuracy measure of a financial flow;
- a measure which is used to *stand for* another;
- one measure which stands for another measure, and which is also of low accuracy.

For example, the cost of a visit to the doctor may be assessed at £150. Since the actual cost of each visit may vary and is usually unknown, this may be described as a proxy of the cost. A visit to the doctor may also be regarded as a measure of health (or illness) and in this sense also, the aggregated costs of visits to the doctor may be described as a proxy for health.

Using visits to the doctor as a measure of health is an example of a quantification of an outcome. Quantification is usually the first step to monetization. Monetization, of course, also entails the further step of converting the number into financial units, such as pounds or dollars.

The real problem is not so much one of definition, but of how to put financial values on things which don't already have them – unlike visits to the doctor. There are two basic approaches:

- market behaviour: analyse closely related prices to derive the prices desired;
- stakeholders: ask stakeholders about appropriate prices.

Market behaviour-based methods, often called 'revealed preferences' rely on relevant, existing markets. One method is to analyse the component factors which contribute to the price of something. For example a house near a national park may be more costly than an otherwise identical one which is in a town. Of course this requires some statistical sophistication, as the price of the town house may also result from the fact that it is near a railway station. Nevertheless with a sufficient, and appropriately varied, population of prices, it is possible to calculate through regression analysis how far one component, such as proximity to a park, influences prices. Firmly based in economic theory, this method is called hedonic pricing. Of course it assumes that there are no distorting externalities in the market under study. If there are, they will also affect the calculated component prices.

Another method is to study the additional price which people will pay for the enjoyment of a clean beach, for example. This is usually reduced to travel costs, which again ignore externalities. A further method is to discover the costs which would have been incurred in *preventing* some social or environmental harm from occurring in the first place. For example, the costs of an effective road traffic safety training programme in schools and additional road-side measures could be used to put a price on avoiding accidents. While the costs of the proposed method of prevention may be fairly clear from the market, the thought experiment which determines the prevention scenario is by definition counter-factual and so subject to much uncertainty. Also this method is likely to underestimate the costs to the individual: for the family of a child killed on the roads, their value is very likely to outweigh, at least subjectively, the costs of any such programmes.

A significant variation on this technique is to ascertain the costs which *restoring* the damage would incur. This has the advantage that it focuses attention on the damage done and the practical availability of current technologies to remedy the situation. However while this method makes some sense in relation to environmental impacts, it makes much less sense when talking about social impacts, such as road accident injuries.

Asking stakeholders what they think prices should be is widely used and appears to be more appropriately participative. However, such methods are also subject to distortions. People affected by an airport development, for example, may be asked how much they would be *willing to pay* to have it stopped. This is typically done using a questionnaire; there may be little informed discussion of the pros and cons which might be associated with the scenario in which the development were stopped, ranging perhaps from reduced carbon emissions to no land clearance and reduced noise. There is also a built-in bias towards lower prices. This can be seen from the alternative method which is to ask how much someone might be *willing to accept* not to object to the proposed development. When 'willingness to accept' questions are asked, the responses lead to significantly higher prices.

Yet this discussion presupposes that the kinds of techniques used deliver credible ways to measure social impact. When there are real financial flows, SROI certainly produces a far more complete picture of impact than the typical business case, which uses analogous techniques to capture shareholder impact alone. However, when this is not the case, great care should be used in any claims made regarding the accuracy and completeness of the measurement made.

Working with SROI

Ignoring the practice of calculating Economic Rates of Return, what does SROI look like in practice? This section will not provide a checklist, which is not necessary especially given the numerous guides which already exist. Instead it will briefly set out the approach which NEF recommends (Lawlor, Neitzert et al., 2008) and has illustrated elsewhere (Lawlor, Murray et al., 2008). In addition, Appendix III gives an example of what the method produces based on a typical real world case. After that some of the issues which its practical use has raised are discussed.

The NEF approach has four stages. The first stage is described as 'boundary setting and impact mapping'. It involves firstly being clear about what is to be covered by the SROI analysis, particularly whether it is a specific project or the whole organization, and identifying the stakeholders involved. One of the strengths of this approach is the emphasis on engaging with stakeholders to discover from them what should be measured. This culminates in the development of a 'theory of change' which captures the architecture of the impact the organization has and contributes to the assumptions made about attribution and deadweight.

The second stage concerns collecting data and establishing financial values and proxies. The third is concerned with constructing the financial models and spreadsheets. This includes the issue of sensitivity analysis, which is an important technique to test how far the specific results of the modelling depend on the precise values of the various assumptions used.

The final stage concerns reporting and embedding. In order to make SROI a useable technique, the way the model and the data collection systems on which it depends are made part of the normal process of management, the easier it will be to repeat the process. A key part of this embedding is the reporting of results to stakeholders and its internal communication within the organization.

The majority of SROI exercises have been done for mission-oriented organizations, such as charities and social enterprises, with a significant proportion focusing on employment and training projects. While this community has been welcoming of the technique, a number of important issues have been raised. One of these is the fear that funders will be drawn to SROI figures, because they appear to be hard data, and may therefore ignore other measures and more qualitative appraisals. Although this outcome is unlikely (Andrews, 2008), the fear of it may be a barrier to a more widespread uptake in the social sector.

Related to this obstacle is a concern about comparability. This centres on whether it is permissible to compare the SROI figure from one organization with that from another. After all, it could be argued that this is precisely what financial investors do with financial ROI. Yet these are legitimate concerns, given the variation in the scope of application of the technique from organization to organization, the variety of approaches to SROI and the degree of judgement with which the evaluation of social outcomes are made.

12

Social Footprint

ONE INDICATOR TO RULE THEM ALL?

Is it necessary to have many social indicators, one for each of the many aspects of social impact? The advantages of this approach centre on its ability to reflect the apparent diversity of social impacts caused by any one organization. However, the disadvantage is that comparison between organizations becomes far more complicated. So is it really necessary?

Is it possible to find some overall indicator of organizational social impact? In relation to ecological impact, this problem has been addressed through the development of the 'ecological footprint', described below. The question for this chapter is how far it is possible to define and measure an analogous indicator, the 'social footprint' which may be useful to gauge the social impact of companies and other social entities.

LEARNING FROM THE ECOLOGICAL FOOTPRINT

The idea of an ecological footprint was derived from that of carrying capacity. The concept of carrying capacity was developed to define the maximum biological population, and its resulting biological load, which a given area of land might continuously support. It is intended to be related to sustainability and is typically measured as a population level per unit area, which can be supported by the land. A footprint approach reverses this ratio to consider the quantity of land which a given population requires. The concept of 'ecological footprint' for a population was defined by Mathis Wackernagel and William Rees (Wackernagel and Rees, 1996) as:

> *the area of ecologically productive land (and water) in various classes – cropland, pasture, forests, etc – that would be required on a continuous basis:*
> * *to provide all the energy/material resources consumed, and*
> * *to absorb all the wastes discharged*

- *by that population with prevailing technology*, wherever on
  Earth that land is located.

(Wackernagel and Rees, 1996, pp51–52).

Much work has taken place in applying and using the concept to assess overall ecological impact in practical ways. It has been applied to regions, cities, organizations (Lenzen, Lundie et al., 2003) and to products. The concept of the ecological footprint remains extremely compelling because it provides an indicator which appears to be obviously related to overall sustainability through the interactions of the demands of different ecological processes. What the ecological footprint captures is the *command over land*, or ecological resources, of the population concerned.

It is important to appreciate, however, that the concept of the ecological footprint is not generally claimed to be an indicator of *sustainability* itself, at least directly. As a quantity of land needed by a given population, it captures the contribution to overall ecological load exerted by that population. As a comparative measure of different populations it can also reflect the relative intensity of such ecological demand. The principal reason why such a measure cannot be a direct measure of sustainability, is that sustainability is a property of a system as a whole, rather than of any given entity within that system. Knowledge of the system as a whole may suggest certain limits which should not be breached, thus giving rise to 'sustainability indicators', see for example (Smith and Zhang, 2004; Meadows, Randers et al., 2005). One important consequence of this is that an ecological footprint that fits within what nature can offer, strictly speaking, does not *on its own* somehow imply sustainability, although it is a powerful precondition for sustainability.

As a practical indicator the ecological footprint has a number of important characteristics, which may be regarded as tests for effective footprint indicators. These 'footprint conditions' are that the proposed footprint is:

- possible to calculate to a reasonable degree of approximation;
- related unambiguously to impact; for the ecological footprint, an increase in a footprint will imply an increasing command over ecological resources;
- able to provide comparisons between different applications; through the ecological footprint, the ecological impacts of different populations have been applied to a wide variety of 'populations', including countries, cities, organizations and products.

It is important to emphasize the crucial role which land (or more generically, perhaps, space) plays in the formulation of an ecological footprint. The role of land is that so many, if not all, ecological processes are mediated through it. In Wackernagel and Rees's words, 'Land area not only captures the Earth's finiteness, it can also be seen as a proxy for numerous essential life-support functions from gas exchange to nutrient recycling' (Wackernagel and Rees, 1996, p56).

The ecological footprint has its challenges. From a practical perspective, the calculation of a specific footprint is not a trivial task; in particular only direct land requirements have usually been calculated, the land requirement for the production of capital inputs has often been ignored. Some of the other practical problems include the assumptions concerning the sustainability of the land required for uses such as agriculture and the most appropriate way to include the requirements for sea and air.

There are also inherent limitations to an indicator which so highly aggregates information from a wide variety of ecological processes, however legitimately. Nevertheless, land is the central aspect of an ecological footprint and this serves to reflect, systematically (Holmberg, Lundqvist et al., 1999), humanity's impacts on the environment. Of course an ecological footprint, being a single indicator, does not separately reflect the different contributions arising from the various factors influencing it. In this sense it cannot capture all aspects of environmental impact. Neither can it dictate how the requirement for a quantity of land should be achieved (Lenzen and Murray, 2003). The ecological footprint has been criticized on these grounds, but this is to criticize it for what it does not attempt to do.

As we have seen, in recent years the proposition that sustainable development is only ecological (or environmental) in nature has been questioned and the idea that it involves more than just an ecological dimension has become widely accepted. Similarly for companies, the notion of the 'triple bottom line' (Elkington, 1998; Henriques and Richardson, 2004) makes explicit the idea that the contribution to sustainability of an organization involves at least a social as well as an environmental dimension. Yet there is no indicator equivalent to the ecological footprint for social impact. The following sections of this chapter propose how such an indicator, sharing similar characteristics to those identified above for the ecological footprint, can be derived.

A SOCIAL FOOTPRINT IN THE FOOTSTEPS OF THE ECOLOGICAL FOOTPRINT?

The point has often been made that social systems (and within them economic systems) are merely aspects of ecological systems; without a natural world there can be no society, whereas the reverse does not hold. Much of the practical work on 'sustainable development' has been on specific impacts and their relationship to ecological changes resulting from particular economic development projects, for example by the World Bank (WB, 2003). So if social impact is an important component of sustainability, perhaps the concept of an ecological footprint can be extended to include social aspects, rather than developing a measure of the social aspects as a separate indicator, the social footprint.

Adding weight to this perspective, social and environmental issues are interconnected. Social issues relate to ecological issues in two key ways:

- social well-being is required if adverse environmental impacts are to be allocated sufficient resources and systematically addressed;

- adverse environmental impacts can form an important component of social issues. In both developed and less developed societies, environmental impacts such as pollution or the availability of natural resources are socially skewed.

Possible candidates for integration into such an expanded footprint might include some sort of derivative of the UNDP's Human Development Index (UNDP, 2009) or some measure of social equity. Each of these measures appears to capture the extent to which a population has achieved important social outcomes. They are also calculable, and so satisfy the first condition for footprint indicators identified above.

The Human Development Index is in fact a 'composite index' or assembly of heterogeneous measures (including literacy and life expectancy, for example). As a result, the relationship, or more precisely the linearity of the relationship, with social sustainability may not be clear. It is possible for different countries to achieve the same index score for entirely different reasons (as might be argued for their ecological footprints). It is therefore difficult to draw detailed lessons from comparisons between two such countries with the same index score.

Social equity on the other hand can be calculated as a homogeneous measure. It may be assessed through measuring access to resources, i.e. social and environmental goods, and exposure to social and environmental 'bads' (see McLaren, Bullock et al., 1998) for example. Income distribution, for example, can provide a measure directly reflecting one aspect of social equity and, it could be argued, also a proxy measure for other aspects of social equity. Social equity might therefore be a candidate for integrating with an ecological footprint. In practice, this could be achieved by in some way weighting an ecological footprint with an indicator of social equity, such as the distribution of income for the relevant population.

While it may be possible to calculate, the major problem with integrating social issues into a broader indicator is that it will exacerbate the aggregation of information, which as we have seen is already an issue with the ecological footprint. This is another aspect of the debate concerning weak and strong forms of sustainability, which hinges on whether an adverse impact of one kind may be 'made up' by positive impacts of another kind. In other words, is it valid to trade off improved social equity, say, for environmental degradation and still have an acceptable outcome? To integrate a social footprint indicator into a 'larger' indicator will inevitably presuppose that such trading off is permissible. Conversely, should such trading off be viewed as justified, then a separately developed social footprint indicator could still provide the means to do that as a separate exercise.

It can be concluded that while it may be possible to develop such a footprint indicator combining ecological and social measures, it is not clear whether it would unambiguously indicate the scale of impact. It would therefore meet the first, but not the second or third of the footprint conditions outlined above.

If the Human Development Index, or some measure of social equity, is not to be used as part of an enhanced ecological footprint indicator, could either of them be used on their own to form a social footprint indicator? This is problematic as each of these measures are 'outcome measures', capturing what is desirable for society. However the sources or origins of these outcomes are not directly captured. It is therefore difficult to apportion the outcomes to anything less than large populations, typically at a national level. As social footprint indicators, they would be relatively inflexible – at least in comparison to the ecological footprint.

A measurement technique explicitly called a 'social footprint' has been developed by Mark McElroy (Baue, 2006; McElroy, 2008b) of the Center for Sustainable Innovation (McElroy, 2008a). The central idea is that social unsustainability can be measured by comparing the gaps between the social resources required and the social resources produced by people. With this approach, activities, rather than specific outcomes or performance is what may be termed sustainable or unsustainable. The domain in which such measures may be sought is termed 'anthro capital' which is taken to include social, human and constructed capital. It then becomes possible, for example, to analyse the production of primary education versus the need for it such that a ratio of less than 1 will reflect an unsustainable lack of universal education.

While this approach confronts the need for a simple indicator head on and does recognize that what are usually called social, human and economic capital do have something in common, it also suffers from some problems. The principal one is that while the technique does produce simple measures, it would produce a great many of them, one for each kind of impact, even for a single company. The converse of this is that there is no way of deriving an overview of the complete social impact of a company. A further problem is that there appears to be no way to determine what the target social outcome should be. The example of universal primary education is well-chosen as it is uncontentious. The distribution of a company's income in the form of wages between different grades of staff, for example, is far more contentious.

SPACE, TIME AND THE SOCIAL FOOTPRINT

The Human Development Index, social equity and McElroy's footprint measure all lack a single factor which is in turn closely connected to the multiple aspects of social impact. For ecological footprints there is such a factor: land, or space, more generically. The most immediate difficulty for a social footprint is that social processes are not so closely bound up with land – although of course land may often have tremendous social significance.

Is some other factor available? At first sight, the idea seems fraught with problems. The nature of social impacts seems to have so many qualitatively different aspects – consider status and esteem, social networks and the density of relationships or wealth and its distribution, for example. How could a single indicator capture all of that? Of course, as noted above, a single number *cannot* integrate the measures of many different variables and at the same time reflect the contribution of each of them. However this is not what the ecological footprint does either (in relation to ecological impacts). The ecological footprint takes advantage of the relationship of one factor to the many different kinds of ecological impact. The final footprint measure only includes in a derivative sense the vastly different kinds of ecological consequences of human behaviour. It captures the central dependency of all the different kinds of ecological impact on a single resource. Is it possible to find a corresponding factor with the same function in relation to social impacts?

One possibility is that the appropriate factor for social impact is *time*. Time can be regarded as central to social processes in the way land can be regarded as central to ecological processes. Time can serve a parallel function for an indicator of social impact to that of land for environmental impact. The use of time as the basis for the indicator also captures the essential human commitment to a social relationship far better than can an indicator based, for example, on market relationships.

Why is time so central to social process? At a theoretical level, time is an essential element of social process; as Anthony Giddens has pointed out, social structures and institutions are only manifested across time. 'The study of day-to-day life is integral to analysis of the reproduction of institutionalized practices. Day-to-day life is bound up with the repetitive character of reversible time – with paths traced through time-space and associated with the constraining and enabling features of the body' (Giddens, 1984).

On a more intuitive level, time may be felt to be important to critical social issues such as the practical expression of human rights. For example, the right to freedom from slavery is essentially a right to enjoy one's own personal time. It may be possible to articulate other human rights in this way, as the 'availability' of a person to themselves. In a more distant sense, other positive social goods such as health (or self-esteem) can also be understood as the time (or quality time) that a person has available for themselves.

This is not to forget that there are a number of senses in which time is related to social and ecological processes in very straightforward ways. Time is factored into the ecological footprint through the rate at which physical processes occur and therefore affects the quantity of land needed to provide the environmental services required by a population. Time is also required for social processes in this sense. And in the trivial sense that any process will occupy space to some degree, space is also required for social processes.

THE FOOTPRINTS OF ROBINSON CRUSOE

If time is to form the core of a social footprint indicator, how can the time relevant to social processes be measured in a practical way? Robinson Crusoe (Defoe, 2007), a story written by Daniel Defoe, provides a helpful starting point to illustrate how the concept of a social footprint might work in practice. Robinson Crusoe was shipwrecked and marooned on an island. He had some supplies, including a gun, but he had to fend for himself. At first he thought he was alone, but then discovered that there was another human on the island, whom he named 'Man Friday'. Had Man Friday not emerged, Robinson Crusoe may not have needed more land than he had: we can assume that his footprint was no more than that of the island together with some of its local waters.

At this stage also, socially, although he was most certainly lonely, his day-to-day activities filled his time and provided everything he needed (or at least all he got). He also had 24 hours in a day and provided for himself in that time. We can define his social footprint as the 24 hours (or more precisely, 'person-hours' per day), that he had available.

When Man Friday emerged, the human ecological load on the island would have been re-calculated as about double that of Robinson Crusoe alone. However, assuming they both could have survived indefinitely, their total ecological footprint would still have been less than that of the island.

However, when Man Friday arrived, Robinson Crusoe and he entered into a social relationship. In the story, Robinson Crusoe becomes Man Friday's master. What this meant in practice was that some of Man Friday's time was devoted to Robinson Crusoe's interests and commanded by him. If we assume that half of Man Friday's time was devoted to Robinson Crusoe, then the time Robinson Crusoe will have available to himself is greater. His social footprint is now 36 hours per day.

What this captures is the extent to which Man Friday's time was not his own, reflecting his subservience to Robinson Crusoe. A social footprint thus adequately captures Robinson Crusoe's command over the time of others. Of course, this should not be taken to imply that the only socially acceptable solution is complete individual autonomy. Robinson Crusoe might specialize in fishing and Man Friday in gathering fruit. If each shared the results of their work with the other, their social footprints might each remain at 24 hours per day.

SOCIAL FOOTPRINT AND EMBODIED LABOUR

The time reflected in a social footprint is related to the notion of 'embodied labour' as developed in Marxian theories. Marx (1974) was concerned with relating the product prices and profits achieved by the owners of capital to the quantity of labour expended in their production. This quantity of labour has been termed embodied labour; it is further divided into the direct (labour) time embodied in the production of commodities and the indirect time embodied in the production of the capital goods used to manufacture those commodities. Marx's purpose was to show that that those who expended the labour deserved its fruits.

However, while the social footprint indicator might include embodied labour in its calculation, its purpose is not to analyse the distribution of profits, but of time. Its use would not therefore run into the 'transformation problem' of finding the function which converts time to price and thereby profit. The social footprint indicator might nevertheless make use of the distinction between direct and indirect time in calculating social footprints.

More broadly, a social footprint as measured by time and the corresponding embodied labour are also different because:

- the social footprint calculation need not be confined to the time involved in economic production. Just as relevant to certain social footprints may be the time devoted to maintaining a household and to leisure;
- the time involved in a social footprint of an economic production process will not, in general, be contributed by employees alone, as will be shown below. A social footprint for a production process, however, might be said to measure total embodied time.

WHOSE FOOTPRINT? WHOSE TIME?

Having established the principles of the calculation of social footprint with the Robinson Crusoe example, how would a modern, real world example look? There are perhaps two key questions: whose footprint is to be calculated and whose time should be taken into account?

The ecological footprint defines a boundary for the population whose footprint is to be established. The boundary is typically, but not invariably, delineated by a spatial limit – this may be a city or a country, for example. For a social footprint, it would seem appropriate to use a social institution to define the boundary of the 'population'. In a sociological sense, an institution is a series of processes replicated over time.

How could the social footprint of a retail company, for example, be calculated? The social footprint of a retail company should reflect the time invested in that company by all its stakeholders. That would include, for example:

- the time expended by suppliers in making and delivering the products it sells;
- the time spent by managers and staff in devising promotions, stocking shelves and other activities (the embodied direct labour);
- the time spent by customers in purchasing its products;
- the time expended by company analysts in making recommendations to shareholders.

To make the outline calculation simpler, we can assume that the retail company's only stakeholders are farmers supplying apples. The social footprint may then be calculated as follows:

1 for supplier 'a', obtain the total number of hours expended over a year on:
  - the planting and care of the apple trees;
  - the harvesting of the apples;
  - the arrangement of transport to the retailer;

- an apportionment of time spent on capital works, e.g. maintaining fences.
2 divide the total hours per year by 365 to give the average daily time commitment related to supplier 'a';
3 repeat steps 1 and 2 for each supplier;
4 add all the supplier footprints together to obtain the retailer's social footprint.

To take into account other stakeholders, the social footprint would then need to be summed across all its stakeholders and expressed as stakeholder-hours per hour. In other words the social footprint will capture the time invested in an organization each day.

In calculating actual social footprints, it is important to bear in mind the effects of different production methods will mean that a footprint is not necessarily directly proportional to corresponding economic output. One of the consequences of including embodied labour within the footprint calculation is that the time expended in production is dependent on the level of technology employed in the production process. Higher technology generally enables greater rates of productivity. Other things being equal, this will tend to lower the social footprint. This reflects the fact that the corresponding social relationships will be altered by a given new technology.

Of course, just as with the calculation of an ecological footprint, there are questions for the social footprint about where the boundary of the time to be included should be drawn. Should all the labour required to produce all the capital goods be counted in the embodied labour, for example? And practically, it will of course be onerous to calculate the total embodied labour within all the capital goods involved in the production of even an apple, considering all the capital equipment involved, from conveyor belts to integrated circuit board manufacturing equipment for tractors.

FOOTPRINTING SUSTAINABILITY

Finally, it may be useful to clarify the relationship of footprint indicators to sustainability (considered as a system-level concept) rather than their relationship to impact. While it may not be practical to calculate in any detail the ecological footprint for the world's total population, if it were found to be greater than the total available land (as is certainly the case), then there is clearly a condition of absolute ecological unsustainability. This would occur should the entire global population attempt to live at the same level of material well-being that the Western world currently enjoys. Should the global footprint in this situation be greater than the available land, this would of course not mean that more land had somehow been created, but that natural capital was being depleted at a greater rate than it was being created.

There are two reasons why a smaller ecological footprint is thought to be more sustainable than a larger one. The first is that the world is shared; so it is more likely to be possible for all populations to co-exist with each other (including non-human ones) if any given human footprint is reduced. The second is that it is assumed that ecological resources are produced, to a first level of approximation, through the natural workings of ecological systems and without a human contribution. In other words the assumption is that a human population only draws upon external ecological resources; it does not contribute to them. On this assumption, it follows that a larger footprint is always 'worse' than a smaller footprint, since it uses more such resources. However, it may be observed that it is not entirely true that all ecological impacts of humans have to be negative; some of the uses to which humans put land might be regarded as positive, such as restoring natural habitats.

It is possible that a parallel condition of global unsustainability might prevail for social reasons. In a situation in which the global population ceased to undertake productive work at all, we would encounter social unsustainability. It is possible, over a short period, for human activity and consumption to command more embodied time than is being produced over that period. In that situation, human consumption would be drawing on social resources at a greater *rate* than they were being created. In terms of time, this would mean that the global social footprint was greater than 24 hours per day. Of course, it is not possible to sustain this situation for a very extended period: it is socially unsustainable.

Are there reasons to think a smaller social footprint is also more sustainable than a larger one? Given that social resources (just as ecological resources) must be shared, it would follow that there will at least be some pressure for larger social footprints to be reduced, otherwise conflicts for resources will result. However, social footprints differ from ecological footprints because social resources are produced by the human population itself, not by external systems. This includes, for example, positive social resources, such as knowledge and learning. So while a larger social footprint will reveal a larger command of time, it may also permit a greater rate of consumption of social resources. Under some circumstances this may therefore enable a society to exist for a longer time in a situation in which social resources were being consumed, unsustainably, faster than they were being produced.

FOOTPRINTS IN PRACTICE?

Does a social footprint indicator satisfy the three practical 'footprint conditions' set out at the start of this chapter? It is, in relation to the first condition, clearly possible to calculate, given suitable assumptions as to the boundaries of concern. In relation to the second condition, it appears clear that the social footprint of an organization will increase with the command of the population or organization over the time of others. The scale of its social impact, which will be composed of a variety of different social effects (both good and bad) will also increase as a result. However the correspondence of a larger social footprint with a greater degree of unsustainability is weaker than for ecological footprints. In relation to the third condition, it is possible to calculate a social footprint for various different 'populations' or organizations. A social footprint, therefore, should satisfy the three conditions for a footprint indicator identified above.

What can social footprints, calculated on this basis be used for? The situation is similar to that for ecological footprints. For example, the average Canadian's footprint has been calculated at 4.7 hectares. *On its own* this says nothing about the sustainability of Canadians. Yet the ecological footprint becomes very interesting when used to compare the footprints of peoples in different places. So while not actually measuring sustainability, an ecological footprint leads to greater insight into the way ecological resources are *allocated*. This allocation is extremely relevant to the practical achievement of sustainability.

Similarly, a social footprint figure becomes interesting when used to compare how time is allocated between organizations. In addition, social footprint calculations can be used to compare how time is allocated between different stakeholder groups of the same organization. Where such social imbalances are significant, they are likely to decrease social sustainability, since an undue influence of one social group on another easily gives rise to resentments. This kind of analysis may be done at a number of different levels and should give an insight into power relationships as expressed by how far the time of one group is commanded by another. For example:

- Considering a national social footprint, how does the time commanded by different imports compare to the relative costs of those imports?
- How is an organization's management time allocated between stakeholder groups? Is this proportionate to the stakeholder time devoted to the organization?
- Considering a personal social footprint, is it bigger than 24 hours? This would mean that the individual has a disproportionate quantity of time at their command. (As was the case in one of the Robinson Crusoe scenarios considered above.)

The time-based social footprint described in this chapter can provide useful insights into corporate impact, even if it cannot, on its own, convey whether that impact is 'good' or 'bad'. But it is unlikely that any indicator can capture *all* aspects of either ecological or of social impact. Nevertheless, it is very useful to have high-level indicators which are systematically related to the scale of ecological impact on the one hand and to the scale of social impact on the other.

13

Accounting for Social Impact

FINANCIAL ACCOUNTING FOR SUSTAINABILITY

If a company is to manage its sustainability contribution, including its social impact, it must measure and account for it. Therefore, a coherent system of accounting needs to be developed for the ecological and social dimensions of sustainability. Some work has been undertaken to do this in relation to income accounting (Bent, 2005), but very little on true capital accounting. One particular difficulty with such a sustainability capital accounting is that, unlike the global level at which capital is an asset, at the level of the individual company, capital is a liability which is owned and therefore (in the logic of the market) priced by another party – which is the immediate motive to account for it. Of course, only very recently have mechanisms been introduced to price carbon emissions; the great majority of ecological factors involved in sustainability remain almost wholly un-priced. The pricing of social factors is perhaps even more problematic, as it would seem to require the commercialization of a whole range of human experience which has hitherto been largely outside the marketplace. The pricing of some forms of intellectual property, to take just one example, is still a very controversial issue.

One of the more fundamental points about this approach, however, is that it assumes that the model of financial accounting is adequate to the task of sustainability accounting. This chapter will review what that model of sustainability accounting might look like.

ACCOUNTING FOR SUSTAINABILITY

To 'give an account' has two meanings. The accounting metaphor therefore has two branches: one concerns a strict and systematic quantitative counting characteristic of financial accounting, which may cover social or economic indicators; the other a less structured story telling. Both branches are important. The counting branch can yield firm information and a firm foundation for evidence-based policy making.

Yet the counting branch can only describe what it can count, which as we have seen, is a limited subset of the important issues. The story-telling branch has to cover everything else. The principal story to be told, from a financial point of view, is whether the business is a 'going concern'. But from a sustainability perspective, the story needed is obviously much wider and less defined.

Such narrative can be a support to values-based policy making. In previous chapters it has emerged in issues such as the degree of participation in social impact analysis. In previous years it was called the 'voice of the stakeholder' and was an important feature of social auditing. Today it appears, in somewhat degenerate form, as the near ubiquitous 'case study'. Its merits are the richness and insight it can convey (see Chapter 6). Its dangers, that it can be unrepresentative and misleading.

Both branches are the result of a concern to communicate with a stakeholder. For traditional financial accounting, that stakeholder is the shareholder. For environmental and social accounting, the set of stakeholders will typically be much wider. There are interesting philosophical questions as to how far these two approaches can be integrated, but it seems clear that they are mutually complementary (Gray, Dey et al., 1997).

It is also important to be clear on the extent that we are looking for a framework which deals with social issues on their own terms, or in their 'native' or most applicable units. Financial accounts are expressed in units of currency, such as pounds or dollars. This is the native unit for financial accounts; there is no better unit to use for them. However, for environmental accounts, there are many units, each of which is the one most applicable for a given issue. 'Tonnes of CO_2 equivalent', for example, is the native unit for measuring climate changing discharges to the atmosphere. But of course there are many other units for different environmental issues, such as 'litres of water', 'kg of SO_2', and the 'population per hectare' of a given species. This means, as Schaltegger and Burritt have pointed out, that environmental accounting is simply a subset of the overall project of accounting (Schaltegger and Burritt, 2000).

For social impact, the situation is similar. That is, social accounting can be thought of as another subset of the overall project of accounting for a company or other organization. As with environmental accounting, the native units of a social account are many. These may include customer satisfaction percentages, violations of human rights, the usual terms of payment of suppliers and many others. Some would go further and see social accounting as equivalent to the overall accounting project and position financial accounting as a subset (Gray, Owen et al., 1996, p11). However, it is only necessary to establish the differences rather than the hierarchy.

Previous chapters have dealt with aspects of narrative and native unit accounting. They have actually covered the record-keeping aspect of accounting; they have only tangentially covered the equivalents of the profit and loss account and they have not dealt with the balance sheet aspect at all. But there have been serious attempts to develop an overall, formal framework to account for sustainability based on traditional financial accounting concepts. The end of this chapter will present an approach to this goal.

In order to describe what a social accounting framework based on the financial model might look like, there are several important and related issues concerning traditional financial accounting frameworks which must be addressed:

- internal and external accounting;
- revenue and capital accounting.

INTERNAL, EXTERNAL AND FULL COST ACCOUNTING

Internal or direct accounting describes what companies already do. The principal task of traditional financial accounting is to measure expenditures and income from whatever source, including social and environmental ones. However, these are typically 'hidden' or 'silent' in that they are not explicitly gathered together and presented as part of the social or environmental impact of an organization. For example, companies will record any fines associated with pollution or anti-competitive behaviours, but will not often present these altogether as part of an accounting for sustainability. From a practical and motivational point of view it is very helpful simply to collect together such items – they will often form a powerful business case for improving sustainability performance.

External accounting captures the impacts organizations cause which are not captured in traditional accounting. They exist as a result of market imperfections. From an orthodox economist's point of view, almost all markets can be said to be imperfect. The reason they are imperfect is that the prices for goods and services are affected by externalities. As we have seen in the chapter on SROI, for example, externalities are directly connected to unsustainability. Within the financial accounting system, this issue is reflected in the idea of 'full cost accounting'.

Full cost accounting is actually just what its name suggests, an attempt to find a way to allocate the full costs to market prices, including those from environmental and social impacts. Once this is done, at least according to economic theory, then the free market would spontaneously deliver sustainable outcomes. As ever with economics, the theory might work, but the practice seems unattainable. The issues with full cost accounting (Bebbington, Gray et al., 2001) include determining what the actual costs are and imposing them on existing market participants.

Various means have been proposed to accomplish these ends. One is the radical privatization approach which has been described by David Pearce (Pearce, Markandya et al., 1989). This entails creating ownership rights in environmental assets such that they are valued by the marketplace. However, there are real issues with the social consequences of privatizing environmental resources. In general, distributing or withdrawing ownership is also distributing or withdrawing power. For example, the privatization of water resources can very readily lead to deprivation of those in society who cannot afford water under a privatized regime.

Another approach is to make use of taxes, grants, quotas and other market interventions to guide the market to do what it is currently not doing. A simple example would be the imposition of taxes on 'environmental bads'. However, this can also create tremendous social impacts, as the demonstrations across much of the world in the face of the 2008 spike in fuel prices (which the market produced without any intervention) showed. There is also an argument that environmental taxes may drive companies to countries where there is less onerous taxation.

A further approach is the development of shadow prices to calculate the true environmental and social costs of current market activity. One problem with this approach is how to make use of such prices to change behaviour. Unless the achievement of environmentally and socially sound outcomes is what the market is already seeking, then it is hard to see how knowing how much an outcome should cost is actually going to alter the behaviour of market participants. What is really required is precisely such a change in market participants so that sustainable outcomes are sought. A further problem is that the significant costs involved in calculating shadow prices are unlikely to be willingly borne by a company in most situations, unless they form part of a business case which also has significant consequences at a regional or national level.

However, if we are seeking to understand what the impact of a particular company may be, then only the shadow approach is actually of use, since this is the only one which gets down to the level of specific products and services and tries to quantify the social and economic dimensions of economic activities. And it is also important to realize that full cost accounting as a whole is an attempt to rectify the *financial* accounting framework to support sustainability; it is not an attempt to provide a systematic accounting for social impact.

REVENUE, CAPITAL AND NATIVE UNIT ACCOUNTING

Revenue accounting provides a record of revenue expenditures and expenses, which can be summarized in the profit and loss account. Capital accounting provides a snapshot of the state of capital resources at a given point in time. But when does expenditure count as revenue and when is it capital? One organization (East Sussex, 2008) defines the difference in these monetary accounting terms, with corresponding definitions for income, in this way:

- Capital expenditure – invests for the long-term improvement of services and buys more expensive items that will last longer than a year. Examples include buildings, roads and vehicles.
- Revenue expenditure – provides services and buys items that will be used within a year. Examples include salaries, heating, lighting and small items of equipment.

Table 13.1 *Stocks and Flows of Sustainability – Some Examples*

	Revenue (Flow)	Capital (Stock)
Economic	Purchase of stamps	Purchase of franking machine
Environmental	Annual production of carbon dioxide	Total, net quantity of carbon dioxide produced by a company over its lifetime
Social	Average annual number of contacts with customers	Total contacts with all customers

Moving from a traditional financial framework to a sustainability framework requires generalizing this distinction. In general, revenues are flows and capital is a stock, or accumulation, of flows. This is actually harder to see in relation to monetary or social accounts than it is with environmental accounts, although the principles are the same. The annual production by a company of CO_2 should be reflected as an environmental flow, or revenue. The change in environmental capital is the net total production of carbon dioxide over the life of the company. That will be the capital amount which the company has drawn down but not re-paid. While its measurement will be different, similar principles could apply to social capital. Table 13.1 sets out a series of capital and revenue items for economic, environmental and social issues for comparison.

It is important to distinguish environmental capital, as an accumulation of flows, from environmental sources and sinks. The term 'natural capital' is sometimes used to refer to a property of the eco-system. In this sense it may refer to the carbon absorption capacity of the planet, for example. In this usage, natural capital is clearly something valuable and which has been overwhelmed by human activity, but it may not be something which is directly affected by a company's production of CO_2. On the other hand, some activities of a company, such as removing forest cover, may directly affect the size of the planetary carbon sink. This would need to be accounted for separately from the production of carbon. Cutting down a forest would count as a withdrawal or destruction of environmental capital by the company. Part of this is also the destruction of an ecological carbon sink.

While social accounting and environmental accounting are different projects to that of shareholder accounting, there is an interesting area in which they overlap. If management invests in a customer relationship system or in an energy reduction programme, this may entail expenditure on IT or other systems that may count as either capital or revenue expenditure. These expenditures will be captured in the financial accounts, including any financial consequences of the social and environmental impacts. However their full effects will not be captured in the financial accounts. The full social or environmental accounts, however, will capture the actual social or environmental effect itself (e.g. the reduction in carbon dioxide); this will most likely be in sets of accounts for which the native units are not monetary.

A FRAMEWORK FOR SUSTAINABILITY ACCOUNTING

The model which Forum for the Future, an environmental NGO, has developed is set out in Figure 13.1. This compares the scope of traditional financial accounting with sustainability accounting, as expressed in:

- the three components of sustainability;
- revenue and capital accounting;
- internal and external accounting.

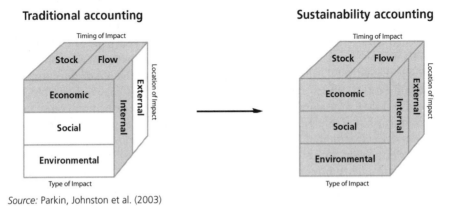

Source: Parkin, Johnston et al. (2003)

Figure 13.1 *Accounting for Sustainability*

By drawing on traditional approaches to capital financing, such an accounting model can be used to help change organizational behaviour. For example, the depletion in environmental or social capital should be provided for, just as it would in relation to the depreciation of an economic asset, such as office machinery. Of course, there is no legal compulsion to do so, nevertheless a few organizations have begun to maintain such 'shadow accounts'. At one stage, Bulmers, which produces cider, began to maintain accounts which captured the adverse social costs of alcohol on society (Bent, 2005).

According to Forum for the Future, moving from traditional accounting to sustainability accounting requires adjustment and extension to the primary accounting statements in the following ways:

- *Restatement of the profit and loss account to show costs and benefits relating to economic, social and environmental performance (internal sustainability accounting).*
- *Extension of the profit and loss account to encompass the external costs and benefits to the environment, society and the economy, which are not traditionally taken into account (external sustainability accounting).*

184

- *Extension of the balance sheet to take account of the full range of assets (including intangible assets such as brands, human capital or reputation as they relate to sustainability); and 'shadow' liabilities (including liabilities relating to sustainability risks) of the organisation.*

(FFF, 2002, pp23–24)

Very few companies have even attempted to provide this kind of full, formal financial account of their sustainability impacts. The Forum for the Future has made some systematic attempts (FFF, 2002; Howes, 2003; Parkin, Johnston et al., 2003) to work out its own impacts and that of some other organizations.

The key practical steps involved are:

1   identification of the most significant impacts;
2   identification of a sustainable level of impact;
3   evaluation of the impacts in financial terms;
4   preparation of formal accounts.

For any given company this represents a considerable programme of work. The identification of significant impacts is still only at its earliest stage in many companies. The identification of a sustainable level of impact is an even harder goal, although the work of Mark McElroy provides a model for how this may be done for social impacts (McElroy, 2008b).

The value of sustainability accounting from a company perspective is that it would provide better quality information and a far more secure basis for decisions relating to sustainability – in its environmental, social as well as economic senses. This short sketch of the dimensions of a sustainability accounting framework has really only served to show how much further theoretical and practical work needs to be done before a sustainability accounting framework could be considered complete.

14

The Elusiveness
of the Social Revisited

This book has spanned the way social impact can be captured and presented. This chapter will discuss how the various approaches relate to each other. Overall, three main kinds of approach have been covered:

- narrative accounts, in Chapters 5 and 6;
- social indicators, in Chapters 7, 8 and 9;
- economic indicators (of social impact) in Chapters 10 and 11.

Chapters 12 and 13 considered two approaches to developing techniques which integrate social impact on the one hand and sustainability accounting on the other.

Of the three main approaches to capturing social impact, narrative accounting is the richest approach. It brings the voice and subjective experience of the stakeholder directly to the attention of the reader. Of course it has its disadvantages as it can easily be manipulated and is hard to quantify. But it provides the most meaningful account of the social and conveys the sense of subjectivity which is the hallmark of 'the social'.

If narrative accounting is the most meaningful, under what conditions can other forms be useful? Theoretically, following Giddens (1984, p285), it is possible to dispense with narrative accounting and make use of social indicators, when dealing with:

- generalized characteristics;
- characteristics familiar to the reader;
- a focus on institutional analysis or on individuals validly treated in aggregate or as 'typical' in some way.

Of course, in practice, care must be taken that these conditions are not abused. Nevertheless, there are valid applications of social indicators. The most obvious relate to human rights. Human rights describe key areas in which there is a

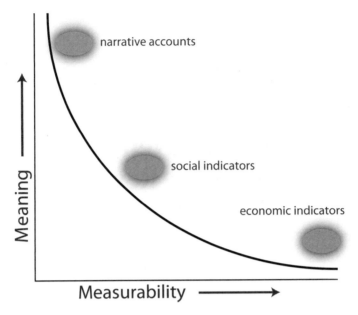

Figure 14.1 *Meaning Versus Measurability*

broad global agreement as to how all people should be treated. For some, this broad consensus covers not only the validity of the indicators, but also what acceptable performance against these indicators is. That is there is no need for any appeal to narrative accounting in order to describe acceptable social performance – the dangers of distortion which narrative accounting presents, make any contribution from that quarter too dangerous.

In general then, social indicators are therefore obviously meaningful and offer considerable precision, but are clearly not as rich a source of social insight as narrative accounting. Economic indicators go one step further: they are capable of being even more precise than other social indicators, but (especially where they are not the native social units) offer significantly less meaning in return. The overall relationship between the different approaches is therefore one in which meaningfulness is traded against precision and measurability, as illustrated in Figure 14.1.

However, the relationship between different means of accounting is not fixed. Because social accounting is a social process, it is likely to change and develop as stakeholders not only enter into the process but also change it. As stakeholders become more informed about the issues in their relationship with a company, their approach may become increasingly articulate and sophisticated. For example, colonists could famously buy large tracts of land in Australia for 'a string of beads' when they first arrived; that was because the original inhabitants did not know what the colonists were doing. That situation is very different today. The descendants of the original inhabitants are very aware of their heritage and how it was taken from them. They make use of every instru-

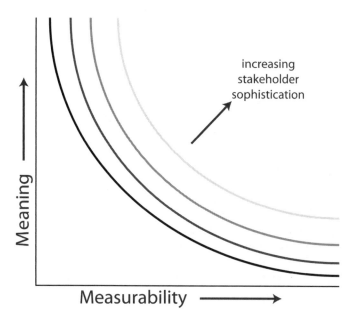

Figure 14.2 *Evolution of Meaningfulness*

ment of the modern state to pursue their claims. This progression is illustrated in Figure 14.2.

It might even be argued that some economic indicators, such as GDP, have attained a mystical status in modern politics. That is, GDP is not only a well-defined and measurable economic indicator, it is also one which is meaningful to large segments of people. Yet the respect in which it is measurable is not the same as the respect in which it is meaningful. It is meaningful because it symbolizes well-being in some general and vague way, not because of its technical relationship to national income. So in the end it will never be possible to turn economic indicators into narrative insight.

Overall, an adequate account of the social impact of any company would need to reflect:

- the complexity of social impact, while providing some structure to the account of the impact;
- various procedures and relevant measurement techniques that currently exist, without claiming that the limits of the currently measurable are also the limits of its social impact;
- significance and subjectivity of stakeholders;
- gaps in the company's understanding of its impact.

At the moment, while there are many different techniques which capture something of the nature of social impact, there is no method or technique which does it all, or brings them all together in a unified way. For that reason, all organizations, including companies, should address their social impacts with care, seeking the best combination of tools possible. That should include at least some part of each of the three approaches covered in this book.

There is no universally valid set of social issues that is also complete. Because social issues are continually changing and because stakeholder involvement is crucial to their legitimacy and authority, any pre-defined set of issues, and their indicators, must be provisional. In the end, the understanding, assessment and boundaries of corporate impact are continually negotiated between a company and its stakeholders. Measurement is a vital part of that process, but always only a part. This might all make it seem too difficult for a company to be bothered with: why spend time and money on such a hazy area of governance? Why raise so many additional questions without obvious answers?

There is no easy response to this with a guaranteed business case. Yet understanding corporate social impact is likely to become ever more central to the many companies whose ability to succeed economically will increasingly depend on a deliberate co-operation with stakeholders. The very discipline of discovering its social impacts will enable a company to remain awake to the issues on which its survival may depend.

Appendix I

Market Research

Market research has been defined as 'the systematic collection analysis and interpretation of information relevant to marketing decisions' (Hague, Hague et al., 2008, p11). Market research relates to social impact in two ways:

- A key element of all markets are consumers or organizational customers. These are always stakeholders of the organization that is trying to sell something. So market research ought in theory to provide important information about these stakeholders and therefore about the social impact of the organization.
- When companies research their stakeholders to try to understand their social impacts, they often use the techniques of market research.

Market research arose out of the need to cope with the increasing competition between large companies in the USA in the 1930s. Interestingly, the main technique used initially was observation of what people actually bought in shops together with a close attention to shelf space and stock levels. The reason this was the preferred technique was that it was not thought that people would respond honestly if simply asked directly about their buying habits. While there is a real insight underlying this approach, it is interesting that market research had its origins in distrust of a stakeholder vital to any business.

After World War II, market research adopted the techniques of sociology and began to measure people's 'attitudes', that is, their propensities to behave in a certain way and to include what they said as well as what they did. In more recent years the basic techniques have not altered, but the ubiquitous use of computers has meant that far more sophisticated statistical analyses have become routine. In recent years, the use of observation has come somewhat back into vogue. This time, however, it is usually undertaken by 'mystery shoppers' who engage in ordinary retail transactions and report back or record every detail of their experience, so that organizations can understand how they treat their consumers. It is also undertaken by anthropologists, using techniques developed to understand cultures very different from their own. The heart of such anthropological techniques is that of long term immersion and participation by the researcher in the culture under study.

However, mainstream market research relies on a set of techniques which owe more to the clipboards and questionnaires familiar to most of us. Before examining such techniques in a little more detail, it is worthwhile pointing out that market research divides into consumer and business branches – that is the analysis of customers which might either be individuals or organizations. However, many of the actual techniques used are very similar. Those techniques have for many come to be the major tools of the stakeholder engagement trade, so it is important to understand how they work and their advantages as well as their shortcomings.

The two principal sets of techniques are called quantitative research and qualitative research. Quantitative techniques, as the name suggests, are designed to get numerical answers susceptible to statistical analysis. This will answer questions such as 'what proportion of customers (say they) will buy product X?' Information for quantitative analysis can be gathered through highly structured questionnaires and interviews and observation. This is possible if the specific issues for which analysis is required are already understood – such as discovering customer reaction to a proposed price rise.

Where the issues to be analysed are not already understood, then qualitative techniques need to be used. These deal in 'softer' data, although, confusingly, the results can sometimes be expressed as percentages of 'people who thought that...'. Information for qualitative analysis can be gathered through:

- open-ended question on questionnaires;
- focus groups;
- unstructured interview techniques.

Whereas quantitative techniques are primarily concerned with analysing known issues, qualitative techniques are useful for discovering new issues. In market research, qualitative techniques are often used as an input to the quantitative research.

From the point of view of understanding social impact, qualitative techniques are the most significant, since often the detail of the impact an organization has on a customer is unknown. And of course the technique need not be confined to understanding customers alone. 'Market research', as we have seen, was derived from social science; it is relevant, or can be adapted to many different stakeholder groups. The main impediment is cost.

Appendix II

Analysis of GRI
Social Indicators

Aspect (area of impact)	Indicator	Classification
Employment	LA1 Total workforce by employment type, employment contract, and region. (Core)	Substantive
Employment	LA2 Total number and rate of employee turnover by age group, gender, and region. (Core)	Substantive
Employment	LA3 Benefits provided to full-time employees that are not provided to temporary or part-time employees, by major operations. (Additional)	Substantive
Labor/Management Relations	LA4 Percentage of employees covered by collective bargaining agreements. (Core)	Substantive
Labor/Management Relations	LA5 Minimum notice period(s) regarding significant operational changes, including whether it is specified in collective agreements. (Core)	Substantive
Occupational Health & Safety	LA6 Percentage of total workforce represented in formal joint management-worker health and safety committees that help monitor and advise on occupational health and safety programs. (Additional)	Process
Occupational Health & Safety	LA7 Rates of injury, occupational diseases, lost days, and absenteeism, and number of work-related fatalities by region. (Core)	Substantive
Occupational Health & Safety	LA8 Education, training, counselling, prevention, and risk-control programs in place to assist workforce members, their families, or community members regarding serious diseases. (Core)	Process
Occupational Health & Safety	LA9 Health and safety topics covered in formal agreements with trade unions. (Additional)	Process
Training & Education	LA10 Average hours of training per year per employee by employee category. (Core)	Substantive
Training & Education	LA11 Programmes for skills management and lifelong learning that support the continued employability of employees and assist them in managing career endings. (Additional)	Process
Training & Education	LA12 Percentage of employees receiving regular performance and career development reviews. (Additional)	Substantive

Aspect (area of impact)	Indicator	Classification
Diversity & Equal Opportunity	LA13 Composition of governance bodies and breakdown of employees per category according to gender, age group, minority group membership, and other indicators of diversity. (Core)	Substantive
Diversity & Equal Opportunity	LA14 Ratio of basic salary of men to women by employee category. (Core)	Substantive
Investment & Procurement Practices	HR1 Percentage and total number of significant investment agreements that include human rights clauses or that have undergone human rights screening. (Core)	Process
Investment & Procurement Practices	HR2 Percentage of significant suppliers and contractors that have undergone screening on human rights and actions taken. (Core)	Process
Investment & Procurement Practices	HR3 Total hours of employee training on policies and procedures concerning aspects of human rights that are relevant to operations, including the percentage of employees trained. (Additional)	Process
Non-discrimination	HR4 Total number of incidents of discrimination and actions taken. (Core)	Substantive
Freedom of Association & Collective Bargaining	HR5 Operations identified in which the right to exercise freedom of association and collective bargaining may be at significant risk, and actions taken to support these rights. (Core)	Process
Child Labour	HR6 Operations identified as having significant risk for incidents of child labor, and measures taken to contribute to the elimination of child labor. (Core)	Process
Forced & Compulsory Labour	HR7 Operations identified as having significant risk for incidents of forced or compulsory labor, and measures to contribute to the elimination of forced or compulsory labor. (Core)	Process
Security Practices	HR8 Percentage of security personnel trained in the organization's policies or procedures concerning aspects of human rights that are relevant to operations. (Additional)	Process
Indigenous Rights	HR9 Total number of incidents of violations involving rights of indigenous people and actions taken. (Additional)	Substantive
Community	SO1 Nature, scope, and effectiveness of any programs and practices that assess and manage the impacts of operations on communities, including entering, operating, and exiting. (Core)	Mainly process
Corruption	SO2 Percentage and total number of business units analyzed for risks related to corruption. (Core)	Process
Corruption	SO3 Percentage of employees trained in organization's organization's anti-corruption policies and procedures. (Core)	Process
Corruption	SO4 Actions taken in response to incidents of corruption. (Core)	Process
Public Policy	SO5 Public policy positions and participation in public policy development and lobbying. (Core)	Mainly process
Public Policy	SO6 Total value of financial and in-kind contributions to political parties, politicians, and related institutions by country. (Additional)	Process
Anti-competitive Behavior	SO7 Total number of legal actions for anti-competitive behavior, anti-trust, and monopoly practices and their outcomes. (Additional)	Substantive

Aspect (area of impact)	Indicator	Classification
Compliance	SO8 Monetary value of significant fines and total number of non-monetary sanctions for non-compliance with laws and regulations. (Core)	Process
Customer Health & Safety	PR1 Life cycle stages in which health and safety impacts of products and services are assessed for improvement, and percentage of significant products and services categories subject to such procedures. (Core)	Process
Customer Health & Safety	PR2 Total number of incidents of non-compliance with regulations and voluntary codes concerning health and safety impacts of products and services during their life cycle, by type of outcomes. (Additional)	Substantive
Product & Service Labeling	PR3 Type of product and service information required by procedures, and percentage of significant products and services subject to such information requirements. (Core)	Process
Product & Service Labeling	PR4 Total number of incidents of non-compliance with regulations and voluntary codes concerning product and service information and labeling, by type of outcomes. (Additional)	Substantive
Product & Service Labeling	PR5 Practices related to customer satisfaction, including results of surveys measuring customer satisfaction. (Additional)	Mainly process
Marketing Communications	PR6 Programs for adherence to laws, standards, and voluntary codes related to marketing communications, including advertising, promotion, and sponsorship. (Core)	Process
Marketing Communications	PR7 Total number of incidents of non-compliance with regulations and voluntary codes concerning marketing communications, including advertising, promotion, and sponsorship by type of outcomes. (Additional)	Substantive
Customer Privacy	PR8 Total number of substantiated complaints regarding breaches of customer privacy and losses of customer data. (Additional)	Substantive
Compliance	PR9 Monetary value of significant fines for non-compliance with laws and regulations concerning the provision and use of products and services. (Core).	Process

Source: adapted from (GRI, 2006)

Appendix III

SROI Case Study

This appendix is based on the work of Adam Richards of Liverpool John Moores University who conducted the SROI analysis described below. Names of the participating organizations have been changed.

SUMMARY

The Regional Housing Group provides social housing to its tenants. It also operates the New Chance scheme, offering all tenants the opportunity for a package to furnish their homes. This is then paid for by the tenants usually via their welfare benefits over a three year period.

The social return on investment (SROI) analysis focused on the costs and benefits created as a result of Regional Housing's New Chance scheme, considering those of significance to the tenant and the organization. Such an analysis aids organizations to better prove the value creation beyond simply financial profit, and identify areas for improvement.

Although the result of the SROI is a ratio of monetized social value (NPV of benefits/NPV of investment), there is much more to the story. It is important that qualitative statements are included within the report to indicate those areas that cannot be monetized. SROI can be described as the start of a conversation to better understand the creation of social value.

The value of the New Chance scheme was projected for five years beyond the initial year's investment, therefore six years in total from 2007, capturing all areas of the scheme's created-value. The final SROI ratio is 2.11:1, suggesting that for every £1 invested, there is a social return of £2.11.

Sensitivity analysis was conducted on the results, revealing the changes when altering one variable within the analysis. Alterations to the assumptions revealed little change in the ratio result, suggesting that the assumptions incorporated are robust and reasonable. As expected however modification to the number of tenants within the scheme reveals the most (only) significant change.

The social benefits created include improved disposable income (through financial savings made in comparison to alternative retailers and the avoidance of credit options), the creation of a home, arrears and void costs avoided, improved confidence, increased time to undertake alternative activities (such as seek employment), guaranteed revenue through repayments, improved stakeholder relations and improvements to the sustainability of tenancies.

REGIONAL HOUSING – NEW CHANCE SCHEME

Regional Housing Group is a family of housing organizations that provide some 15,000 homes across the region. The Group's mission to 'make a difference' is demonstrated by their strategic objectives and the commitment to use their skills and resources for 'sustainable, economic and social improvement, tackling poverty and inequality.'

The New Chance Scheme is designed to allow tenants the opportunity to furnish their homes quickly and with good quality furniture. Regional Housing provides a package of furniture to tenants. Regional Housing then hires the furniture for three years, using in most cases welfare benefits to cover the costs through rental charges and maintenance and repair costs.

All new tenants are offered the opportunity for a furnished home, with options of three levels of furnished accommodation:

1   just carpets;
2   just furniture;
3   both furniture and carpets.

The investigation was only concerned with those tenants that were recipients of furniture from packages from a particular supplier; tenants receiving only carpets were excluded from this study. Over three years approximately 211 furnished properties were included in this study.

SROI ANALYSIS

The New Chance scheme is particularly suited to SROI analysis, owing to the creation of both economic and non-economic value for both the tenants and Group. Those areas of value creation that can be assigned a monetary value, such as the avoidance of alternative higher priced goods and credit options, provide information for the cost-benefit final ratio of return. However, it must be remembered that those outcomes producing less-tangible outcomes such as improved well-being and quality of life for tenants and improved Group-tenant relationships cannot be monetized and are therefore beyond the scope of the ratio of return. Although such areas are commented upon and may be of equal significance to those monetized, such an understanding does indicate that the SROI ratio of return will be an under-estimation of the true value created by the New Chance scheme.

Understanding how value is created for different stakeholders is crucial to the development of the SROI analysis. Determining the inputs required, leading to the direct outputs of the New Chance scheme and longer-term outcomes, whilst appreciating the impact of the organization (those outcomes Regional Housing can take credit for) is essential.

IDENTIFYING STAKEHOLDERS

Stakeholder engagement is central to the SROI process, owing to the necessity to highlight both the immediate goals and longer term objectives (impacts) of the New Chance scheme. Regional Housing is committed to such engagement, demonstrated by their Equality and Diversity Strategy, developed in conjunction with a range of stakeholders in order to offer excellent customer satisfaction, thereby fostering vibrant communities with improved quality of life.

There are a number of stakeholders that are of interest to Regional Housing, including the following:

- staff;
- customers;
- board of directors;
- the state (local and national Government);
- external auditors;
- competitors;
- suppliers;
- local communities;
- the environment;
- partner organizations.

For the purpose of this analysis only the tenants and Regional Housing Group are considered as key stakeholders and were included within the investigation. Although further benefits and costs for other stakeholders will undoubtedly have been created by the New Chance scheme, it was important in the initial stages of analysis to focus on those areas of greatest significance.

In order to understand this information, a stakeholder impact map is constructed, detailing the cause and effect chains that lead to value creation, as illustrated in Table III.1.

Table III.1 *From Input to Impact*

Stakeholder	Input	Activity	Output	Outcome	Impact
Tenant	Home	Acceptance of furniture package	1. Avoidance of higher cost alternative retailers. 2. Avoidance of unfavourable credit options. 3. Avoid delay of ownership.	1. Increased disposable income. 2. Furnish home quicker. 3. Creation of a 'home.'	1. Increased personal/family wealth. 2. Avoidance of arrears costs. 3. Avoidance of higher alternative accommodation costs. 4. Remain in property for longer duration. 5. Time to spend doing something other than purchase furniture. 6. Improved job prospects (increased available time). 7. Improved quality of life. 8. Ownership of items would not have otherwise owned. 9. Increased confidence. 10. Provision of safe environment for family.
Regional Housing Group	Financial investment	Provision of furniture package	1. Tenants move into property quicker. 2. Tenant repayments.	1. Reduction of incurred void costs. 2. Improved customer satisfaction. 3. Guaranteed income.	1. Financial saving. 2. Improved sustainability of tenancy. 3. Keep Regional Housing's voice to a minimum. 4. Improved relationship with tenants and potential customers. 5. Economic benefit.

Materiality

All of the issues illustrated in the stakeholder impact map arose from discussions with a member of staff at Regional Housing and a survey distributed to tenants.

Although some of the impacts outlined are unsuited to monetization, it must be remembered that they are of equal significance to the investigation and are necessary to fully appreciate the value created by the New Chance scheme. The chief impact excluded from further (quantitative) analyses was the outcome of the creation of a home (and all associated impacts) for the tenants.

Having outlined the impacts of the scheme, the next step was to identify suitable indicators that could effectively quantify and ultimately monetize the appropriate outputs, outcomes and impacts. This information is summarized by the indicator map in Table III.2.

Table III.2 *Indicator Map*

Stakeholder	Input indicators	Outputs	Output indicators	Outcomes	Outcome indicators	Impacts	Impact indicators
Tenant	N/A	Avoidance of higher cost alternative retailers. Avoidance of unfavourable credit options. Avoid delay of ownership.	Tenant's opinion of alternative cost to purchase identical furniture. Comparative savings made by avoiding credit subject to proportion of tenants that would select credit options. Average length of time to find alternative items of furniture – 31.91 weeks (tenant responses).	Increased disposable income. Furnish home quicker.	Net value of savings for annual tenants on scheme. Tenants responses of where to select credit options (catalogue, credit cards & bank loan). Proxy value equated to ownership of furniture (per week) based on value of furniture [actual + perceived extra cost] and 3 years ownership (156 weeks / £1954.48). Multiplied by average delay in ownership.	Increased personal/family wealth. Avoidance of arrears costs. Avoidance of higher alternative accommodation costs.	Savings made subject to 5% deadweight. 91.30% of tenants responded that they would accept unfurnished tenancy – this figure is used for following 2 proxies: Based on cheapest one-bed property at Regional Housing, and average rate charges for region. Arrears assumed for 7 weeks – average duration to receive Community Care Grant. Also assumed 5% arrears rate. Half of 5% tenants in arrears are assumed to enter both private and hostel accommodation. Regional average used for private accommodation. Actual figure used for hostel price and average length of stay.
Regional Housing Group	Number of tenancies receiving furniture as part of New Chance scheme.	Tenants move into property quicker. Tenant repayments	Service charge calculated by standard industry calculation over 3 years repayment.	Reduction of incurred void costs. Guaranteed income.	Assumed frequency of voids is 5%. Rental charge subject to 4% assumed bad debt.	Financial saving. Improved sustainability of tenancy.	Overall deadweight value of 5%. Reduction in void costs based on tenant survey — 48.48% of tenants would remain in furnished tenancy for longer than unfurnished alternative.

Attribution

Considerations of attribution determine what proportion of benefit individuals or organizations can be credited with. In this particular case, Regional Housing assumed all financial risk, working independently to create value. It is therefore reasonable to assume that Regional Housing was responsible for all value created, and as such there were no requirements to consider attribution.

NON-MONETIZED BENEFITS CREATED

Tenants

A number of areas of value creation were uncovered during this investigation, including those previously illustrated in the stakeholder impact map (Table III.1), such as increased confidence, improvements in job prospects owing to the reduced need to search for furniture, ownership of furniture items that would not have ordinarily been the case, the provision of a safe environment for family members and increased quality of life. Although a number of the proxies used do go some way to cover some of these areas (e.g. increased wealth could act as a proxy for increased quality of life), they still require explicit consideration.

A number of tenants also stated that if they had not moved into their home when they did their only realistic alternative was to become homeless. Although a reduction in homelessness cannot be attributed solely to the possession of furniture, there is a clear relationship. It is a commonly known practice among tenants to accept an unfurnished property whilst still renting alternative accommodation. This may continue for a number of weeks until the tenant can afford to furnish the new property at which point they may be in a position to move in. However by this stage (whether moved in or not) they will have incurred rental arrears, which in many cases forces the tenant to give up the property (or become evicted). Such a situation has long-lasting consequences; not only have they lost their home, they are now considered high risk by landlords and will probably face the situation of being unable to rent from a registered social landlord, therefore being left with the options of private landlords, hostels, friends or family or, in the most extreme cases, homelessness. Such benefits are also clearly not restricted to the tenants themselves, homelessness and associated social issues are of economic significance to the state.

Regional Housing Group

Those benefits of the New Chance scheme to Regional Housing that are not appropriate for monetization include improvements in customer relationships. Although a reduction in void costs and the belief that tenants will remain in properties for longer periods can be considered as proxies for such benefits, it would be unwise to consider this the total benefit. Considerations of positive word-of-mouth marketing of Regional Housing to potential customers, along with further stakeholders in the community and beyond are also significant.

Tenants generally cover their repayments with welfare income and so do not have to worry about further financial commitment through taking part in the scheme. Being in an improved financial position reduces the likelihood of running into difficulties that may require the Group's intervention.

Overall, it must be remembered that the SROI analysis will underestimate the true value created, owing to the inability to monetize all impacts. Not only are there clear economic advantages to the scheme, the social benefits are numerous and significant. The benefits will also extend beyond the tenants and Group; the local economy will benefit from increased disposable income of tenants, whilst the social capital of participants will similarly improve.

FINDINGS

Regional Housing Group's New Chance scheme creates a range of both economic and social benefits to both tenants and the organization. The value created reveals a ratio of return of 2.11:1, thereby indicating that for each £1 invested there are social returns (over the course of the whole analysis) of £2.11, whilst the payback for the initial investment is just over 5 months.

Value is created for the organization through regular rental income, a reduction in void costs, improved stakeholder relationships and overall improved sustainability of tenancies that will also clearly have a number of additional benefits, such as the opportunity time and cost saving from a reduction in administrative responsibilities.

As expected, the recipients of the scheme receive the majority of created-benefits, in the form of: a financial saving in comparison to alternative retail options, avoidance of potentially expensive credit options, possession of furniture much sooner and a reduction in the likelihood of incurring arrears and alternative accommodation costs. Furthermore, the creation of a 'home' improves self confidence and happiness, allows for possession of items that would not have otherwise been owned, the provision of a safe and comfortable space for family and friends to visit and increased time available to spend doing other activities, such as seeking employment.

Alteration to the number of tenants in receipt of the furniture package can be considered the most significant factor within this analysis. As would be expected, increases in the number of tenants utilizing the scheme provides the greatest potential for further value creation. The sensitivity analysis suggests that alteration to other variables will not revise the ration of return by a significant amount. This implies confidence in the robustness of any assumptions made, within an acceptable range.

Bibliography

AccountAbility (2003) *AA1000AS – Assurance Standard*, AccountAbility, London

AccountAbility (2006a) *The Materiality Report – Aligning Strategy, Performance and Reporting*, AccountAbility, BT, LRQA, London

AccountAbility (2006b) *Stakeholder Engagment Standard – Exposure Draft*, AccountAbility, London

Adidas (2008) 'Supply Chain Code of Conduct', Retrieved September, 2008, from www.adidas-group.com/en/sustainability/suppliers_and_workers/code_of_conduct/default.asp

AI (2006) *Undermining Freedom of Expression in China – The Role of Yahoo!, Microsoft and Google*, Amnesty Interational (UK), London

Andrews, C. (2008) 'Go Figure', Retrieved May, 2008, from www.charitytimes.com/pages/ct_features/september07/text-features/ct_september07_feature1_go_figure.htm

Aristotle (1968) 'De interpretatione', in R. McKeon (ed) *The Basic Works of Aristotle*, Random, New York

Assist (2008) 'Assist Social Capital', Retrieved August, 2008, from www.social-capital.net/index.php?SK=727e02c316adb001c86abb795fd5a90e&W21ID=117

BabyMilkAction (2008) 'Baby Milk Action', Retrieved March 28, 2008, from www.babymilkaction.org/pages/boycott.html

Barrientos, S. and Smith, S. (2007) *The ETI Code of Practice – Do Workers Really Benefit?* IDS, Brighton

Baue, B. (2006) 'Social Footprint Introduces Simple Elegance in Measuring Corporate Sustainability Performance', *Sustainability Investment News*. Retrieved from www.socialfunds.com/news/article.cgi/article1968.html

Bebbington, J., Gray, R., Hibbitt, C. and Kirk, E. (2001) *Full Cost Accounting – An Agenda for Action*, ACCA, London

Bent, D. (2005) 'Towards a monetised triple bottom line for an alcohol producer', *Environmental Management Accounting Network (EMAN) proceedings* (Sustainability Accounting and Reporting), www.leuphana.de/umanagement/projekte/eman/eman-global/

Berelson, B. (1952) *Content Analysis in Communication Research*, Free Press, Glencoe

Berle, A. A. and Means, G. C. (1933) *The Modern Corporation and Private Property*, Macmillan, New York

Blowfield, M. and Murray, A. (2008) *Corporate Responsibility – A Critical Introduction*, OUP, Oxford

Bourdieu, P. and Wacquant, L. (1992) *An Invitation to Reflexive Sociology*, University of Chicago Press, Chicago

BP (2008) 'Sustainability Review 2007: Our key priorities Safety People Performance', Retrieved August, 2008, from www.bp.com/liveassets/bp_internet/globalbp/STAGING/global_assets/e_s_assets/downloads/bp_sustainability_review_2007.pdf

Braun, J. v. (1995) *Employment for Poverty Reduction and Food Security*, International Food Policy Institute, Washington DC

Brown, G. and Harris, T. (1978) *Social Origins of Depression*, Tavistock, London

BT (2003) *Just Values – Beyond the Business Case for Sustainable Development*, BT, Forum for the Future, London

BT (2007) *The Economic Impact of BT in the United Kingdom*, BT, London

Cadbury (2008) 'Responsible Cocoa Farming', Retrieved September, 2008, from www.cadbury.com/ourresponsibilities/ethicaltrading/cocoasourcing/Pages/responsiblecocoafarming.aspx

CC (2009) 'About Us', Retrieved January, 2009, from www.competition-commission.org.uk/about_us/index.htm

CEOP (2008) *Strategic Overview*, Child Exploitation and Online Protection Centre, London

Chandler, G. (2002) 'Let's not fool ourselves with the business case', *Ethical Performance*, vol 4 no 1, May

CIA-USA (2007) *The World Fact Book*, CIA, Washington

CIPS (2008) *Taking the Lead: A Guide to More Responsible Procurement Practices*, London, Chartered Insititute of Purchasing and Supply, Traidcraft, London

Clay, J. (2005) *Exploring the Links Between International Business and Poverty Reduction – A Case Study of Unilever in Indonesia*, Oxfam, Novib, Unilever, Indonesia

Coleman, J. (1988) 'Social capital in the creation of human capital', *American Journal of Sociology*, vol 94(Supplement) ppS95–S120

ConsumerAffairs (2005) 'Consumer Group Sues Sony BMG', Retrieved May, 2008, from www.consumeraffairs.com/news04/2005/sony_eff.html

Davies, N. (2008) *Flat Earth News*, Chatto & Windus, London

Dearne, K. (2008) *Not Easy Being Green, but Audits Help*, Australian IT, Surry Hills

Defoe, D. (2007) *Robinson Crusoe*, Penguin, London (first published 1719)

Deshingkar, P. (2006) *Internal Migration, Poverty and Development in Asia*, Asia 2015, IDS, ODI, Brighton

Deumes, R. (2008) 'Corporate risk reporting: a content analysis of narrative risk disclosures in prospectuses' *Journal of Business Communication*, vol 45, no 2, pp120–157.

Doane, D. and A. Holder (2007) *Why Corporate Social Responsibility is Failing Children*, SCF, CORE, London

DPA (2008) 'Say Something' Retrieved August, 2008, from www.davies communications.com/downloads/davies_brochure.pdf

DTI (1999) *Modern Company Law for a Competitive Economy: The Strategic Framework*, Company Law Review Steering Group, London

Durie, S., Hutton, E. and Robbie, K. (2008) *Investing in Impact – Developing Social Return on Investment*, Forth Sector, Edinburgh

East Sussex (2008) 'Capital and Revenue Expenditure', Retrieved October, 2008, from www.eastsussex.gov.uk/yourcouncil/finance/budget/expenditure/.

EC (2001) *Promoting a European framework for Corporate Social Responsibility*, European Commission, Brussels

EC (2002) *Directive 2002/14/EC*, European Commission, Brussels

EC (2003) *Directive 2002/96/EC of the European Parliament and of the Council of 27 January 2003 on Waste Electrical and Electronic Equipment (WEEE)*, European Commission, Brussels

EC (2008) The Stakeholder Engagment Summit 2008 – Brochure, Ethical Corporation, London

Elkington, J. (1998) *Cannibals with Forks: The Triple Bottom Line of 21st Century Business*, New Society Publishers, Gabriola Island, BC, Stony Creek, CT

Elkington, J. and Hartigan, P. (2008) *The Power of Unreasonable People*, Harvard Business School Press, Boston

EP (2006) 'Equator Principles', from www.equator-principles.com/index.shtml

Esty, E., Lysy, F. and Ferman, C. (2003) *An Economic Framework for Assessing Development Impact*, Harvard Business School Press, Cambridge

ETI (2008) 'Ethical Trading Initiative', Retrieved September, 2008, from www.ethicaltrade.org/

Euromonitor (2004) 'Innovation Drives Growth in Cosmetics and Toiletries', Retrieved March 28, 2008, from www.euromonitor.com/Innovation_drives_growth_in_ cosmetics_and_toiletries

Euromoney (2005) *National Oil Companies*, Petroleum Economist, www.euromoney.com

ExxonMobil (2008) 'Educating Women and Girls', Retrieved August, 2008, from www.exxonmobil.com/Corporate/Files/Corporate/Women_Girls_brochure.pdf

FCACP (2008) 'The Financial Coalition Against Child Pornography – Fact Sheet', Retrieved September, 2008, from www.missingkids.com/missingkids/servlet/ PageServlet?LanguageCountry=en_US&PageId=403

FFF (2002) *Sustainability Accounting in the Construction Business*, Forum for the Future, London, Carillion, Castella

FLA (2005) 'Workplace Code of Conduct.' Retrieved May, 2006, from www.fairlabor.org/all/code/index.html

Ford (2007) 'Materiality Matrix', Ford Motor Company Sustainability Report 2006/7. Retrieved April, 2008, from www.ford.com/aboutford/microsites/ sustainability-report-2006-07/impactsMaterialityMatrix.htm

Freeman, E. R. (1984) *Strategic Management: A Stakeholder Approach*, Pitman, Boston

Friedman, M. (2007) 'The social responsibility of business is to increase its profits', *Corporate Ethics and Corporate Governance*, Springer, Berlin, pp173–178

G8 (2007) 'Ministers' Declaration: Reinforcing the International Fight Against Child Pornography', Retrieved September, 2008, from www.g-8.de/Content/EN/_ Anlagen/2007-05-24-g8-justiz-innen-start-erklaerung-en,property=publicationFile

GC (2008) 'The Global Compact', from www.unglobalcompact.org/

Giddens, A. (1984) *The Constitution of Society: Outline of the Theory of Structuration*, Polity Press, Cambridge

Gilpin, D. R. (2008) 'Narrating the organizational self: reframing the role of the news release', Public Relations Review vol 34 no 1, pp9–18

Gramsci, A. (1971) *Selections from the Prison Notebooks*, Lawrence and Wishart, London

Gray, R., Dey, C., Owen, D. Evans, R. and Zadek, S. (1997) 'Struggling with the praxis of social accounting: stakeholders, accountability, audits and procedures', *Accounting, Auditing & Accountability Journal*, vol 10, no 3, pp325–364

Gray, R., Owen, D. and Adams, C. (1996) *Accounting & Accountability: Changes and Challenges in Corporate Social and Environmental Reporting*, Prentice Hall, London

Greenhill, R. (2006) *Real Aid 2 – Making Technical Assistance Work*, Action Aid, Johannesburg

Greenhill, R. and Watts, P. (2005) *Real Aid – An Agenda for Making Aid Work*, Action Aid, Johannesburg

GRI (2005) *GRI Boundary Protocol*, Global Reporting Initiative, Amsterdam

GRI (2006) *Global Reporting Initative – Sustainability Reporting Guidelines Version 3*. GRI, Amsterdam

GRI (2008a) 'Global Reporting Initiative', Retrieved September, 2008, from www.globalreporting.org/Home

GRI (2008b) 'Reporting Framework', Retrieved April 3, 2008, from www.globalreporting.org/ReportingFramework/ReportingFrameworkDownloads/

Grumiau, S. (2001) *Commercial Sexual Exploitation of Children: The Situation in Thailand, Cambodia and the Philippines. What can the trade union movement do to help?* ICFTU, Brussels

Guha, K. (2007) 'US "wary" of sovereign wealth funds', *Financial Times*, London, 20 June

Hague, P., Hague, N. and Morgan, C-A. (2008) *Market Research in Practice*, Kogan Page, London

Halpern, D. (2005) *Social Capital*, Polity Press, Cambridge

Han, S.-K. and Breiger, R. L. (1999) 'Dimensions of corporate social capital: towards models and measures', in S. Gabbay and R. Leenders (eds) *Corporate Social Capital and Liability*, Kluwer Academic Publications, London

Harbinson, R. (2007) *Development Recast: A Review of the Impact of the Rio Tinto Ilmenite Mine in Southern Madagascar*, Panos London, London

Hawken, P. (2007) *Blessed Unrest: How the Largest Movement in the World Came into Being and Why No One Saw It Coming*, Viking, New York

Henriques, A. (2001) 'Civil society and social auditing', *Business Ethics – A European Review*, vol 10, no 1, pp40–44

Henriques, A. and Richardson, J. (2004) 'CSR, sustainability and the triple bottom line', in A. Henriques and J. Richardson (eds) *The Triple Bottom Line – does it all add up?* Earthscan, London

Henriques, A. (2007) *Corporate Truth: The Limits to Transparency*, Earthscan, London

Henriques, A. and Laerke-Engelschmidt, P. (2007) *Environmental Management Report: Focus on Sustainability and its Implications for CSR*, BSI, London

Henschel, B. (2003) *The Assessment of Commercial Sexual Exploitation of Children: A Review of Methodologies*, ILO, UNICEF, World Bank Group, Geneva.

HIIK (2008) *Conflict Barometer 2008*, Heidelberg Institute for International Conflict Research, Heidelberg

Holmberg, J., Lundqvist, U. et al. (1999) 'The ecological footprint from a systems perspective of sustainability', *International Journal of Sustainable Development and World Ecology*, vol 6 pp17–33

Home Office (2008) 'Child Protection', Retrieved September, 2008, from http://police.homeoffice.gov.uk/operational-policing/crime-disorder/child-protection-taskforce

Honda (2004) 'Honda's Economic Impact on Ohio', Retrieved July, 2008, from www.ohio.honda.com/ohio/econ.cfm

Hopkins, M. (2003) *The Planetary Bargain*, Earthscan, London

Hopkins, M. (2006) *Corporate Social Responsibility & International Development*, Earthscan, London

Howes, R. (2003) 'Environmental cost accounting – coming of age?' in A. Henriques and J. Richardson (eds) *The Triple Bottom Line – Does it All Add Up?* Earthscan, London

HRW (2002) *Tainted Harvest: Child Labor and Obstacles to Organizing on Ecuador's Banana Plantations*, Human Rights Watch, New York

IAIA (2003) *Social Impact Assessment – International Principles*, International Association for Impact Assessment, Hobart

IASC (2007) *A Guide Through International Financial Reporting Standards*, IASB, London

ICJ (2008) *Facing the Facts and Charting a Legal Path, Report of the International Commission of Jurists Expert Legal Panel on Corporate Complicity in International Crimes*, 1 International Commission of Jurists, Geneva

ILO (1999) *Worst Forms of Child Labour Convention*, ILO, Geneva, C182

Insight (2004) *Buying Your Way into Trouble? The Challenge of Responsible Supply Chain Management*, Insight Investment, Acona, London

IOM (2008) *Athens Ethical Principles Follow Up. Global Eye on Human Trafficking*, Geneva, International Organization for Migration, Geneva, 3

IPEC (2003) *Investing in Every Child: An Economic Study of the Costs and Benefits of Eliminating Child Labour*, Geneva, ILO

Ireland, P. (1996) 'Capitalism without the capitalist: the joint stock company share and the emergence of the modern doctrine of separate legal personality', *Journal of Legal History*, vol 17 no 1, pp40–72

ISO (2008) *Guidance on Social Responsibility*, ISO, Geneva, WD 4.2

Jackson, T., Marks, N., Ralls, J. and Stymmer, S. (1997) *Sustainable Economic Welfare in the UK 1950–1996*, New Economics Foundation, London

James, O. (2007) *Affluenza – How to be Successful and Stay Sane*, Vermillion, London

Kapstein, E. (2008) *Measuring Unilever's Economic Footprint: The Case of South Africa*, INSEAD, London

Kay, J. (2008) *Drowning by Numbers*, RSA Journal, London

Kendall, C. (2008) 'A new law of nature', *Guardian*, London

Keynes, J. M. (2007) *The General Theory of Employment, Interest and Money*, Palgrave Macmillan (first published 1936), Basingstoke

Kingsmill, D. (2003) *Accounting for People*, DTI, London

Krugman, P. (2008) *Poverty is Poison*, New York Times, New York

Labov, W. (1997) 'Some further steps in narrative analysis', *The Journal of Narrative and Life History*, vol 7, nos 1–4, pp395–415

Labov, W. and Waletzky, J. (1967) 'Narrative analysis: oral versions of personal experience', in J. Helm (ed) *Essays on the Verbal and Visual Arts*, University of Washington Press, Seattle, pp12–44

Lawlor, E., Neitzert, E. and Nicholls, J. (2008) *Measuring Value: A Guide to Social Return on Investment (SROI)*, New Economics Foundation, London

Lawlor, E., Murray, R., Neitzert, E. and Sanfilippo, L. (2008) *Investing for Social Value – measuring social return on investment for the Adventure Capital Fund*, New Economics Foundation, London

Layard, R. (2003) *Happiness: Has Social Science a Clue?* LSE, London

LBG (2009) 'The London Benchmark Group', Retrieved April, 2009, from www.lbg-online.net/

Leenders, R. and Gabbay, S. (1999) *Corporate Social Capital and Liability*, Kluwer Academic Publications, London

Leipziger, D. (2003) *The Corporate Responsibility Code Book*, Greenleaf, Sheffield

Lenzen, M. and Murray, S. (2003) *The Ecological Footprint – Issues and Trends*, University of Sydney, Sydney

Lenzen, M., Lundie, S., Bransgrove, G., Bullock, S. and Sack, F. (2003) 'Assessing the ecological footprint of a large metropolitan water supplier: lessons for water management and planning towards sustainability', *Journal of Environmental Planning and Management*, vol 46, no 1 pp113–141

Lewis, C. S. (2001) *The Abolition of Man*, Zondervan (first published 1943), Grand Rapids

Liu, J. (1999) 'Social capital and covariates of reoffending risk in the Chinese context', *International Criminal Justice Review*, vol 9 pp39–45

Lustig, N. C. and McLeod, D. (1997) 'Minimum wages and poverty in developing countries: some empirical evidence, in S. Edwards and N. Lustig (eds) *Labor Markets in Latin America*, Brookings Institution Press, Washington DC

Lysy, F. J. (1999) *Assessing Development Impact*, IFC, Washington

Macgillivray, A. (2004) 'Social capital at work: a manger's guide', in A. Henriques and J. Richardson (eds) *The Triple Bottom Line: Does it All Add Up?* Earthscan, London

Malinowski, B. (1929) *The Sexual Life of Savages in North-Western Melanesia: An Ethnographic Account of Courtship, Marriage and Family Life Among the Natives of the Trobriand Islands*, British New Guinea, Halcyon House, New York

Marr, A. (2005) *My Trade: A Short History of British Journalism*, Pan, London

Marx, K. (1974) *Capital*, Lawrence & Wishart (first published 1867), London

Maslow, A. H. (1943) 'A theory of human motivation', *Psychological Review*, vol 50, pp370–396

McElroy, M. (2008a) 'Center for Sustainable Innovation', Retrieved October, 2008, from www.sustainableinnovation.org/the-social-footprint.html

McElroy, M. (2008b) 'Social footprints: measuring the social sustainability performance of organizations',, PhD, University of Groningen,.Groningen

McLaren, D., Bullock, S. and Yusuf, N. (1998) *Tomorrow's world: Britain's share in a sustainable future*, Earthscan, London

Meadows, D., Randers, J. and Meadows, D. (2005) *Limits to Growth – The 30-year Update*, Earthscan, London

MMSD (2002) *Breaking New Ground – Mining, Minerals and Sustainable Development*, IIED, WBCSD, London

Nestlé (2008a) *Creating Shared Value*, Nestlé, Vevey

Nestlé (2008b) *Group Performance*, Nestlé, Vevey

Nordhaus, W. D. and Tobin, J. (1973) 'The measurement of economic and social performance', *Studies in Income and Wealth*, M. Moss, NBER, vol 38, pp509–532

Nordlinger, J. (2004) *The New Colossus*, National Review, New York

OECD (2000) *Guidelines for Multinational Enterprises*, Organisation for Economic Cooperation and Development, Paris

OECD (2001) *The Well-being of Nations: The Role of Human and Social Capital*, OECD, Paris

OECD (2004) *Stakeholder Involvement Techniques: Short Guide and Annotated Bibliography*, OECD (NEA), Paris

OFWAT (2008) 'Protecting your Interests', Retrieved 24th March, 2008, from www.ofwat.gov.uk/aptrix/ofwat/publish.nsf/Content/protecting_interests280905

Olsen, S. and A. Lingane A. (2003) *Social Return on Investment: Standard Guidelines*, National Social Venture Competition, Berkeley

ONS (2007) 'Internet Access', Retrieved August, 2008, from www.statistics.gov.uk/CCI/nugget.asp?ID=8

ONS (2008) 'Social Capital', Retrieved August, 2008, from www.statistics.gov.uk/socialcapital/

Owen, R. and Sweeting, A. (2007) *Hoodie or Goodie? The Link Between Violent Victimisation and Offending in Young People: A Research Report*, Victim Support, BMRB Social Research, London

Oxfam (2004) *Trading Away Our Rights*, Oxfam International, Oxfam

Parkin, S., Johnston, A., Buckland, H., Brookes, F., While, E., Howes, R., Richardson, J. and Bent, D. (2003) *Accounting for Sustainability: Guidance for Higher Education Institutions, Forum for the Future*, Higher Education Partnership for Sustainability, London

Pearce, D. W., Markandya, A. and Barbier, E. B. (1989) *Blueprint For a Green Economy*, Earthscan, London

Peirce, C. S. (1868) 'On a new list of categories', *Proceedings of the American Academy of Arts and Sciences*, vol 7, pp287–298

Phillips, K., Hamden, K. and Lopez, E. (2004) 'Gauging the Impact of the San Antonio Toyota Plant.' Retrieved July, 2008, from www.dallasfed.org/research/vista/vista0401.html

Prahalad, C. K. and Hart, S. (2001) 'The fortune and the bottom of the pyramid' *Strategy and Business*, 26

Prasad, M. (2007) 'Child Labour in BT Cotton Fields', Retrieved September, 2008, from www.timesnow.tv/NewsDtls.aspx?NewsID=1962

Propp, V. (1977) *Morphology of the Folktale*, University of Texas Press (first published 1928), Austin

Putnam, R. (1993) *Making Democracy Work: Civic Traditions in Modern Italy*, Princeton University Press, Princeton

Putnam, R. (1995) 'Bowling alone: America's declining social capital', *Journal of Democracy*, vol 6, pp65–78

Putnam, R. (2000) *Bowling Alone: The Collapse and Revival of American Community*, Simon & Schuster, New York

REDF (2001) *SROI Methodology*, REDF, San Francisco

REDF (2008) 'About REDF', Retrieved July, 2008, from www.redf.org/about-intro.htm

Robbins, P. (2008) 'IWF Annual Report highlights persistent core of child sexual abuse websites', Retrieved September, 2008, from www.iwf.org.uk/media/news.229.htm

Robins, N. (2006) *The Corporation that Changed the World*, Pluto Press, London

Roche (2006) 'AIDS Technology Transfer Initiative', Retrieved 22nd February, 2009, from www.roche.com/sus_acc_tti.pdf

Roche (2007) *Roche Annual Report 2006*, Roche, Basel

RTZ (2007) *Social and Communities Fact Sheet*, Rio Tinto, London

Ruggie, J. (2006) *Promotion and Protection of Human Rights: Interim Report of the Special Representative of the Secretary-General on the Issue of Human Rights and Transnational Corporations and Other Business Enterprises*, OHCHR, Geneva

Ruggie, J. (2007) *Human Rights Impact Assessments – Resolving Key Methodological Questions*, UN General Assembly, New York

Ruggie, J. (2008) *Protect, Respect and Remedy: A Framework for Business and Human Rights*, UNHCR, Geneva

Saatchi (2008) 'Kevin Roberts', Retrieved March 28, 2008, from www.saatchi.com/worldwide/kevin_roberts.asp

Sacks, J. (2002) *The Money Trail*, NEF, London

Sacks, J. (2009) 'Taking (local) economic impact seriously', Personal communication

Saget, C. (2001) *Is the Minimum Wage an Effective Tool to Promote Decent Work and Reduce Poverty? The Experience of Selected Developing Countries*, ILO, Geneva

SAI (2008) 'Social Accountability International', Retrieved September, 2008, from www.ethicaltrade.org/

Sala-i-Martin, X. (2002) *The Disturbing 'Rise' of Global Income Inequality*, NBER, Cambridge

Schaltegger, S. and Burritt, R. (2000) *Contemporary Environmental Accounting: Issues, Concepts and Practice*, Greenleaf, Sheffield

Schleiermacher, F. (1998) *Hermeneutics and Criticism and Other Writings*, Cambridge University Press, Cambridge

Scholten, P., Nicholls, J., Olsen, S. and Galimidi, B. (2006) *Social Return on Investment: A Guide to SROI Analysis*, Lenthe, Amstelveen

SEC (2008) 'Social Enterprise Definitions', Retrieved April, 2008, from www.socialenterprise.org.uk/Page.aspx?SP=1878

Sen, A. K. (2001) *Development as Freedom*, Oxford University Press, Oxford

Servadio, G. (1976) *Mafioso: A History of the Mafia from its Origins to the Present Day*, Stein & Day, New York

Seymour, A. (1998) 'Aetiology of the sexual abuse of children: an extended feminist perspective', *Women's Studies International Forum*, vol 21, no 4, pp415–427

Sharp (2008) 'CSR Procurement', Retrieved May, 2008, from http://sharp-world.com/corporate/eco/customer/csr/index.html

Sherbourne, C. D., Hayes, R. D. and Wells, K. B. (1995) 'Personal and psychological risk factors for physical and mental health outcomes and course of depression amongst depressed patients', *Journal of Consulting and Clinical Psychology*, vol 63, no 3, pp345–355

Silk, T. (2004) 'Corporate philanthropy and law in the United States: a practical guide to tax choices and an introduction to compliance with anti-terrorism laws', *International Journal of Not-for-Profit Law*, vol 6, no 3, available at www.icnl.org/knowledge/ijnl/vol6iss3/art_2.htm

Smith, A. (1999a) *The Wealth of Nations: I-III*, Penguin (first published 1776), London

Smith, A. (1999b) *The Wealth of Nations: IV-V*, Penguin (first published 1776), London

Smith, E. T. and Zhang, H. X. (2004) 'Developing key water quality indicators for sustainable water resources management', 77th Annual Water Environment Federation Technical Exhibition and Conference, Water Environment Federation, Alexandria, Virginia,

Smith-Doerr, J., Owen-Smith, J., Koput, K. K., and Powell, W. W. (1999) 'Networks and knowledge production: collaboration and patenting in biotechnology', in S. Gabbay and R. Leenders (eds) *Corporate Social Capital and Liability*, Kluwer Academic Publications, London

Stefanoni, S. (2003) *Save the Children UK's Engagement with Children as Stakeholders*, One World Trust, London

Stern, N. H. (2007) *The Economics of Climate Change: The Stern Review*, Cambridge University Press, Cambridge

Stoeckl, N. (2007) 'Using surveys of business expenditure to draw inferences about the size of regional multipliers: a case-study of tourism in Northern Australia', *Regional Studies*, vol 41, no 7 pp917–931

Swedlove, F. (2008) *Chairman's Summary – Paris Plenary*, Paris, Financial Action Task Force, Paris

Tainter, J. (1990) *The Collapse of Complex Societies*, Cambridge University Press, Cambridge

Therivel, R. (2004) *Strategic Environmental Assessment in Action*, Earthscan, London

Toshiba (2008) 'Vision & Policies', Retrieved May, 2008, from www.toshiba.com/csrpub/jsp/home/ToshibaVision.jsp

Traidcraft (2006) *Buying Matters*, Traidcraft, London

Traidcraft and Impactt (2008) *Material Concerns: How Responsible Sourcing Can Deliver the Goods for Business and Workers in the Garment Industry*, Traidcraft Exchange, Newcastle

UK (2006) *Charities Act 2006*

UN (1989) 'Convention on the Rights of the Child', Retrieved from http://www2.ohchr.org/english/law/crc.htm

UN (2008) 'What are the Millennium Development Goals?', Retrieved April, 2008, from www.un.org/millenniumgoals/

UNCTAD (2001) World Investment Report 2001, Promoting Linkages, UNCTAD, Geneva

UNDP (2009) 'Statistics of the Human Development Report', Retrieved January, 2009, from http://hdr.undp.org/statistics/

UNICEF (2008) 'The Challenge', Retrieved March 28, 2008, from www.unicef.org/programme/breastfeeding/challenge.htm

UNICEF (2008) 'Child Labour', Retrieved September, 2008, from www.unicef.org/protection/index_childlabour.html

USA (1969) *National Environmental Policy Act*, Washington, USA

Uzzi, B. and Gillespie, J. J. (1999) 'Corporate social capital and the cost of financial capital: an embeddedness approach', in S. Gabbay and R. Leenders (eds) *Corporate Social Capital and Liability*, Kluwer Academic Publications, London

Visa (2007) *Card Payments: Clamping down on child abuse. Reputation Matters. D. Luchtenberg*, Visa Europe, London

Vodafone (2008) *One Strategy: Corporate Responsibility Report*, Vodafone, Newbury

Wackernagel, M. and Rees, W. (1996) *Our Ecological Footprint: Reducing Human Impact on the Earth*, New Society Publishers, Gabriola Island

Wallerstein, I. (1974) *The Modern World-System, vol. I: Capitalist Agriculture and the Origins of the European World-Economy in the Sixteenth Century*, Academic Press, New York

Wallerstein, I. (1980) *The Modern World-System, vol. II: Mercantilism and the Consolidation of the European World-Economy, 1600–1750*, Academic Press, New York

Wallerstein, I. (1989) *The Modern World-System, vol. III: The Second Great Expansion of the Capitalist World-Economy, 1730–1840s*, Academic Press, New York

WalMart (2007) *Annual Report*, Arkansas

WalMart (2008) 'Renewable Energy' retrieved February 2008, from http://walmart-stores.com/GlobalWMStoresWeb/navigate.do?catg=347

WB (2003) *Social Analysis Sourcebook: Incorporating Social Dimensions in to Bank-Supported Projects*, World Bank, Washington

WB (2005) *World Development Report 2006: Equity and Development*, World Bank, Washington

WB (2008a) 'Measuring Social Capital', Retrieved August, 2008, from http://go.world-bank.org/A77F30UIX0

WB (2008b) 'Overview: Social Capital', Retrieved August, 2008, from http://go.world-bank.org/C0QTRW4QF0

WEF (2006) *Blended Value Investing*, World Economic Forum, Geneva

WI (2003) 'Rich-poor gap growing', in *Vital Signs 2003*, Washington, Worldwatch Institute, Washington, pp88–89

Willman, J. (2008) 'Sovereign wealth funds grow by 18%', *Financial Times*, London, 31 March

Wood, D. J. (2006) 'Transforming business citizenship: experiments in sustainable capitalism', *Politeia*, vol 22, no 86, pp257–271

Woodward, D. P. (1999) 'Multinational enterprise, employment, and local entrepreneurial development: Coca-Cola in South Africa', Columbia, Division of Research and the Faber Center for Entrepreneurship, Moore School of Business, University of South Carolina

Wray, R. (2007) 'China overtaking US for fast internet access as Africa gets left behind', *Guardian*, London, 14 June

Wright, M. and Hooper, S. (2001) *Break it Down, Open it Up... Green Futures*, Forum for the Future, London

WV (2002) *No Child of Mine – Opening the World's Eyes to the Sexual Exploitation of Children*, World Vision UK, Milton Keynes

WVS (2005) 'World Values Survey Questionnaire', Retrieved August, 2008, from www.worldvaluessurvey.org/

Index